AF599039

THE
Old Testament
HANDBOOK

Old Testament Handbook

Brentwood, Tennessee

Interior design by Faceout Studio, Jeff Miller and Paul Nielsen

Style	ISBN
Charcoal Cloth-over-Board	978-1-0877-8724-4
Sand Cloth-over-Board	978-1-4300-8582-9

DEWEY: 220.02
SUBHD: BIBLE—HANDBOOKS, MANUALS, ETC.

Printed in China
3 4 5 6 7 8 9 10 11 — 30 29 28 27 26 25
RRD

Contents

Letter from the Publisher

The Bible has a lot to say about beauty and how beauty might serve as a means leading to the praise and worship of God. In fact, just looking at the Old Testament narratives involving the construction of the tabernacle and the temple, we come to realize that there is a lot of specificity and detail surrounding their craftsmanship. The detail of these designs and the level of craftsmanship involved were not merely meant to create a place that instructs God's people—those designs and the beautiful creations that resulted were also meant to point the congregation to God's glory. When the Lord told Moses, "Make holy garments for your brother Aaron," he said to make these "for glory and beauty" (Exod 28:2). In other words, these craftsmen and artisans of the Old Testament were instructed to complete their tasks for the combined effect of both glory and beauty.

Unfortunately, too often the notion of beauty is overlooked in Christian culture. However, it is good to be reminded that the medium should always be commensurate with the message. Since Christians have the most beautiful message, the one found in the pages of Scripture, it is incumbent upon us to create beautiful mediums that relay that message in hopes that they also point others to the glory of God.

The *Old Testament Handbook* before you seeks to do just that in a creative and informative way. Intended to be used as a stand-alone reference work and/or companion to individual Bible reading and study, the *Old Testament Handbook* focuses on presenting important biblical themes, theological concepts, and individual book summaries in a visually compelling way. Its presentation of synthesized biblical material through intentional design and infographics helps deepen one's understanding of the historical, literary, and theological context of each book of the Old Testament. Features include the following:

- One-Sentence Summaries
- Book Introductions, Outlines, and Genre Indicators
- Word Studies
- Maps
- Timelines
- Charts and tables connecting Christ and key themes across Scripture
- Infographics about key figures and events
- Key Verses and Key Quotes

The *Old Testament Handbook* is intended to enhance your reading and understanding of the beauty found within the pages of the Old Testament and ultimately point you to "God's glory in the face of Jesus Christ" (2 Cor 4:6).

Andy McLean
Publisher

God's Timely and Inspired Word

INTRODUCTION: THE COMPOSITION AND CANON OF THE OLD TESTAMENT

People approach the Bible in a range of ways. Some people treat it as a collection of disconnected stories, others as an antiquated moral handbook. For some, the Bible functions as a cryptic codebook about modern-day political affairs and "end-time" events. Then there are those who treat it as a theological encyclopedia with a specific chapter and verse providing a straightforward answer to any question we might have. Yet others treat the Bible like a devotional grab bag, the equivalent of a spiritual vending machine waiting to satiate your "Quiet Time" fix.

While these approaches to the Bible might not apply to you or someone you know precisely, these sweeping descriptors are nonetheless useful for seeing that *the way people conceive of the Bible affects what they expect from it*. In other words, your definition of the Bible determines how you read the Bible and connect it with the real world and everyday life. Rather than imposing our own preferences and expectations on the Bible (as all of us are prone to do to some extent), we should instead allow the biblical literature to lead us as we consider its claims and observe its nature. This is especially the case with the Old Testament (OT), which consists of the first 39 books of our Bible. Two crucial questions will accordingly assist us in figuring out how best to conceive of the OT: (1) What is the OT? (2) Where did it come from? As we probe these two questions, we will craft a more optimal definition of what the Bible is: *God's timely and inspired Word*.

Before moving forward, let's consider the meaning of these two key adjectives within the definition: *timely* and *inspired*. The latter term, *inspired*, refers to the process by which the Holy Spirit supernaturally and concurrently worked in the human authors of Scripture to produce the message God desired down to the words themselves. The apostle Paul described the entirety of the OT in this way when he wrote, "All Scripture is inspired by God" (2 Tim 3:16). The apostle Peter provided further insight about the reality of inspiration by noting that "no prophecy ever came by the will of man; instead, men spoke from God as they were carried along by the Holy Spirit" (2 Pet 1:21). When these two passages are considered together, we are left to conclude that both the authors (redactors) and the texts they wrote were inspired. In other words, inspired authors produced inspired texts. What men wrote, the Holy Spirit wrote; what Scripture says, God says. Therefore, Scripture, and specifically the Old Testament, is God's inspired Word.

This brings us to the former term, *timely*. When applied to the Bible, the word *timely* applies in multiple senses. First, God's Word is timely because it is the record of God's speech and revelatory acts that occurred in time and space (2 Kgs 17:13; Jer 7:25; Dan 9:6; Hos 12:10; Luke 1:1–4; Heb 1:1–2; cp. Acts 26:26–27). It is a timely Word from an eternal God, a message that acts upon and speaks to creatures, events, and circumstances within history. Second, God's Word is "timely" in that God has delivered his message to his people at the "right" time historically and culturally befitting his redemptive purposes (Deut 30:11–16; cp. Rom 5:6; Gal 4:4). Just as with daily manna in the wilderness, God faithfully provides for his people what they need when they need it, and this extends to written, verbal revelation. Third, God's Word is forever "timely" because it is always relevant for God's people and for humanity in general (Gen 1:26–30; 2:15–17; Pss 1–2; 1 Cor 10:6–11).

As authoritative verbal revelation, God's Word should be the primary source for our knowing who God is and what life is about.

As counterintuitive as it might seem, we will begin our exploration of the nature of Scripture by considering where the OT came from before examining what it is. Looking at the second question first will give us a more well-rounded answer to the first question.

THE MAKING OF THE OLD TESTAMENT: A PERSONAL PROJECT TURNED COMMUNITY PROJECT

The composition and production of the OT was in a true sense something of a personal project turned into a community project—God involving his people in the process of committing his Word to writing. God's personal project of making himself known to his creatures became a historical process that would entail the meaningful agency of his creatures. Accordingly, we can think of the OT as a type of community project where God enlisted prophets, priests, kings, and scribes, mostly from among Israel, to partner with him in the composition of his literary Word.

Part of this community project included revisions and updates that occurred at a later time than the original writing. These revisions were no less inspired by the Spirit, however, and were made for subsequent generations to ensure accessibility and understanding, resulting in anachronistic references to locations and historical figures that might not have existed at the time of the original setting of a book (see Gen 22:14; 36:31–43; Judg 1:10; 1 Sam 9:9).

While prominent religious figures known as prophets wrote the bulk of the biblical content as we know it, others played a role in the preservation and compilation of Scripture. This was not a process where substantive alterations to content took place, and the observed differences that exist among manuscript copies do not affect or alter doctrine. Nonetheless, the recording of biblical history is more complex than it might seem, as is the case for any written historical accounts. Yet, when it comes to the Bible, the authors and redactors of Scripture were kept from making any factual errors because of the Holy Spirit's superintending work.

Events and their ensuing written accounts are not the same thing. Written accounts describe and interpret events that have already taken place; in other words, any telling of an event is a retelling. The Bible is no exception to this rule. However, our confidence in the accuracy and infallibility of the biblical records lies in the fact that we are receiving the *inspired* record of these events (2 Tim 3:14–17; 2 Pet 1:19–21; cp. Rom 15:4). The OT is not an exhaustive detailing of events but rather a God-guided, God-centered, curated retelling of important events in human history that pertain to God's plans and purposes for the world and especially for his covenant people, Israel. The OT functions largely as a God-given interpretation of Israel's history, including God's own self-revealing actions.

Accordingly, the inspired retelling of these stories and events involves several steps to get from the original event to the final form of the written text—namely, the recording of the event followed by the inspired writing, providentially guided redacting, and careful copying of the text.

PHASE ONE:

Events ▸ Oral Histories/Eyewitness Records ▸ Inspired Author ▸ Inspired Original Text

PHASE TWO:

Inspired Original Text ▸ Inspired Ancient Redactors ▸ Inspired Augmented Text

PHASE THREE:

Inspired Augmented Text ▸ Providentially Preserved Inspired Text

By following the Bible's lead as we observe its nature and origin, we see indicators of this editorial process within the biblical witness itself. In the book of Exodus we see the first mention of a biblical figure, Moses, being instructed to write something down: "The LORD then said to Moses, 'Write this down on a scroll as a reminder and recite it to Joshua'" (Exod 17:14). This passage, among others, associates Moses with the written record of events presented throughout the rest of the Pentateuch that was to be passed down to future generations (see Deut 31:24–26; 34:10–12).

However, there are obviously events that predate Moses recorded in the Bible, events that concern the origin of the universe and early human history and extending to the lives of Israel's patriarchs. We can reasonably infer that Moses took these narratives from the written accounts available to him, which themselves had been passed down orally until the advent of written language. We see evidence of these sorts of accounts being acknowledged and preserved in what are often called *toledoth*, or "family records," passages (see Gen 2:4; 5:1; 6:9; 10:1; 11:10,27; 25:12,19; 36:1,9; 37:2).

Similar patterns of editorial and compilation work can be seen in other parts of the Bible, such as in the wisdom books (see Prov 1:1; 25:1; 35:1) along with the Historical Books and Prophets (see Josh 10:13; 2 Sam 1:18; 1 Kgs 11:41; 14:19; 15:7; 1 Chr 9:1; Jer 36:32; see also the apparent parallel thematic arrangements within the Minor Prophets: Joel 3:16/Amos 1:12; Amos 9:12/Obad 1–2; Jonah/Nahum). Again, this does not compromise the Bible's claims about its supernatural inspiration; rather, it shows the humble and conventional lengths that God was pleased to go to in order to speak to his people through a collection of texts that would exist throughout all generations.

After all, if God was pleased to rule the world through human beings (e.g., Gen 1:26–30; Ps 8:4–8), then does it not seem plausible that he would use mundane human processes to communicate to us? If God invites humanity to partner with him and under him in *rulership*, then does it not seem fitting that he would also use humans in a similar manner as partners in *revelation*? God's personal project of revealing himself and his purposes to

GOD'S SPIRIT GUIDING THE PROCESS

PRIMEVAL AND PATRIARCHAL ERAS
Theologically significant events ocurring from creation to roughly 1800 BC

▶ **ORAL HISTORIES OF THESE ERAS**
Oral histories arose among early peoples who sought to preserve knowledge of key events. In the patriarchal age, Abraham and his descendants would have taken great care to pass down knowledge of God, his covenant promises, and key events in the lives of the Hebrew clan. God's sovereign Spirit ensured that these histories were uncorrupted by error.

▶ **EARLY WRITTEN RECORDS OF THESE ERAS**
When elementary alphabets were invented, oral histories were set down in writing. Under God's guidance the biblical patriarchs would have taken great care to pass down accounts of their dealings with God. Through men such as Joseph, these records came down to Moses.

▶ **MOSES**
Drawing from the reliable histories available to him, and guided by God, Moses infallibly wrote a theologically driven early history of earth in the book of Genesis.

▶ **MINOR EDITING**
Done under the care of God's providence in the centuries after Moses wrote Genesis, mindful priests and redactors, also under the inspiration of the Holy Spirit, updated the text without modifying its meaning. This helped keep the text accessible to later generations of Hebrews, whose language and life situations differed significantly from those of Moses and the era about which he wrote.

DIVINE INSPIRATION
God commissioned Moses to write, guided his search through the histories, and supernaturally directed every word he wrote. Similarly, God sanctioned, inspired, and guided later authors and redactors to compose the other books of Scripture.

humanity is once again something of a personal project become community project. As any book in the modern day goes through a sequence of professional editing during the months before it becomes published, likewise the OT underwent inspired redaction and some providentially directed scribal polishing over its centuries of becoming the body of sacred literature we know today. This documented process is nothing to cause us alarm but rather informs our doctrine of biblical inspiration and the comprehensive scope of God's providence in dispensing his Word.

THE RECEPTION OF THE OLD TESTAMENT: WHY OUR CANON IS ON TARGET

Moving from the historical nature and development of the OT as a literary composition, we can now turn to the question "What is the OT?" Specifically, we will consider why we can be confident that we recognize the right books as Scripture. We are moving from looking at the *timely* nature of God's Word, in the sense of the wise and favorable timing in which it was given to God's people, to looking at the corporate heeding of its *inspired* nature as authoritative canon.

When considering the canon of Scripture (the officially accepted collection of books), people's minds often divert to church councils and so-called lost Gospels. However, those are issues that might be discussed when dealing with the New Testament (NT) canon. The OT canon is a bit of a different story. While the NT canon was recognized when parallel consensus emerged among most churches spread around the Mediterranean, the writings of the OT were already being accepted as they were produced from within the Jewish community.

What Christians call the OT, the Jewish community (and much of the academic world) calls the Hebrew Bible, and historically, this body of literature was known as *TaNaK*: *Torah* (Law); *Nevi'im* (Prophets); *Ketuvim* (Writings). TaNaK, consisting of 24 books, is the same as the 39 books that make up what Protestants regard as the OT; they are simply arranged and grouped differently. Sometimes grouped as 22 books to correspond with the number of letters in the Hebrew alphabet, the books of TaNaK are attested to in various ways over the course of Jewish history, including in both extrabiblical Jewish literature and the NT.

Most notably, we see Jesus refer to this threefold division of Scripture (Luke 24:44–47; using "Psalms" to refer to the Writings), giving us a clear idea of what he regarded as the scope of the canon. Additionally, the Jewish historian Josephus noted that copies of these particular books were kept in the temple. As reflected in the NT, there seemed to be no major dispute among the mainstream Jewish religious bodies over which books were authoritative. The Pharisees and the Sadducees both accepted this same standard canon (despite the mistaken notion that the Sadducees only accepted the Pentateuch).

The consensus concerning the canon that was already in place before the time of Jesus's public ministry stems from the precedent set by Moses, who authored the foundational books of the Torah (or Pentateuch), with subsequent prophets and historians building on this foundation, beginning with Joshua, Moses's successor, and extending to the prophets, priests, scribes, chroniclers, and sometimes kings in cases like David and Solomon.

While there is no recorded process that tells us how the Jewish people went about measuring each individual book, we see in their later history that they differentiated the books recognized as Scripture from other religious and historical writings. There is little evidence to suggest that any pocket of the Jewish community regarded the books of the Apocrypha as being Scripture. Belief that the Apocrypha belonged within the OT canon was a later Christian phenomenon, an idea opposed by the most renowned biblical scholars such as Origen and Jerome. Part of the reason that some Christians during the early centuries of the church came to identify the books of the Apocrypha as part of the

TORAH (LAW)	*NEVI'IM* (PROPHETS)	*KETUVIM* (WRITINGS)
Genesis	Joshua	Psalms
Exodus	Judges	Proverbs
Leviticus	1–2 Samuel	Job
Numbers	1–2 Kings	Song of Songs
Deuteronomy	Isaiah	Ruth
	Jeremiah	Lamentations
	Ezekiel	Ecclesiastes
	Book of the Twelve	Esther
		Ezra–Nehemiah
		Daniel
		1–2 Chronicles

canon of Scripture was because the Greek translation of the OT, the Septuagint (LXX), included these books. Because the Septuagint functioned as the common convention for their access to the OT, Christians eventually lost the distinction that the Jewish community made between the noncanonical books and the Hebrew Bible.

The Jewish sect of the Essenes possessed writings that came to be known as part of the Pseudepigrapha (e.g., 1 Enoch, Jubilees, etc.), some of which were found among the libraries of the Dead Sea Scrolls. However, they seemed to have treated these writings differently than the standard canonical writings of the OT. Further, for the whole of TaNaK, only five books received any notable discussion as to their canonicity—Ezekiel, Proverbs, Ecclesiastes, Song of Songs, and Esther. These discussions were about continuing to recognize this set of books, not about adding them into the canon anew.

Though the council at Jamnia discussed the matter of canon in AD 90, the meeting merely confirmed what was already accepted as Scripture among the Jewish community. Only two books were debated, yet still affirmed: Ecclesiastes and Song of Songs. Functionally, the Jewish people had stopped expecting further revelation from God by the time of the Maccabees, around the second century BC. When Daniel and Esther were completed, likely the final books, they were added to the collections containing the books belonging to the threefold division and thus regarded as Scripture.

Because neither the larger Jewish community, nor Jesus, nor the NT authors accepted any writings outside of the 24 books of the Hebrew Bible, early Christians came to recognize only these books as part the OT. As noted above, the 39 books making up the Protestant OT canon contain the same content as the 24 books of TaNaK; they are just divided up differently. In response to the Protestant Reformation, the Roman Catholic Church, in 1546 at the Council of Trent, officially deemed the books of the Apocrypha to be part of the canon. By contrast, Protestant Christianity appears to be on solid historical ground for limiting its OT canon to the 39 books. Our canon is on target, so to speak.

CONCLUSION

When the historical development and literary form of the OT are considered carefully, it becomes more difficult to impose our modern-day conventions on its theological claims. Knowing some of the most important details about what the OT is and where it came from enables us to accept it for what it is: *God's timely and inspired Word*. The content in the *Old Testament Handbook* aims to keep in step with this premise. The literary analysis, word studies, timelines, tables, and infographics exist to enable the reader to better understand and more deeply appreciate Scripture on its own terms: as God's timely and inspired Word.

Genesis

Genre | **HISTORICAL NARRATIVE**

As a book of beginnings, Genesis presents God's creation of the universe, humanity's fall into sin, and God's promise to bring blessing and restoration to his good but corrupted world through the family of Abraham.

INTRODUCTION

AUTHOR Since pre-Christian times authorship of the Torah, the five books that include the book of Genesis, has been attributed to Moses. Even though Genesis is technically anonymous, both the Old and New Testaments unanimously recognize Moses as the Torah's author (Josh 8:35; 23:6; 1 Kgs 2:3; 8:9; 2 Kgs 14:6; 23:25; 2 Chr 23:18; 25:4; 30:16; 34:14; 35:12; Ezra 3:2; 6:18; Neh 8:1; 9:14; Dan 9:11,13; Mal 4:4; Mark 12:19,26; Luke 2:22; 20:28; 24:44; John 1:17,45; 7:19; Acts 13:39; 15:21; 28:23; Rom 10:5; 1 Cor 9:9; Heb 10:28). At the same time, evidence in Genesis suggests that minor editorial changes dating to ancient times have been inserted into the text (see Gen 14:14; 36:31; cp. Judg 18:29).

BACKGROUND Genesis, the first book of the Torah, provides both the universal history of humankind and the patriarchal history of the nation of Israel. The first section (chaps. 1–11) is a general history commonly called the "primeval history," showing how all humanity descended from one couple and became sinners. The second section (chaps. 12–50) is a more specific history commonly referred to as the "patriarchal history," focusing on the covenant God made with Abraham and his descendants: Isaac, Jacob, and Jacob's 12 sons. Genesis unfolds God's plan to bless and redeem humanity through Abraham's descendants. The book concludes with the events that led to the Israelites being in the land of Egypt.

MESSAGE AND PURPOSE God is the sovereign Lord and Creator of all things. God is infinite in power, and his control over human history is so complete that even the worst of human deeds can be turned to serve his benevolent purposes (50:20). Evil and sin did not originate with God. Sin entered the world at a specific place and time in history. Adam and Eve chose freely to disobey God, fell from innocence, and lost their freedom. Sin resulted in death, both physical and spiritual, and led to a world of pain and struggle. Further, Genesis is a narrative of relationships, and certainly relationships grounded in covenants with God. These covenants provide a unifying principle for understanding the whole of Scripture and define the relationship between God and man. The heart of that relationship is found in the phrase "They will be my people, and I will be their God" (Jer 32:38; cp. Gen 17:7–8; Exod 6:6–7; Lev 26:12; Deut 4:20; Jer 11:4; Ezek 11:20). God's covenant with Abraham is a major event both in Genesis and throughout the Bible.

SUMMARY The book of Genesis is the great book of beginnings in the Bible. True to the meanings of its Hebrew and Greek names (Hb. *bere'shith*, "In Beginning" [based on 1:1]; Gk. *Geneseos*, "Of Birth" [based on 2:4]), Genesis permits us to view the beginning of a multitude of realities that shape our daily existence: the creation of the universe and the planet earth; the origins of plant and animal life; and the origins of human beings, marriage, families, nations, industry, artistic expression, religious ritual, prophecy, sin, law, crime, conflict, punishment, and death.

STRUCTURE Genesis is chiefly a narrative. From a narrative standpoint, God is the only true hero of the Bible, and the book of Genesis has the distinct privilege of introducing him. God is the first subject of a verb in the book and is mentioned more frequently than any other character in the Bible. The content of the first 11 chapters is distinct from the patriarchal stories in chapters 12–50. The primary literary device is the catchphrase "these are the family records."

Outline

I. Creation of Heaven and Earth (1:1–2:3)
- A. Creator and creation (1:1–2)
- B. Six days of creation (1:3–31)
- C. Seventh day—day of consecration (2:1–3)

II. The Human Family in and outside the Garden (2:4–4:26)
- A. The man and woman in the garden (2:4–25)
- B. The man and woman expelled from the garden (3:1–24)
- C. Adam and Eve's family outside the garden (4:1–26)

III. Adam's Family Line (5:1–6:8)
- A. Introduction: Creation and blessing (5:1–2)
- B. "Image of God" from Adam to Noah (5:3–32)
- C. Conclusion: Procreation and perversion (6:1–8)

IV. Noah and His Family (6:9–9:29)
- A. Righteous Noah and the corrupt world (6:9–12)
- B. Coming judgment but the ark of promise (6:13–7:10)
- C. Worldwide flood of judgment (7:11–24)
- D. God's remembrance and rescue of Noah (8:1–14)
- E. Exiting the ark (8:15–19)
- F. Worship and the word of promise (8:20–22)
- G. God's covenant with the new world (9:1–17)
- H. Noah's sons and future blessing (9:18–29)

V. The Nations and the Tower of Babylon (10:1–11:26)
- A. Table of Nations (10:1–32)
- B. Tower of Babylon (11:1–9)
- C. Family line of Abram (11:10–26)

VI. Father Abraham (11:27–25:11)
- A. Abram's beginnings (11:27–32)
- B. The promissory call and Abram's obedience (12:1–9)
- C. Abram and Sarai in Egypt: Blessing begins (12:10–13:1)
- D. Abram and Lot part: Promises recalled (13:2–18)
- E. Abram rescues Lot: Abram's faithfulness (14:1–24)
- F. Covenant promises confirmed (15:1–21)
- G. Abram's firstborn son, Ishmael (16:1–16)
- H. Covenant sign of circumcision (17:1–27)
- I. Divine judgment and mercy (18:1–19:38)
- J. Abraham and Sarah in Gerar: Promises preserved (20:1–18)
- K. Abraham's promised son: The birth of Isaac (21:1–21)
- L. Treaty with Abimelech (21:22–34)
- M. Abraham's test (22:1–19)
- N. Family line of Rebekah (22:20–24)
- O. Sarah's burial site (23:1–20)
- P. A wife for Isaac (24:1–67)
- Q. Abraham's death and burial (25:1–11)

VII. Ishmael's Family Line (25:12–18)

VIII. Isaac's Family: Jacob and Esau (25:19–35:29)
- A. Struggle at birth and birthright (25:19–34)
- B. Isaac's deception and strife with the Philistines (26:1–35)
- C. Stolen blessing and flight to Paddan-aram (27:1–28:9)
- D. Promise of blessing at Bethel (28:10–22)
- E. Laban deceives Jacob (29:1–30)
- F. Birth of Jacob's children (29:31–30:24)
- G. Birth of Jacob's herds (30:25–43)
- H. Jacob deceives Laban (31:1–55)
- I. Struggle for blessing at Peniel (32:1–32)
- J. Restored gift and return to Shechem (33:1–20)
- K. Dinah, deception, and strife with the Hivites (34:1–31)
- L. Blessing and struggle at birth (35:1–29)

IX. Esau's Family (36:1–8)

X. Esau, Father of the Edomites (36:9–37:1)

XI. Jacob's Family: Joseph and His Brothers (37:2–50:26)
- A. The early days of Joseph (37:2–36)
- B. Judah and Tamar (38:1–30)
- C. Joseph in Egypt (39:1–23)
- D. Joseph, savior of Egypt (40:1–41:57)
- E. The brothers' journeys to Egypt (42:1–43:34)
- F. Joseph tests the brothers (44:1–34)
- G. Joseph reveals his identity (45:1–28)
- H. Jacob's migration to Egypt (46:1–27)
- I. Joseph, savior of the family (46:28–47:12)
- J. Joseph's administration in Egypt (47:13–31)
- K. Jacob's blessings (48:1–49:28)
- L. The death and burial of Jacob (49:29–50:14)
- M. The final days of Joseph (50:15–26)

WORD STUDY

zera'

Hebrew pronunciation: [ZEH ra]

CSB translation: seed, offspring

Uses in Genesis: 59
Uses in the OT: 229

Focus passage: Genesis 12:7

Zera' appears 15 times with related *zara'* (*sow;* Exod 23:10). *Zera'* means *seed* (Num 24:7), *seedtime* (Gen 8:22), *crop* (Deut 22:9), or *grain* (Isa 23:3). *Zera'* indicates human or animal *seed* (Jer 31:27), *semen* (Lev 22:4), or *offspring* (Gen 3:15; 46:6). It signifies *children* (Lev 22:13) or *son* (1 Sam 1:11), *descendants* (Ps 18:50), *heirs* (2 Kgs 11:1), *family* (1 Kgs 11:14), and *people* (Isa 61:9). It connotes *brood* (Isa 1:4), *line* or *bloodline* (Gen 19:32), *lineage* (Num 16:40), or *ancestral families* (Ezra 2:59). *Zera'* implies *fertile* (Ezek 17:5). *Zara'* (56x) also denotes sowed *seed* (Gen 26:12), *plant, become pregnant* (Lev 12:2), *conceive* (Num 5:28), and *have offspring* (Nah 1:14). It functions figuratively (Hos 8:7). Participles with *zera'* indicate *seed-bearing* (Gen 1:12,29). *Zerua'* (3x) is *sowing, what is sown,* or *vegetables* (Dan 1:12).

'erets

Hebrew pronunciation [EHR ehtz]

CSB translation: land

Uses in Genesis: 311
Uses in the OT: 2,505

Focus passage: Genesis 28:4,12–14

'Erets is one of the most common and flexible OT nouns, whose meanings seem derived from the idea of *land* (Gen 2:5). Often it refers to nations such as the *land of Israel. 'Erets* denotes *area, region, homeland, country,* or *earth,* the latter often in conjunction with "heaven" to represent the whole world (Gen 1:1; 20:1; 21:23; 30:25; 34:1). *'Erets* means *district* (1 Chr 13:2). It is *soil* (Lev 27:30) or *dirt* (Jer 17:13) but may suggest the *land's produce* (Lev 27:30). *'Erets* can involve *distance* (Gen 35:16), the surface of the *ground* (Judg 6:37), or private property (Gen 23:15). *'Erets* indicates the *whole earth* (Ps 66:4) or *every land* (Gen 41:57) as the inhabitants of the earth. It describes the depths of the *earth* (Isa 44:23) and, with modifiers, the *underworld* (Ezek 26:20). "People of the *land*" can connote *common people* (Lev 4:27). "Field of the *land*" indicates *open fields* (Lev 25:31).

parah

Hebrew pronunciation [pah RAH]

CSB translation: be fruitful

Uses in Genesis: 15
Uses in the OT: 29

Focus passage: Genesis 47:27

Parah means be *fruitful* (Gen 1:22) or *sprout* (Isa 45:8). In some verses the sense is to have *plenty of fruit* (Isa 17:6; 32:12). *Parah* refers to many offspring or descendants, appearing as *become numerous* (Exod 23:30) or *increase* (Jer 3:16). This sense was applied to a mother with numerous children (Ps 128:3). It regularly stands alongside other verbs with similar meanings. Exodus 1:7 lists four in a row to emphasize that God blessed Israel as he originally intended to bless creation (Gen 1:22,28). In 15 verses *parah* occurs together with *rabah* meaning *fruitful and multiply.* Israelites linked the two verbs (Gen 28:3) in imitation of the Lord's repeatedly stressed intention for his creation (e.g., Gen 8:17; Lev 26:9; Ezek 36:11). Participles denote *fruitful* or *bearing fruit* (Deut 29:18). Causative verbs indicate *make fruitful* (Ps 105:24).

Genesis Timeline

BEGINNING

2166–1991 BC
Abraham

2100
Job

2100
Construction of Ziggurat at Ur in Sumer

2091
Abraham moves from Haran to Canaan.

2085
Destruction of Sodom and Gomorrah

2081
God's covenant with Abraham

2080
Ishmael is born.

2066–1886
Isaac

2006–1859
Jacob

2000
Chinese create first zoo, Park of Intelligence.

2000
Babylonians and Egyptians divide days into hours, minutes, and seconds.

2000
Mesopotamians learn to solve quadratic equations.

2000
Code of medical ethics, Mesopotamia

2000
Courier systems of communication are developed in both China and Egypt.

1915–1805
Joseph

1900
Benjamin is born; Rachel dies.

1900
Potter's wheel is introduced to Crete.

1900
Use of the sail in the Aegean

1900
Egyptian town of El Lahun gives evidence of town planning with streets at right angles.

1900
Mesopotamian mathematicians discover what later came to be called the Pythagorean theorem.

1898
Joseph is sold into Egypt.

1800
Musical theory, Mesopotamia

1800
Multiplication tables, Mesopotamia

1800
Babylonians develop a catalog of stars and planets.

END

Creation: Day by Day

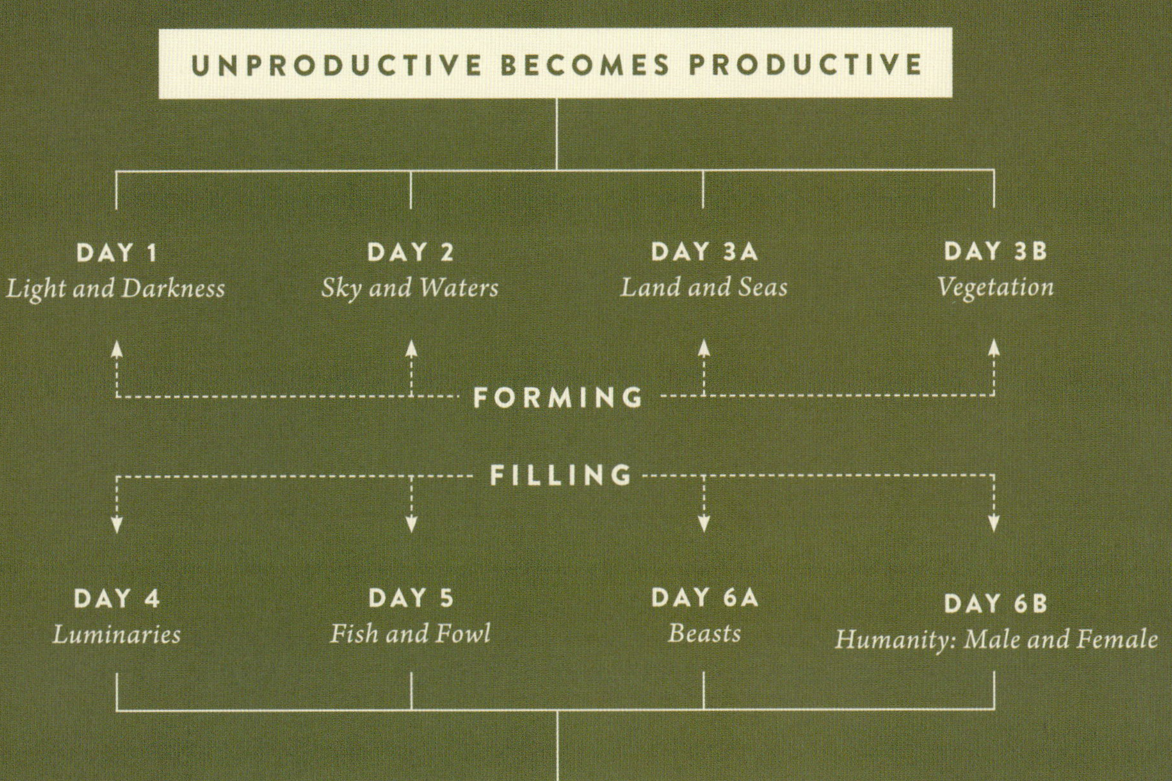

Early Covenants

COVENANT	KEY PLAYERS	SCRIPTURE	DESCRIPTION OF THE PROMISE
Creation (sometimes called "covenant of works")	God and mankind (Adam and Eve)	Genesis 1:26–30; 2:16–17	Man was created in the image of God and told to be fruitful, multiply, fill the earth, and subdue it. Life (blessing) or death (curse) offered based on Adam's obedience to the command not to eat from the tree of the knowledge of good and evil.
Noahic	Noah and all his descendants and every living creature	Genesis 9:1–17	God made a promise to not repeat the great flood, with the rainbow as the covenant sign. Humanity is still expected to be fruitful, multiply, fill the earth, and rule it.
Abrahamic	Abraham, Isaac, and Jacob and their descendants	Genesis 12:1–3; 15; 17	God promised to give the land (Canaan), offspring (nations and kings), and blessing (a great name and blessing to others) to Abraham, Isaac, Jacob, and their descendants. Circumcision was given as the covenant sign.
Mosaic (old)	The people of Israel	Exodus 6:2–8; 19–24; ; 31:16	God redeemed and liberated the Israelites from bondage based on his promises to Abraham and his descendants. The covenant established blessing for obedience and curse for disobedience (agricultural plight, military defeat, exile from the land). The Sabbath was given as a permanent covenant sign.

Directives to Adam and Noah

DIRECTIVE	ADAM / GARDEN	NOAH / FLOOD
Be fruitful and multiply	Genesis 1:28	Genesis 9:1
Rule over the creatures	Genesis 1:28	Genesis 9:2
Curse the ground	Genesis 3:17	Genesis 8:21
Eat of the plants	Genesis 1:29	Genesis 9:3
Dietary restrictions	Genesis 2:17	Genesis 9:4
Light and seasons	Genesis 1:14	Genesis 8:22
God made man in his image	Genesis 1:27	Genesis 9:5–6
Animal bloodshed for atonement	Genesis 3:17–21	Genesis 8:20–21

Noah and Jesus

NOAH	JESUS
The Recipient of God's Favor *(Gen 6:8)*	The Means of God's Favor *(Eph 1:3–14)*
A Righteous Man *(Gen 6:9)*	The Righteous One *(1 John 2:1)*
Built an Ark for His Family in Obedience to God *(Gen 6:14–22)*	Suffered Death for Sinners in Obedience to God *(Gal 1:3–4)*
Saved through the Waters of God's Judgment *(Gen 6:17–18)*	Suffered God's Judgment for Sin to Save Sinners *(1 Pet 3:18)*
The Rainbow: • The Sign of God's Covenant with the World Not to Destroy the World by Water Again *(Gen 9:9–17)* • The "War Bow" of God Aimed Up into the Heavens	**The Cross:** • The Sign of Fulfillment of God's Promise to Take Away the Sin of the World *(Col 2:13–14)* • The Promised Curse of Sin Fell upon Jesus Nailed to a Tree
Shamed in His Drunkenness *(Gen 9:20–23)*	Shamed Only in His Sacrifice for Sin *(Heb 4:15; 12:2)*
Continued the Curse of Sin after the Flood *(Gen 9:20–29)*	Ended the Curse of Sin with His Death and Resurrection *(1 Cor 15)*

Salvation through Judgment

JUDGMENT	THE EVENT	THE MEANS	SALVATION
The Wicked	The Flood *(Gen 6–9)*	Floodwater	Noah and His Family
The Egyptians	The Exodus *(Exod 1–15)*	The Plagues and the Red Sea	The Israelites
Judah and Jerusalem	The Exile *(2 Chr 36)*	The Babylonians	The Remnant
Sinners/Jesus Christ	The Cross *(Rom 5)*	God's Wrath on Our Substitute	Believers in Christ
God's Enemies	The Final Judgment *(2 Thess 1)*	God's Wrath and Hell	God's People

Abraham's Migration

TAURUS MOUNTAINS
Haran
Tigris
River
PADDAN-ARAM
CYPRUS
MEDITERRANEAN SEA
Euphrates
River
Susa
CANAAN
Bethel
Jerusalem
DEAD SEA
Ur
0 40 80 120 160 200 Miles
0 40 80 120 160 200 Kilometers
GULF OF SUEZ
GULF OF AQABA

• City
ABRAHAM'S MIGRATION ROUTE
ABRAHAM'S ALTERNATIVE MIGRATION ROUTE

Birthright and Blessing

A CHILD'S BIRTHRIGHT

In Genesis we learn that Esau forfeited his birthright to his brother, Jacob, for the sake of a meal of lentil stew and bread (Gen 25:27–34).

The birthright consisted of the special privileges that belonged to the firstborn male child in a family. Prominent among those privileges was a double portion of the estate as an inheritance. If a man had two sons, his estate would be divided into three portions, and the older son would receive two. If there were three sons, the estate would be divided into four portions, and the oldest son would receive two. The oldest son also normally received the father's major blessing.

A FATHER'S BLESSING

The unique concept of the spoken word, especially in the context of worship or other formal settings, is important for understanding the significance of blessings. According to Old Testament thought patterns, the formally spoken word had both an independent existence and the power of its own fulfillment. The word once spoken assumed a history of its own and had the power to ensure its fulfillment (see Isa 55:10–11). Formal words of blessing, like the blessing of Joseph's sons, also had the power of self-fulfillment (Gen 48:17–22).

When Isaac mistakenly blessed Jacob rather than Esau, he could not recall the blessing, for it existed in history (Gen 27:18–41); it had acquired an identity of its own. Blessing (and cursing) released superhuman powers that could bring to pass the content of the blessing.

Family of Abraham

TERAH *Gen 11:26*

- **HARAN** *Gen 11:27*
  - **LOT** *Gen 11:27*
    - **SECOND DAUGHTER** *Gen 19:36–38*
      - **BEN-AMMI** *Gen 19:36–38*
    - **FIRST DAUGHTER** *Gen 19:36–38*
      - **MOAB** *Gen 19:36–38*
  - **ISCAH** *Gen 11:29*
  - **MILCAH** *Gen 11:29*
- **NAHOR** *(Gen 11:27)* — married MILCAH
  - with MILCAH: *seven other sons*
  - with MILCAH: **BETHUEL** *Gen 22:21–23*
    - **LABAN** *Gen 24:29*
    - **REBEKAH** *wife* *Gen 24:15*
- **REUMAH** *concubine* *Gen 22:24*
  - **FOUR SONS** *Gen 22:24*
- **HAGAR** *concubine* *Gen 16:1–16*
  - **ISHMAEL** *Gen 16:15*
    - *twelve sons* *Gen 25:12–16*
- **KETURAH** *wife* *Gen 25:1*
  - *four other children*
  - **MIDIAN** *Gen 25:2*
    - *five children*
  - **JOKSHAN** *1 Chr 1:32*
    - *two children*
- **ABRAM** *(Abraham)*
- **SARAI (SARAH)** *wife* *Gen 11:29*
  - **ISAAC** *Gen 21:1–7* — married REBEKAH

GENESIS

ZILPAH
concubine
Gen 30:9–13

BILHAH
concubine
Gen 30:1–8

RACHEL
wife
Gen 29:1–30:24

LEAH
wife
Gen 29:21–30

JACOB (ISRAEL)

ESAU
Father of the Edomites
Gen 36:1–43

ASHER *eighth son* — *three sons*
- **SERAH**
- **BERIAH**

GAD *seventh son* — *seven sons*

NAPHTALI *sixth son* — *four sons*

DAN *fifth son* — *one son*

BENJAMIN *twelfth son* — *ten sons*

JOSEPH *eleventh son*
- **MANASSEH**
- **EPHRAIM**

DINAH

ZEBULUN *tenth son* — *three sons*

ISSACHAR *ninth son* — *four sons*

JUDAH *fourth son* — *five sons*

LEVI *third son*
- **MERARI**
- **KOHATH**
- **GERSHON**

SIMEON *second son* — *six sons*

REUBEN *first son* — *four sons*

GENESIS

Dreams in Genesis

In the ancient Near Eastern world dreams were real. They were not an extension of one's conscious or unconscious mind. Dreams were the world of the divine and the demonic. Dreams had meaning too. They often revealed the future. They could show the dreamer the right decision to make. People even went to temples or holy places to sleep in order to have a dream that would show them the decision to make.

The dreams of common people were important to them, but the dreams of kings and of holy men or women were important on a national or international scale.

Not every dream needed to be interpreted. To note this we can distinguish three types of dreams:

- A simple message dream (Joseph, concerning Mary and Herod, in Matt 1–2)
- A simple symbolic dream (when the symbolism was clear enough for the dreamer and others to understand it; Joseph in Gen 37)
- Complex symbolic dreams (which needed the interpretive skill of someone with experience of an unusual ability in interpretation; Nebuchadnezzar in Dan 2; 4)

It's important to note that dreams were neither foolproof nor infallible in the Bible (Jer 23:28; 27:9; Zech 10:1–2). Thus, while dreams were often used by God to reveal his will, there is a warning, too, not to rely on this method to know the will of God.

SIMPLE MESSAGE DREAMS

God stops Abimelech from having relations with Abraham's wife, Sarah (Gen 20:1–7).

Jacob flees from his brother, Esau (Gen 28:12–14).

God tells Jacob to return to his native land (Gen 31:1–17).

God warns Laban not to bless or curse Jacob (Gen 31:22–24).

SIMPLE SYMBOLIC DREAMS

Joseph's dreams signify that his parents and brothers will bow to him (Gen 37:1–10).

COMPLEX SYMBOLIC DREAMS

Pharaoh's cupbearer dreams that he will be restored to his position (Gen 40:9–10).

Pharaoh's baker's dream proclaims he will die (Gen 40:16–19).

Pharaoh's dream about his cows reveals seven years of abundance (Gen 41:1–4).

Pharaoh's grain dream forewarns of famine (Gen 41:5–7).

Path to Reconciliation

Many similarities exist between Jacob and his son Joseph. While each took different paths, they both fought throughout their lives for the very best that God had promised for them. Each ended their lives by reconciling with their siblings and receiving covenant blessings from God.

JACOB	JOSEPH
The son of Isaac and Rebekah *(Gen 25:19)*	The son of Jacob and Rachel *(Gen 30:22–24)*
His parents waited years before having Jacob and his twin, Esau *(Gen 25:21–22)*.	Jacob waited 14 years before marrying Rachel *(Gen 29:18–30)*, and then Rachel was infertile for many years *(Gen 30:22)*.
Rebekah had two sons, Jacob and Esau *(Gen 25:23–26)*.	Rachel had two sons, Joseph *(Gen 30:23–24)* and Benjamin *(Gen 35:18)*.
Flees from his brother, Esau, after cheating Esau out of his birthright *(Gen 27:41–45)*	Sold into slavery by his brothers *(Gen 37:12–36)* but eventually received his older half-brother's birthright *(Gen 49:3–4,22–26)*
Lived in a foreign land *(Bethel; Gen 28:10–22)*	Lived in a foreign land *(Egypt; Gen 39:1; 45:26)*
Received two dreams from God *(Gen 28:12; 30:25–31:17)*	Received two dreams from God *(Gen 37:5–7,9)*
Needed Esau's forgiveness for stealing his birthright *(Gen 25:27–34; 33:1–16)*	Needed to forgive his brothers for betraying him *(Gen 37:28)*
A servant to his uncle, trying to earn Rachel's hand in marriage *(Gen 29:20–30)*	A servant to Potiphar and Pharaoh in Egypt *(Gen 39:1)*
Past sufferings shaped his fears: "Everything happens to me!" *(Gen 42:36)*.	Remained faithful to God despite suffering: "God has made me fruitful in the land of my affliction" *(Gen 41:52)*
Bestowed a blessing upon Pharaoh *(Gen 47)*	Receives a blessing from Pharaoh *(Gen 41)*

The Promise of Genesis

The book of Genesis contains a number of promises from God, but taken as a whole, the promise of Genesis to the whole world involves a people, a family, and ultimately points to a person—Jesus Christ, whose sacrifice redeems those who believe (1 Pet 1:18–21).

ADAM (930 years)—Be fruitful, multiply, fill the earth, and subdue it; rule every creature (Gen 1:28).

SETH (912 years) **ENOSH** (905 years) **KENAN** (910 years) **MAHALALEL** (895 years) **JARED** (962 years) **ENOCH** (365 years) **METHUSELAH** (969 years) **LAMECH** (777 years)

NOAH (950 years)—Be fruitful, multiply, and fill the earth; every creature will fear you, and they are under your authority (Gen 9:1–2).

SHEM (600 years) **ARPACHSHAD** (438 years) **SHELAH** (433 years) **EBER** (464 years) **PELEG** (239 years) **REU** (239 years) **SERUG** (230 years) **NAHOR** (148 years) **TERAH** (205 years)

ABRAM/ABRAHAM (175 years)—Go, and I will give you land, offspring, and blessing. All the peoples on earth will be blessed through you (Gen 12:1–3).

ISAAC (180 years)—Stay, and I will be with you; I will give you land, offspring, and blessing. All the nations of the earth will be blessed through you (Gen 26:2–5).

JACOB/ISRAEL (147 years)—I will be with you; I will give you land and offspring. All the peoples on earth will be blessed through you (Gen 28:13–15).

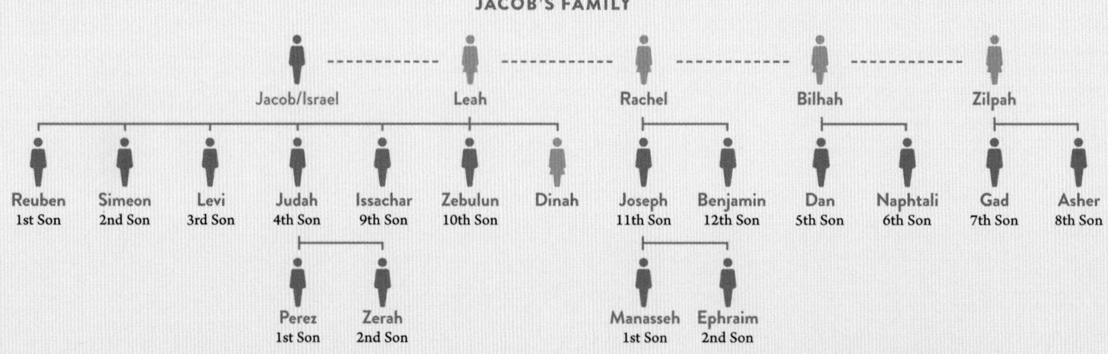

A PROMISED RULER

JUDAH—The scepter will not depart from the tribe of Judah until he whose right it is comes. The obedience of the peoples belongs to him (Gen 49:8–12).

AN EXAMPLE OF BLESSING

JOSEPH (110 years)—The Lord was with Joseph and sent him to Egypt to preserve life for both his family and the nations (Gen 39; 45; 50).

THE PROMISE

JESUS—The second Adam who brings life and blessing (Rom 5). The fulfillment of the protoevangelium, the Seed of the woman to crush the seed of the serpent by his death on the cross for sin and his resurrection to eternal life (1 John 3:8). The One who walked with God in perfect righteousness, miraculously born of a virgin and walked among us as Immanuel, "God is with us" (Matt 1:23). The promised Seed of Abraham who would be a blessing to all the nations through faith in him (Gal 3). The Priest/King in the order of Melchizedek to fulfill the Abrahamic covenant and inaugurate the new covenant with his blood shed for sins (Heb 7–10). The one and only Son of God who would be sacrificed by his Father so that everyone who believes in him will not perish but have eternal life (John 3:16). The true Israel who is the connection between heaven and earth (John 1:51). The Lion from the tribe of Judah, the King to whom the obedience of the peoples rightly belongs (Rev 5:5). The One nailed to a cross and killed by evil people, though, like Joseph, delivered up according to God's determined plan and foreknowledge for the salvation of all who believe in him; he was vindicated in the resurrection and exalted to the right hand of God as both Lord and Messiah (Acts 2:22–36).

Seeing Jesus in Genesis

THE FIRST ADAM Brought Death *(Gen 3)*	**THE SECOND ADAM** Brought Life *(Rom 5)*
THE PROTOEVANGELIUM The Promise of Deliverance from the Serpent *(Gen 3:15)*	**THE FULFILLMENT** Jesus Destroys the Works of the Devil *(1 John 3:8)*
ABEL'S BLOOD Cries Out for Justice *(Gen 4)*	**JESUS'S BLOOD** Proclaims Forgiveness *(Heb 12:24)*
THE FLOOD Ark Rescues Noah's Family *(Gen 6–8)*	**BAPTISM** Christ's Resurrection Rescues Us *(1 Pet 3:20–21)*
THE PROMISE TO ABRAHAM Seed and Blessing to the World *(Gen 12)*	**THE FULFILLMENT IN JESUS** The Seed and Salvation from Sin to the World *(Gal 3)*
THE ALMOST SACRIFICE OF ISAAC "The Lord Will Provide" *(Gen 22)*	**THE CRUCIFIXION OF JESUS** "The Lamb of God" *(John 1:29)*
JACOB'S STAIRWAY (OR LADDER) The Promise of God's Presence *(Gen 28)*	**JESUS IS THE STAIRWAY (OR LADDER)** The Fullness of God's Presence *(John 1:51)*
JOSEPH SUFFERED According to God's Plan *(Gen 50:20)*	**JESUS SUFFERED** According to God's Plan *(Acts 2:23)*
JOSEPH FORGAVE His Brothers *(Gen 45)*	**JESUS FORGIVES** Sinners *(Luke 23:34)*
JOSEPH SAVED People from Famine *(Gen 45)*	**JESUS SAVES** People from Sin *(Acts 2:36–41)*

The Lord Will Provide

	SUBJECT TO DEATH	THE SUBSTITUTE	THE REASON
GENESIS 22	Isaac—Abraham's only son	A Ram	Abraham named the place "The LORD Will Provide," and it was said of that place: "It will be provided on the LORD's mountain" *(Gen 22:14)*.
EXODUS 12–13 (The Passover)	The Firstborn Sons of Israel	An Unblemished Lamb or Goat	The blood on the houses of the Israelites would be a sign to distinguish them; when God saw the blood, he would pass over them *(Exod 12:13)*.
LEVITICUS 16 (The Day of Atonement)	The People of Israel	Animals, Including a Ram	On this day, atonement was made for the Israelites to cleanse them from all their sins so they could be clean before the Lord *(Lev 16:30)*.
REVELATION 5	Sinners	Jesus—"the Lamb of God" *(John 1:29)*	Jesus, the Lamb, was slaughtered in order to redeem people for God by his blood—people from every tribe, language, people, and nation *(Rev 5:9)*.

Joseph's Life

IN PADDAN-ARAM/CANAAN WITH FAMILY—17 YEARS

- Born, the firstborn son of Jacob's favorite wife, Rachel
- Travels with his family back to Canaan (age 6)
- Benjamin, his younger brother, born; Rachel dies
- Given a robe of many colors by his father, a symbol of his favored status (age 17)
- Given two dreams picturing him ruling over his family (age 17)
- Thrown in a pit by his brothers and sold to Midianite traders for 20 pieces of silver (age 17)

IN SLAVERY/PRISON IN EGYPT—13 YEARS

- Sold as a slave to Potiphar in Egypt (age 17)

The Lord was with Joseph (Gen 39:2)

- Promoted to Potiphar's personal attendant, in charge of the whole household
- Falsely accused of sexual misconduct by Potiphar's wife and imprisoned

The Lord was with Joseph (Gen 39:21)

- Given authority over everything under the prison warden
- Becomes personal attendant to Pharaoh's chief cupbearer and chief baker, also in custody (age 28)
- Interprets dreams of cupbearer and baker, which come true three days later (age 28)

WITH AUTHORITY IN EGYPT—80 YEARS

- Called before Pharaoh and interprets his two dreams about coming famine (age 30)
- Elevated to second-in-command over all of Egypt; given a wife, Asenath (age 30)
- Oversees collection of harvest in preparation for famine (age 30–37)
- Joseph's sons, Manasseh and Ephraim, are born
- Oversees the sale of grain during the famine (age 37–44)

71 Years with Family in Egypt

- Reconciled with brothers; reunited with father and family (age 39)
  - *Brothers come for grain; required to bring Benjamin; Simeon imprisoned*
  - *Jacob refuses to send Benjamin until grain runs out; Judah takes responsibility for Benjamin*
  - *Brothers return for grain with Benjamin; Joseph has silver cup placed in Benjamin's bag*
  - *Benjamin accused of theft and sentenced to slavery; Judah asks to substitute himself for Benjamin*
  - *Joseph reveals himself and forgives his brothers; invites his family to come to Egypt*
- Joseph's sons are claimed by Jacob as his own and blessed (age 56)
- Jacob dies and is buried in Canaan (age 56)
- Joseph dies and is buried in Egypt; his bones waiting to be returned to the promised land (age 110)

Exodus

Genre | **HISTORICAL NARRATIVE, LAW**

Recording the foundational event for the Israelite nation, the book of Exodus presents God's dramatic and miraculous intervention to save his people from bondage in Egypt for the sake of establishing them as his covenant people.

INTRODUCTION

AUTHOR The book of Exodus does not state who its author was. It does refer to occasions when Moses made a written record of events that took place and what God had said (17:14; 24:4,7; 34:27–28). The book also contains references to preserving and passing on information. Along with the other four books of the Pentateuch, it has long been considered to be primarily the work of Moses.

BACKGROUND Exodus picks up where the Genesis narrative ended with the death of Joseph around 1805 BC. It quickly moves us forward almost 300 years to a time in Egypt when the circumstances of Jacob's descendants had changed. The Israelites were serving as slaves during Egypt's Eighteenth Dynasty, probably under the pharaohs Thutmose and Amenhotep II. The Israelite slavery ended in 1446 BC. The book of Exodus records the events surrounding the exodus from Egypt and the Israelites' first year in the wilderness, including the giving of the law. The date of the exodus is disputed, but biblical evidence favors 1446 BC.

MESSAGE AND PURPOSE The book of Exodus shows God at work with the goal of having such close fellowship with people that he is described as dwelling among them. He rescued the Israelites in order to make himself known, not only by the exercise of his power but also through an ongoing covenant relationship based on his capacity for patience, grace, and forgiveness. The record of what the Lord did for the Israelites provided grounds for them to recognize him as their God who deserved their complete loyalty and obedience. This record would make clear to the Israelites their identity as God's people and would continue the display of his glorious identity.

SUMMARY The title "Exodus" is an anglicized version of a Greek word that means "departure," in recognition of one of the book's major events—the departure of God's people from Egypt. Exodus could be considered the central book in the Old Testament because it records God's act of saving the Israelites and establishing them as a covenant community, a nation chosen to serve and represent him. Exodus describes the enslavement and oppression of the Israelites; the preparation and call of Moses; the conflict between Yahweh, the God of Israel, and the gods of Egypt (represented by Pharaoh); the exodus of the Israelites; their establishment as a nation in covenant with the Lord; their rebellion; and the Lord's provision for their ongoing relationship, symbolized by his presence at the tabernacle they built for him.

STRUCTURE Exodus is considered a part of the Law, but it is more historical narrative than law. The book is structured around the life and travels of Moses. Sandwiched between the narratives of chapters 1–18 and 32–40 are the establishment of the covenant (chaps. 19–24) and the laws related to the tabernacle and priesthood (chaps. 25–31).

Outline

I. Oppression of God's People in Egypt (1:1–11:10)
   A. Egyptian slavery (1:1–22)
   B. Preparation of the deliverer (2:1–4:31)
   C. Struggles with the oppressor (5:1–11:10)

II. Deliverance of God's People from Egypt (12:1–14:31)
   A. Redemption by blood (12:1–51)
   B. Redemption by divine miracles (13:1–14:31)

III. Education of God's People in the Wilderness (15:1–18:27)
   A. Israel's song of victory (15:1–21)
   B. Testing and trials (15:22–17:16)
   C. Shared leadership under Moses (18:1–27)

IV. Consecration of God's People at Sinai (19:1–34:35)
   A. Acceptance of the law (19:1–31:18)
   B. Breaking of the law (32:1–35)
   C. Restoration of the law (33:1–34:35)

V. Worship of God's People in the Tabernacle (35:1–40:38)
   A. Gifts and workmen for the tabernacle (35:1–35)
   B. Construction and furnishings of the tabernacle (36:1–39:43)
   C. Filling of the tabernacle with God's glory (40:1–38)

WORD STUDY

'ehyeh 'asher 'ehyeh

Hebrew pronunciation: [eh YEH ah SHEHR eh YEH]

CSB translation: I AM WHO I AM

Uses in Exodus: 1
Uses in the OT: 1

Focus passage: Exodus 3:14

'Ehyeh 'asher 'ehyeh is God's statement as he revealed his preferred form of address to be *Yahweh* (Exod 3:14–16). *'Ehyeh* is the first-person form of the Hebrew verb meaning "to be." God may have spoken *'ehyeh 'asher 'ehyeh* as a name in answer to Moses's request in verse 13, but he certainly reduced the words to the name *'Ehyeh*, or *I AM* (v. 14). *Yahweh* seems to be an ancient form of the third-person form of "to be." The third person may have been most suitable for Israelites considering their God. Some scholars interpret *Yahweh* as a causative form like "He Causes to Be," but *'ehyeh 'asher 'ehyeh* favors a meaning like "He Is." Such a translation agrees with the NT portrayal of Christ as the eternally present One (John 8:56). *I AM WHO I AM* suggests God's sovereign freedom to be what he chooses to be.

Yahweh

Hebrew pronunciation: [YAH weh]

CSB translation: Lord, Yahweh

Uses in Exodus: 398
Uses in the OT: 6,828

Focus passage: Exodus 3:15

God told Moses, "I AM WHO I AM." Moses was to tell Israel, "I AM has sent me to you" (Exod 3:14). Then God replaced *I AM* with "***Yahweh***, the God of your fathers, the God of Abraham, the God of Isaac, and the God of Jacob . . . This is my name forever" (Exod 3:15). *Yahweh* is probably a third-person singular equivalent of *I AM*. Its pronunciation was almost lost because Jews considered it so holy that they replaced its vowels with those of other divine names. *Yahweh* communicates God's commitment to deliver Israel in ways that reveal his character. God did not reveal this name to the patriarchs (Exod 6:3), but *Yahweh* occurs in Genesis dialogue (Gen 14:22). Either the meaning was previously unknown, its significance had not been fully appreciated, or Genesis reflects later language. Moses's mother, Jochebed, might have a shortened form of *Yahweh* in her name (*Jo-*) if the name follows later practice.

pesach

Hebrew pronunciation: [peh SAHKH]

CSB translation: Passover

Uses in Exodus: 6
Uses in the OT: 49

Focus passage: Exodus 12:11,21,27,43,48

The first occurrence of ***pesach*** (Exod 12:11) refers either to the *Passover lamb* (Exod 12:21) or to the *Passover Festival* (Exod 12:48). Exodus 12 explains both. *Pesach* usually refers to the festival, but the reference to the *Passover lamb* occurs before and after the exile (Deut 16:2; Ezra 6:20), as well as into the NT era (1 Cor 5:7). The plural of *pesach* indicates the *Passover lambs* needed for the nation (2 Chr 35:6). People "slaughtered" (2 Chr 35:1) and "ate" (2 Chr 30:18) the lamb while "observing" the festival (2 Chr 35:1). *Pesach* seems related to the verb *pasach* ("pass over") in Exod 12:13,23,27. God mercifully *passes over* the people, doors, and houses.

The Route of the Exodus

LOWER EGYPT
Rameses (Qantir)
GOSHEN
On (Heliopolis)
Yam Suph ?
Wilderness of Shur
Yam Suph?
Wilderness of Paran
SINAI
Wilderness of Sin
Rephidim
GULF OF SUEZ
GULF OF AQABA
MIDIAN
RED SEA
AMALEK
Kadesh-barnea
Wilderness of Zin
EDOM (SEIR)
MOAB
CANAAN
AMMON
Jericho
Jerusalem
Heshbon

0 10 20 30 40 50 Miles
0 10 20 30 40 50 Kilometers

- City
- City (uncertain location)
- Mt. Sinai (possible locations)
- NORTHERN ROUTE
- CENTRAL ROUTE
- ALTERNATIVE CENTRAL ROUTE
- SOUTHERN ROUTE
- ALTERNATIVE ROUTE FROM JEBEL MUSA TO KADESH-BARNEA

Exodus–Leviticus Timeline

1500 BC

AARON (1529–1409?) / MOSES (1526–1406)

1570–1303
18th Dynasty of Egypt, includes Thutmose and Amenhotep, traditionally the pharaohs of oppression

1500
Egyptians develop effective pharmaceutical compounds

1500
Shoes worn in Mesopotamia

1500
Plows made of bronze developed in Asia

1500
Bellows used in making glass and in metallurgy

1500
Clay tablet map of the Babylonian city of Nippur

1400 BC

JOSHUA (1490?–1380?)

1479
Battle of Megiddo between Egyptian forces of Pharaoh Thutmose III and a Kadesh alliance, reestablishing Egyptian hegemony in the Levant

1479–1457
Queen Makare Hatshepsut, daughter of Thutmose I, reigned in Egypt during a period of peace and prosperity

1446
Exodus and defeat of Pharaoh at the Red Sea
1446
Passover instituted
1446
God's covenant at Sinai

1445
Tabernacle built and dedicated
1445
Events in Leviticus
1445
Exploration of Canaan by 12 spies

1400
Musical notation, Ugarit
1400
Water clocks invented

The Plagues

THE PLAGUE (OR EVENT)	EGYPT'S FALSE GODS*	SATAN'S COUNTERFEIT	PHARAOH'S HEART	"I AM THE LORD"	ISRAEL'S PROTECTION
AARON'S STAFF BECAME A SERPENT (Exod 7:8–13)	*Wadjet (the snake goddess)*	*Magicians' staffs became serpents, but swallowed by Aaron's staff*	*Pharaoh's heart hardened*	–	–
NILE RIVER TO BLOOD (Exod 7:14–25)	*Hapi (the god of the Nile flood)*	*Magicians also turned water to blood*	*Pharaoh's heart hardened*	*"You will know that I am the LORD" (7:17)*	*All the Egyptians dug for water*
FROGS (Exod 8:1–15)	*Heqet (the frog goddess)*	*Magicians also summoned frogs*	*Pharaoh hardened his heart*	*"There is no one like the LORD our God" (8:10)*	*Frogs only invaded Egyptian homes*
GNATS (Exod 8:16–19)	*Geb (the earth god)*	*Magicians unable to duplicate plague*	*Pharaoh's heart hardened*	*Magicians said, "This is the finger of God" (8:19)*	–
FLIES (Exod 8:20–32)	*Kheprer (the resurrection god, depicted as a beetle)*	–	*Pharaoh hardened his heart*	*"You will know that I, the LORD, am in the land" (8:22)*	*No flies in Goshen, where the Israelites lived*
DEATH OF LIVESTOCK (Exod 9:1–7)	*Apis (the chief bull god)*	–	*Pharaoh's heart was hardened*	–	*None of the Israelites' livestock died*
BOILS (Exod 9:8–12)	*Sekhmet (the patron goddess of physicians)*	*Magicians affected by boils, unable to stand*	*The Lord hardened Pharaoh's heart*	–	*Boils only on the Egyptians*
HAIL (Exod 9:13–35)	*Nut (the sky goddess)*	–	*Pharaoh hardened his heart*	*"The earth belongs to the LORD" (9:29)*	*No hail in Goshen, where the Israelites lived*
LOCUSTS (Exod 10:1–20)	*Min (the patron god of crops)*	–	*The Lord hardened Pharaoh's heart*	*"You will know that I am the LORD" (10:2)*	*Locusts only invaded Egyptian homes*
DARKNESS (Exod 10:21–29)	*Amon-Re (the sun god) and Pharaoh (the son of Re)*	–	*The Lord hardened Pharaoh's heart*	–	*All the Israelites had light where they lived*
DEATH OF THE FIRSTBORN (Exod 11:4–12:42)	*All the gods of Egypt, including Pharaoh's son (12:12)*	–	*The Lord hardened Pharaoh's heart*	*"I am the LORD" (12:12)*	*God passed over the Israelites' houses marked with blood*
THE CROSSING OF THE RED SEA (Exod 13:17–14:31)	*Pharaoh and the Egyptian army*	*Pharaoh's army swallowed by the waters of the Red Sea*	*The Lord hardened Pharaoh's heart*	*"The Egyptians will know that I am the LORD" (14:4)*	*The Israelites walked through the sea on dry ground*

**The Egyptian gods listed here are possible false gods being confronted by the plagues, but certainty is beyond us.*

The Ten Commandments

The first and greatest commandment: Love the Lord your God with all your heart, soul, and mind (Matt 22:37–38; see Deut 6:5).

VERTICAL COMMANDMENTS

FIRST	No Other Gods *(Exod 20:3)*	The Israelites needed to understand that God was to be the exclusive recipient of their worship.
SECOND	No Idols *(Exod 20:4–6)*	God is to be worshipped as he is, not as an image of what people can create.
THIRD	Don't Misuse the Lord's Name *(Exod 20:7)*	God's name is to be revered, not used flippantly.
FOURTH	Remember the Sabbath *(Exod 20:8–11)*	The people were to set aside one day of the week—the Sabbath—as an act of devotion and worship to God.

The second greatest commandment: Love your neighbor as yourself (Matt 22:39; see Lev 19:18,34).

HORIZONTAL COMMANDMENTS

FIFTH	SIXTH	SEVENTH
Honor Your Parents *(Exod 20:12)*	Do Not Murder *(Exod 20:13)*	Do Not Commit Adultery *(Exod 20:14)*
If we love our parents, we will give them the honor they are due.	If we love our neighbor, we will not seek to harm or kill them.	If we love our neighbor, we will not seek an adulterous relationship with someone else.

EIGHTH	NINTH	TENTH
Do Not Steal *(Exod 20:15)*	Do Not Lie *(Exod 20:16)*	Do Not Covet *(Exod 20:17)*
If we love our neighbor, we will respect what God has given them.	If we love our neighbor, we will not lie about them to get them in trouble or to take advantage of them.	If we love our neighbor, we will not be envious of their relationships or their property.

The Tabernacle

EDEN		THE TABERNACLE
Genesis 3:8	God's Presence	Exodus 40
Genesis 3:24	East-Facing Entrance	Numbers 3:38
Genesis 3:24	Guarded by Cherubim	Exodus 26:31–35 (Cherubim Embroidered in the Veil)
Genesis 2:9	Tree of Life	Exodus 25:31–40 (the Golden Lampstand)

INSTRUCTIONS		CONSTRUCTION
Exodus 25:10–22	The Ark and Mercy Seat	Exodus 37:1–9
25:23–30	The Table and Utensils	37:10–16
25:31–40	The Lampstand and Utensils	37:17–24
26:1–37	The Tabernacle Tent	36:8–38
27:1–8	The Altar and Utensils	38:1–7
27:9–19	The Tabernacle Courtyard	38:9–20
28:1–43	The Priestly Garments	39:1–31
30:1–10	The Incense Altar	37:25–28
30:17–21	The Bronze Basin with Stand	38:8
30:22–38	The Anointing Oil and Incense	37:29

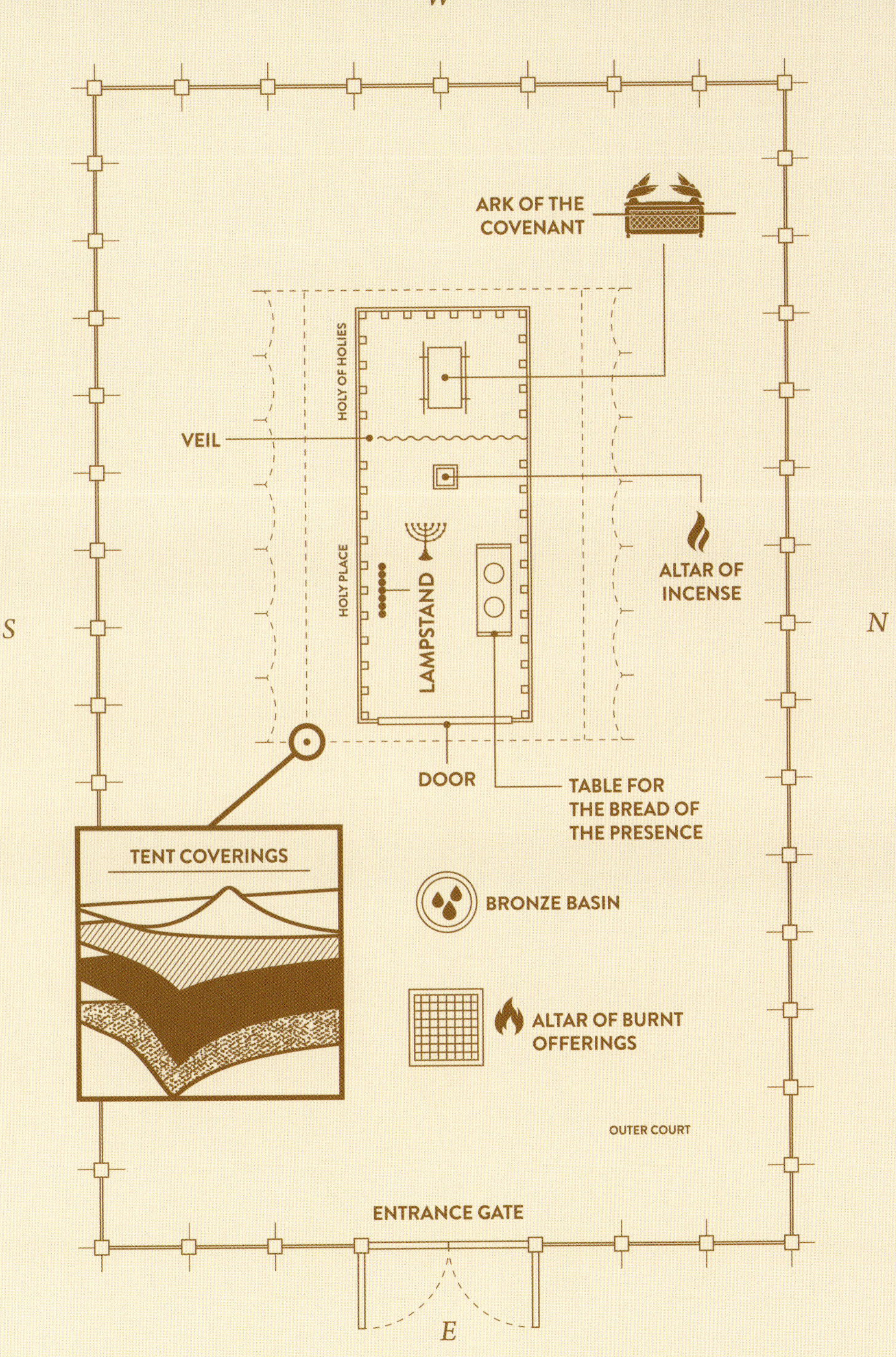

- God showed Moses the pattern for the tabernacle and all its furnishings (Exod 25:9).
- God filled Bezalel and Oholiab with wisdom and skill to complete the work and to teach others who also were given wisdom and skill for the construction of the tabernacle (Exod 35:30–36:2).
- The people of Israel did according to all that the Lord had commanded Moses (Exod 39:32).

Moses's Life

0

Born (Exod 2)

3 Months

- Placed in a basket in the Nile River; found by Pharaoh's daughter (Exod 2)
- Nursed by his mother (Exod 2)
- Later weaned and given to Pharaoh's daughter as her son (Exod 2)

40 Years

- Killed an Egyptian taskmaster beating a Hebrew slave (Exod 2; cp. Acts 7:23–24)
- Fled to Midian (Exod 2)
- Married Zipporah (Exod 2)
- Son Gershom born (Exod 2), and later Eliezer (Exod 18)

80

- Met with Yahweh at the burning bush (Exod 3–4; cp. Acts 7:30)
- Returned to Egypt to confront Pharaoh with the plagues (Exod 4–12)
- The first Passover (Exod 12)
- The exodus and crossing the Red Sea (Exod 12–14)
- Led the Israelites to Mount Sinai (Exod 15–19)
  - *Bitter water made drinkable (Exod 15)*
  - *Manna, bread from heaven, and quail provided (Exod 16)*
  - *Water from the rock (Exod 17)*
  - *The Israelites defeated the Amalekites (Exod 17)*
- Yahweh gave the Ten Commandments and his ordinances (Exod 20–23)
- The covenant ceremony (Exod 24)
- Yahweh gave instructions for the tabernacle and priesthood (Exod 25–31)
- The Israelites worshipped the golden calf (Exod 32)
- Moses witnessed God's glory (Exod 34)

81

- Construction of the tabernacle completed and consecrated (Exod 40)
- Yahweh gave laws and the instructions for sacrifices (Lev 1–Num 10)
- Led the Israelites to the southern edge of the promised land (Num 10)
  - *Miriam and Aaron rebelled against Moses's leadership (Num 12)*
- The Israelites rebelled and rejected the promised land (Num 13–14)
- The Israelites condemned to wander in the wilderness for 40 years (Num 14)
- The Israelites rebelled and were defeated in the promised land (Num 14)

81–119

- Led the people for 38 years in the wilderness (Num 14; 20; 33)
  - *Korah's rebellion (Num 16)*

119

- Miriam's death (Num 20)
- Second water from the rock/Moses and Aaron's disobedience (Num 20)
- Aaron's death (Num 20)
- The Israelites complained/bronze snake (Num 21)
- The Israelites defeated Sihon and the Amorites (Num 21)
- The Israelites defeated Og and the people of Bashan (Num 21)
- Led the Israelites to the eastern edge of the promised land (Num 22)
- Balaam hired to curse Israel, but God turned to blessing (Num 22–24)
- The Israelites rebelled and worshipped Baal of Peor—the work of Balaam (Num 25)
- Joshua chosen to succeed Moses (Num 27)
- The Israelites defeated Midian/killed Balaam (Num 31)

120

- Second proclamation of the law (Deut)
- Moses allowed to see the promised land but not enter it (Deut 3)
- Moses's death on Mount Nebo (Deut 34)

MOSES, A PROPHET	JESUS, THE PROPHET
A very humble man (Num 12:3)	A very humble God-man (Phil 2:5–8)
A faithful servant in God's household (Num 12:7)	A faithful Son over God's household (Heb 3:1–6)
Spoke with the Lord face to face (Exod 33:11)	The face of God's glory (2 Cor 4:6)
Veiled his radiant face, hiding the fading glory (Exod 34:29–35)	Removes the veil, revealing God's everlasting glory (2 Cor 3:13–18)
An unparalleled prophet (Deut 34:10–12)	The promised Prophet (Deut 18:18–19; Acts 3:22–26)

MOSES, A MEDIATOR	JESUS, THE MEDIATOR
Represented God before the people (Exod 20:19) and the people before God (Exod 18:19); interceded for the Israelites (Exod 32; Num 12; 14; 16; 21)	The one Mediator between God and humanity (1 Tim 2:5–6); always lives to intercede for those who come to God through him (Rom 8:34; Heb 7:25)
Mediator of the old covenant (Exod 24:8)	Mediator of the new covenant (Heb 9:15)

Seeing Jesus in the Exodus

YAHWEH, THE LORD "I AM" (Exod 3:14–15)	JESUS "I AM" (John 8:58)
Moses A Mediator *(Exod 32:11–14)*	**Jesus** The One Mediator *(1 Tim 2:5–6)*
Moses A Prophet *(Deut 18:18–19)*	**Jesus** The Prophet *(Acts 3:22–26)*
Israel, God's Firstborn Son Called Out of Egypt *(Exod 4:22–23)*	**Christ, God's Firstborn Son** The Fulfillment *(Matt 2:15)*
The Passover Lamb Protection from the Plague *(Exod 12)*	**Christ, Our Passover** Purification from Sin *(1 Cor 5:7–8)*
Manna Bread from Heaven *(Exod 16)*	**Jesus** The Bread of Life *(John 6)*
The Rock in the Wilderness Struck to Satisfy the People's Thirst *(Exod 17)*	**Jesus** The Rock Struck for Our Salvation *(1 Cor 10:4)*
The Law Given through Moses *(Exod 20–24)*	**Grace and Truth** Come through Jesus Christ *(John 1:17)*
The Tabernacle God's Temporary Dwelling Place with Israel *(Exod 40)*	**Jesus** The Word Became Flesh and Dwelt among Us *(John 1:14)*
Balaam's Blessing A Star from Jacob; a Scepter from Israel *(Num 24:17)*	**Jesus's Birth** Born King of the Jews, Heralded by a Star *(Matt 2:2)*
The Law's Curse Anyone Hung on a Tree Is Under God's Curse *(Deut 21:22–23)*	**The Gospel's Blessing** Christ Became a Curse for Us to Redeem Us *(Gal 3:13–14)*

The Ten Commandments throughout Scripture

COMMANDMENT	PASSAGE	RELATED OLD TESTAMENT PASSAGES	RELATED NEW TESTAMENT PASSAGES	JESUS'S TEACHINGS
You Shall Have No Other Gods before Me	*Exod 20:3; Deut 5:7*	*Exod 34:14; Deut 6:4, 13–14; 2 Kgs 17:35; Ps 81:9; Jer 25:6; 35:15*	*Acts 5:29*	*Matt 4:10; 6:33; 22:37–40*
You Shall Not Make for Yourself an Idol	*Exod 20:4–6; Deut 5:8–10*	*Exod 20:23; 32:8; 34:17; Lev 19:4; 26:1; Deut 4:15–20; 7:25; 32:21; Ps 115:4–7; Isa 44:12–20*	*Acts 17:29; 1 Cor 8:4–6, 10–13; 1 John 5:21*	*Matt 6:24; Luke 16:13*
You Shall Not Misuse the Name of the Lord	*Exod 20:7; Deut 5:11*	*Exod 22:28; Lev 18:21; 19:12; 22:2; 24:16; Ezek 39:7*	*Rom 2:23–24; Jas 5:12*	*Matt 5:33–37; 6:9; 23:16–22*
Remember the Sabbath Day by Keeping It Holy	*Exod 20:8–11; Deut 5:12–15*	*Gen 2:3; Exod 16:23–30; 31:13–16; 35:2–3; Lev 19:30; Isa 56:2; Jer 17:21–27*	*Acts 20:7; Heb 10:25*	*Matt 12:1–13; Mark 2:23–27; 3:1–6; Luke 6:1–11; John 5:1–18*
Honor Your Father and Your Mother	*Exod 20:12; Deut 5:16*	*Exod 21:17; Lev 19:3; Deut 21:18–21; 27:16; Prov 6:20*	*Eph 6:1–3; Col 3:20*	*Matt 15:4–6; 19:19; Mark 7:9–13; Luke 2:51; 18:20; John 19:26–27*
You Shall Not Murder	*Exod 20:13; Deut 5:17*	*Gen 9:6; Lev 24:17; Num 35:33*	*Rom 13:9–10; 1 Pet 4:15*	*Matt 5:21–24; 19:18; 26:52; Mark 10:19; Luke 18:20*
You Shall Not Commit Adultery	*Exod 20:14; Deut 5:18*	*Lev 18:20; 20:10; Num 5:12–31; Deut 22:22; Prov 6:29,32*	*Rom 13:9–10; 1 Cor 6:9; Heb 13:4; Jas 2:11*	*Matt 5:27–30; 19:18; Mark 10:19; Luke 18:20; John 8:1–11*
You Shall Not Steal	*Exod 20:15; Deut 5:19*	*Lev 19:11,13; Ezek 18:7*	*Rom 13:9–10; Eph 4:28; Jas 5:4*	*Matt 19:18; Mark 10:19; 12:40; Luke 18:20*
You Shall Not Give False Testimony	*Exod 20:16; Deut 5:20*	*Exod 23:1,7; Lev 19:11; Pss 15:2; 101:5; Prov 10:18; Jer 9:3–5; Zech 8:16*	*Eph 4:25,31; Col 3:9; Titus 3:2*	*Matt 5:37; 19:18; Mark 10:19; Luke 18:20*
You Shall Not Covet	*Exod 20:17; Deut 5:21*	*Deut 7:25; Job 31:24–28; Ps 62:10*	*Rom 7:7; 13:9; Eph 5:3–5; Heb 13:5; Jas 4:1–2*	*Luke 12:15–34*

Leviticus

Genre | **HISTORICAL NARRATIVE, LAW**

After the Israelites are constituted as a holy people by God, the book of Leviticus provides instructions for how they are to maintain their holiness morally and ceremonially.

INTRODUCTION

AUTHOR Although the book of Leviticus is technically anonymous, the evidence from the Bible and from Jewish and Christian traditions attributes it to the lawgiver Moses (cp. 18:5 with Rom 10:5). Moses was the chief recipient of God's revelation in the book of Leviticus (1:1; 4:1). Elsewhere, Moses is said to have written down revelation that he received (Exod 24:4; 34:28; Mark 10:4–5; 12:19; John 1:45; 5:46).

BACKGROUND About one year passed from the time the Israelites arrived at Sinai until they departed (Exod 19:1; Num 10:11). During that time, Moses received the covenant from the Lord, erected the tabernacle (Exod 40:17), and received all the instructions in Leviticus and in the early chapters of Numbers. This block of material is the continuous narrative extending from Exodus 19 through Leviticus to Numbers 10:11.

MESSAGE AND PURPOSE The message and purpose of Leviticus must be studied in the context of the redemption of Israel from Egypt (Exod 12), the covenant made with Israel (Exod 20–24), and the building of the tent of meeting, or the tabernacle (Exod 25–40). The Lord dwelled among Israel symbolically in the tent of meeting, which stood in the center of the camp's tribal arrangement. In order for the Lord to reside with Israel, it was imperative that the people maintain a holy character and ethical behavior (Lev 11:44–45; 19:2; Deut 23:14; 1 Pet 1:15–16). The purpose of Leviticus was to instruct Israel in holiness so that the Lord might abide among them and bless them.

SUMMARY The book's name comes from the Septuagint (the Greek translation of the Old Testament): "relating to the Levites." This third section of the Pentateuch deals primarily with the duties of the priests and the service of the tabernacle, but it contains other laws as well. Leviticus gives regulations for worship, laws on ceremonial cleanness, moral laws, and holy days.

STRUCTURE Leviticus is primarily a collection of laws, with a little historical narrative. The laws contained in Leviticus can be divided into two groups. First are the commands, or apodictic law. These are both positive commands ("You must . . .") and negative commands ("You must not . . ."). The second type of law is casuistic law. These are case laws using an example of what to do if such and such happened ("If someone . . ."). Some scholars seek to divide the laws further into civil laws, moral laws, and ceremonial laws, but there is no evidence that the Israelites made such a distinction.

Outline

- **I. Laws on Sacrifices and the Priesthood (1:1–7:38)**
  - A. Instructions on different offerings (1:1–6:7)
  - B. Regulations for the priests (6:8–7:38)
- **II. Ordination and Ministry of the Priests (8:1–10:20)**
  - A. Consecration of Aaron (8:1–36)
  - B. Dedication of the tabernacle (9:1–24)
  - C. Warning about immoral priests (10:1–20)
- **III. Laws on Purity (11:1–16:34)**
  - A. Clean and unclean animals (11:1–47)
  - B. Purification for uncleanness (12:1–15:33)
  - C. Regulations for the Day of Atonement (16:1–34)
- **IV. God's Requirements for Holiness (17:1–27:34)**
  - A. Reverence for blood (17:1–16)
  - B. Obedience to the Lord's commands (18:1–22:33)
  - C. Appropriate worship (23:1–26:46)
  - D. Making and keeping vows (27:1–34)

WORD STUDY

qarav

Hebrew pronunciation: [khah RAV]

CSB translation: draw near, present, bring

Uses in Leviticus: 102
Uses in the OT: 280

Focus passage: Leviticus 1:2–3,5,10, 13–15

Qarav, related to *qorban* (*offering*), means *draw* (*come, go, be*) *near, approach* (Gen 47:29). People *come* (*forward, closer, here*). They *get close, step in, advance, approach*, or *reach*. *Qarab* denotes *take place* (Isa 5:19) and *support* (1 Kgs 2:7). People *are about* to act (Gen 12:11) and *are* sexually *intimate* (Deut 22:14). Intensive verbs mean *join* (Ezek 37:17) and *draw* (Hos 7:6). People *submit* cases (Isa 41:21). Causative verbs signify *bring* (*near, forward*), *present, offer*, or *have/let come* (*near, forward*). They imply *join* or *invite* (Jer 30:21). *Qarob* (75x) means *near* (Num 24:17), *close, approaching, soon, brief, almost*, or *just*. It connotes *relative* or *neighbor*. *Qareb* (12x) involves *being about* to (Deut 20:3), *coming* (*near, closer*), *approaching*, or *drawing near*. *Qerab* (9x) is *battle* (Zech 14:3), *war*, or *warfare*. *Qirbah* is *nearness* (Isa 58:2) or *presence*. Another *qarob* (2x) is *warrior* (Ezek 23:5).

kaphar

Hebrew pronunciation: [kah FAR]

CSB translation: cover, make atonement, purge

Uses in Leviticus: 49
Uses in the OT: 102

Focus passage: Leviticus 16:29–34

Akkadian and Arabic cognates mean "wipe on," "wipe away," or "cover." ***Kaphar*** as *cover* occurs with *koper, asphalt* (Gen 6:14). Elsewhere *kaphar* uses other conjugations with different meanings. The intensive verb means *make/provide atonement* (Exod 29:36), *atone for* (Ps 65:3; Dan 9:24), or *wipe out* (1 Sam 3:14). It suggests *appease* (Gen 32:20), *ward off* (Isa 47:11), or *wipe away the guilt of* (Deut 21:8). It denotes *make atonement* or *make atonement for* (Lev 16:10,16). Passive forms also indicate *be atoned for* (Isa 27:9), *dissolved* (Isa 28:18), or *wiped away responsibility* (Deut 21:8). Some verbs connote "ransom" and could possibly derive from a homonym *koper*, "ransom." But this connotation could have developed secondarily because cleansing so often came through substitutionary sacrifice. *Capporet* (27x) indicates *mercy seat* (Lev 16:13), the place of atonement. *Kippuriym* (8x) is *atonement* (Lev 25:9).

qodesh

Hebrew pronunciation: [koh DESH]

CSB translation: sacred, holy, sanctuary

Uses in Leviticus: 92
Uses in the OT: 470

Focus passage: Leviticus 23:2–4, 7–8,20–21,24,27,35–37

This noun regularly functions adjectivally as *holy, sacred, dedicated*, or *consecrated* (Exod 3:5; 12:16; 31:15; Lev 19:24). It denotes *sanctuary* (Exod 28:29) or various parts such as *holy place, sanctuary area*, or *most holy place* (Exod 26:33; 28:43; Lev 16:16). ***Qodesh*** occurs twice in a row to indicate superlatives: *most holy place, especially holy*, and *holiest part* (Exod 26:34; 30:10; Lev 2:3). Singular uses suggest *holiness, what is holy*, or *holy portion* (Exod 15:11; Lev 19:8; Num 6:20). With numbers *qodesh* connotes *holy ones* (Deut 33:2). Plurals can signify *holy offerings, gifts, things*, or *objects* (Exod 28:38; Lev 5:15; Num 4:16). Implicit in *qodesh* are concepts of separateness and consecration (Ezek 42:20). *Holiness* is associated with glory and commands respect or awe (Exod 15:11). God is *holy* as separated from sin. *Holy* things and people belong to God, being set apart from common use (Exod 39:30) for his consecrated purposes (Lev 10:17).

KEY VERSE

"For the life of a creature is in the blood,
and I have appointed it to you to make atonement
on the altar for your lives, since it
is the lifeblood that makes atonement."

LEVITICUS 17:11

KEY QUOTE

The blood has its rich symbolism in sacrifice, first, because it stands for death, secondly because it stands for the death of an individual, substitutionary person, and thirdly because it stands for a death involving suffering.

GEERHARDUS VOS[1]

The Ten Commandments in Leviticus

NO.	EXODUS 20:2–17	LEVITICUS 19
I–II	I am the LORD your God, who brought you out of the land of Egypt, out of the place of slavery. Do not have other gods besides me. Do not make an idol for yourself, whether in the shape of anything in the heavens above or on the earth below or in the waters under the earth. Do not bow in worship to them, and do not serve them; for I, the LORD your God, am a jealous God, bringing the consequences of the fathers' iniquity on the children to the third and fourth generations of those who hate me, but showing faithful love to a thousand generations of those who love me and keep my commands (vv. 2–6).	Do not turn to worthless idols or make cast images of gods for yourselves; I am the LORD your God (v. 4).
III	Do not misuse the name of the LORD your God, because the LORD will not leave anyone unpunished who misuses his name (v. 7).	Do not swear falsely by my name, profaning the name of your God; I am the LORD (v. 12).
IV	Remember the Sabbath day, to keep it holy: You are to labor six days and do all your work, but the seventh day is a Sabbath to the LORD your God. You must not do any work—you, your son or daughter, your male or female servant, your livestock, or the resident alien who is within your city gates. For the LORD made the heavens and the earth, the sea, and everything in them in six days; then he rested on the seventh day. Therefore the LORD blessed the Sabbath day and declared it holy (vv. 8–11).	You are to keep my Sabbaths; I am the LORD your God (v. 3b).
V	Honor your father and your mother so that you may have a long life in the land that the LORD your God is giving you (v. 12).	Each of you is to respect his mother and father (v. 3a).
VI	Do not murder (v. 13).	Do do not jeopardize your neighbor's life; I am the LORD (v. 16b).
VII	Do not commit adultery (v. 14).	Do not debase your daughter by making her a prostitute, or the land will be prostituted and filled with depravity (v. 29).
VIII	Do not steal (v. 15).	Do not steal (v. 11a).
IX	Do not give false testimony against your neighbor (v. 16).	Do not go about spreading slander among your people (v. 16a).
X	Do not covet your neighbor's house. Do not covet your neighbor's wife, his male or female servant, his ox or donkey, or anything that belongs to your neighbor (v. 17).	Do not take revenge or bear a grudge against members of your community, but love your neighbor as yourself; I am the LORD (v. 18).

Hebrew Feasts

NAME	JEWISH CALENDAR (CHRISTIAN CALENDAR)	SCRIPTURE REFERENCE	SIGNIFICANCE
Passover	14–21 Nisan (March/April)	Exodus 12:2–20; Leviticus 23:5	Commemorates God's deliverance of Israel out of Egypt.
Feast of Unleavened Bread	15–21 Nisan (March/April)	Leviticus 23:6–8	Commemorates God's deliverance of Israel out of Egypt. Includes a day of firstfruits for the barley harvest.
Feast of Weeks, or Harvest (Pentecost)	6 Sivan (May/June) (seven weeks after Passover)	Exodus 23:16; 34:22; Leviticus 23:15–21	Commemorates the giving of the law at Mount Sinai. Includes a day of firstfruits for the wheat harvest.
Feast of Trumpets (Rosh Hashanah)	1 Tishri (September/October)	Leviticus 23:23–25; Numbers 29:1–6	Day of the blowing of the trumpets to signal the beginning of the civil new year.
Day of Atonement (Yom Kippur)	10 Tishri (September/October)	Leviticus 23:26–33; Exodus 30:10	On this day the high priest makes atonement for the nation's sin. Also a day of fasting.
Feast of Booths, or Tabernacles (Sukkot)	15–21 Tishri (September/October)	Leviticus 23:33–43; Numbers 29:12–39; Deuteronomy 16:13	Commemorates the forty years of wilderness wandering.
Feast of Dedication, or Festival of Lights (Hanukkah)	25–30 Kislev (November/December) and 1–2 Tebeth (December/January)	John 10:22	Commemorates the purification of the temple by Judas Maccabeus in 164 BC.
Feast of Purim, or Esther	14 Adar (February/March)	Esther 9	Commemorates the deliverance of the Jewish people in the days of Esther.

Priests of Israel

NAME	REFERENCE	IDENTIFICATION
Aaron	*Exodus 28–29*	Older brother of Moses; first high priest of Israel
Abiathar	*1 Samuel 22:20–23; 2 Samuel 20:25*	Son of Ahimelech who escaped the slayings at Nob
Abihu	*See* Nadab and Abihu	
Ahimelech	*1 Samuel 21–22*	Led a priestly community; killed by Saul for befriending David
Amariah	*2 Chronicles 19:11*	High priest during the reign of Jehoshaphat
Amaziah	*Amos 7:10–17*	Evil priest of Bethel; confronted Amos the prophet
Azariah	*2 Chronicles 26:16–20*	High priest who stood against Uzziah, who acted as a prophet
Eleazar and Ithamar	*Leviticus 10:6; Numbers 20:26*	Godly sons of Aaron; Eleazar—Israel's second high priest
Eli	*1 Samuel 1–4*	Descendant of Ithamar; raised Samuel at Shiloh
Eliashib	*Nehemiah 3:1; 13:4–5*	High priest during the time of Nehemiah
Elishama and Jehoram	*2 Chronicles 17:7–9*	Teaching priests during the reign of Jehoshaphat
Ezra	*Ezra 7–10; Nehemiah 8*	Scribe, teacher, and priest during the rebuilding of Jerusalem
Hilkiah	*2 Kings 22–23*	High priest during the reign of Josiah
Hophni and Phinehas	*1 Samuel 2:12–36*	Evil sons of Eli
Ithamar	*See* Eleazar and Ithamar	
Jahaziel	*2 Chronicles 20:14–17*	Levite who assured Jehoshaphat of deliverance from an enemy
Jehoiada	*2 Kings 11–12*	High priest who saved Joash from Queen Athaliah's purge
Jehoram	*See* Elishama and Jehoram	
Joshua	*Haggai 1:1; Zechariah 3*	First high priest after the Babylonian captivity
Nadab and Abihu	*Leviticus 10:1–2*	Evil sons of Aaron
Pashhur	*Jeremiah 20:1–6*	False priest who persecuted the prophet Jeremiah
Phinehas	*Numbers 25:7–13*	Son of Eleazar; Israel's third high priest who stopped a plague
Shelemiah	*Nehemiah 13:13*	Priest during Nehemiah's time; administrated storehouses
Uriah	*2 Kings 16:10–16*	Priest who built a pagan altar for evil King Ahaz
Zadok	*2 Samuel 15; 1 Kings 1*	High priest during the reigns of David and Solomon

Atonement Sacrifices

OFFERING	THE SACRIFICES	SOME DISTINCTIONS	CONTEXTUAL SIGNIFICANCE	FULFILLMENT IN CHRIST'S ATONEMENT
Burnt Offering *(Lev 1; 6:8–13)*	Bull, ram, male goat, turtledoves or pigeons. **UNBLEMISHED**	A whole burnt offering for atonement. The skin belonged to the priest.	Voluntary. Signified propitiation for sin and complete surrender, devotion, and commitment to God.	By his own shed blood on the cross, Jesus gave himself completely for us and obtained our eternal redemption *(Heb 9:12)*.
Grain Offering *(Lev 2; 6:14–23)*	Grain, fine flour, or bread. Offered or made with olive oil, frankincense, and salt. **UNLEAVENED**	A memorial portion (and all the frankincense) burned on the altar. The rest was for the priests.	Voluntary. Signified thanksgiving for firstfruits.	Jesus described his sacrificial death as a service and a blessing, like the death of a grain for the sake of producing a large crop *(John 12:24)*.
Fellowship or Peace Offering *(Lev 3; 7:11–36)*	Any animal from the herd or flock. **UNBLEMISHED**	The fat and certain organs burned on the altar. The rest was for a meal for the offerer and priests.	Voluntary. Symbolized fellowship with God.	Jesus's blood reconciles sinners to one another and to God; he is our peace *(Eph 2:11–14)*.
Sin Offering *(Lev 4:1–5:13; 6:24–30)*	Various animals depending on role and economic status. **UNBLEMISHED**	The fat burned on the altar for atonement for unintentional sins. The rest was for the priests.	Mandatory. Made by one who had sinned unintentionally or was unclean in order to attain purification.	The sin offering burnt outside the camp prefigured Jesus's death on the cross outside the gates of Jerusalem to sanctify the people *(Heb 13:11–12)*.
Restitution or Guilt Offering *(Lev 5:14–6:7; 7:1–6)*	A ram. **UNBLEMISHED**	The fat and certain organs burned on the altar. The rest, plus a fifth of restitution, was for the priests.	Mandatory. Made by a person who had either deprived another of his rights or had desecrated something holy.	Jesus's bloody death cleanses the conscience of a sinner who trusts in him *(Heb 9:13–4)*.

Numbers

Genre | **HISTORICAL NARRATIVE, LAW**

The book of Numbers is primarily a narrative of the Israelites' stay in the wilderness with some laws and regulations interspersed.

INTRODUCTION

AUTHOR As with the other books in the Pentateuch, Numbers is anonymous, but Moses is a central character throughout. Moses kept a journal (33:2), and the phrase "The LORD spoke to Moses" is used over 40 times. It is possible that a few portions were later added by scribes, such as the reference to Moses's humility (12:3) and the reference to the "Book of the LORD's Wars" (21:14). Moses remains the primary writer.

BACKGROUND Numbers continues the historical narrative begun in Exodus. It picks up one month after the close of Exodus (Exod 40:2; Num 1:1), which is about one year after the Israelites' departure from Egypt. Numbers covers the remaining 39 years of the Israelites' stay in the wilderness, from Sinai to Kadesh, and finally to the plains on the eastern side of the Jordan River.

MESSAGE AND PURPOSE The principal character in the book of Numbers is Yahweh, the God of Israel. God accomplished his will even when his people rebelled. He is holy and pure, and he requires such behavior from those who claim him as their God. This is a central theme of the Pentateuch and the book of Numbers. God promised Abram that he would produce a great nation through him (Gen 12:2) and give his descendants the land of the Canaanites and Amorites (Gen 15:1,8–21; 17:8). The two censuses show God's fulfillment of the first promise. The granting of territory to two and a half tribes in Transjordan is the beginning of the land fulfillment.

SUMMARY The English title "Numbers" derives from the Septuagint name "Arithmoi," based on the two military censuses in chapters 1 and 26. The Hebrew title, *Bemidbar*, "In the Wilderness," describes the geographical setting of much of the book—from the Wilderness of Sinai to the arid plains of Moab, across the Jordan River from Jericho.

STRUCTURE The book consists of seven cycles of material, with the repetition of the following types of material: (1) a statement of the historical setting, (2) reference to the twelve tribes of Israel and their respective leaders, (3) matters related to the priests and Levites, and (4) laws for defining the nature of the faithful community. This book of the Pentateuch is primarily narrative with portions of case law interwoven into a vibrant literary fabric.

Outline

I. **First Census and Consecration of Israel at Sinai (1:1–6:27)**
   A. Numbering and arrangement of the people (1:1–2:34)
   B. Choosing of the Levites (3:1–4:49)
   C. Cleansing and blessing of the people (5:1–6:27)

II. **Preparation for Departure to the Promised Land (7:1–10:36)**
   A. Gifts of the tribal leaders (7:1–89)
   B. Consecration of the Levites (8:1–26)
   C. Observance of the Passover (9:1–14)
   D. Movement of the camp (9:15–10:36)

III. **From Mount Sinai to Kadesh (11:1–15:41)**
   A. Disobedience of the people (11:1–14:45)
   B. Miscellaneous instructions and laws (15:1–41)

IV. **Rebellion against Aaron's Priesthood (16:1–19:22)**
   A. Judgment of Korah, Dathan, and Abiram (16:1–17:13)
   B. Duties and revenues of priests and Levites (18:1–32)
   C. Ordinance of the red cow (19:1–22)

V. **From Kadesh to the Plains of Moab (20:1–25:18)**
   A. Rebellion and judgment of Moses and Aaron (20:1–29)
   B. Judgment and healing via snakes (21:1–35)
   C. Balaam's efforts to curse Israel (22:1–24:25)
   D. Campaign of Phinehas against idolatry (25:1–18)

VI. **Second Census and Preparation of the New Generation (26:1–30:16)**
   A. Another counting of Israel (26:1–65)
   B. Inheritance for Zelophehad's daughters (27:1–23)
   C. Instructions to the new generation (28:1–30:16)

VII. **Preparation for Entering the Promised Land (31:1–36:13)**
   A. Vengeance against the Midianites (31:1–54)
   B. Settlement of tribes beyond the Jordan (32:1–42)
   C. Journey from Egypt summarized (33:1–49)
   D. Instructions for division of Canaan (33:50–34:29)
   E. Levitical cities and havens of refuge (35:1–34)
   F. Laws of female inheritance amended (36:1–13)

WORD STUDY

qin'ah

Hebrew pronunciation: [kin AH]

CSB translation: jealousy

Uses in Numbers: 9

Uses in the OT: 43

Focus passage: Numbers 5:14–15,18,25, 29–30

Qin'ah represents *jealousy* (23x, Ezek 5:13), *zeal* (14x, Isa 9:7), or *envy* (2x, Isa 11:13). Two forms of *qin'ah* occur in Ezekiel 8:3. One instance connotes that which is *offensive*; the second means *jealousy*. *Qin'ah* refers to *jealous fury* (Ezek 23:25), *anger* (Ps 119:139), and *jealousy* (Song 8:6). Seven times (Num 25:11) it occurs with related *qinne'* (34x), *be envious* or *jealous* (Gen 26:14; 37:11). People wrongly *envy* others (Prov 23:17). They *are* also *zealous* (1 Kgs 19:14) or *jealous* (Num 11:29) for God. The infinitive indicates *zeal* (2 Sam 21:2). Causative verbs denote *provoke jealousy* or to have jealous anger (Deut 32:16). *Qanna'* (6x, Exod 20:5) and *qano'* (2x, Josh 24:19) both describe God as *jealous*. *Jealousy*, central to his nature (Exod 34:14), was aroused particularly by Israel's worship of false gods (Deut 32:16). He resembled a justly *jealous* husband (Num 5:14–15).

charah

Hebrew pronunciation: [khah RAH]

CSB translation: burn, be angry

Uses in Numbers: 11

Uses in the OT: 93

Focus passage: Numbers 11:1,10,33

Charah has *'ap* ("anger, nose") as its subject 55 times so that *anger burns* (Job 19:11) and people become *incensed* (Num 22:22), *enraged* (Exod 32:19), or *infuriated* (2 Sam 12:5). God's anger *burns* and he sends literal fire (Num 11:1). *Charah* alone denotes *be angry* or *incensed* (Gen 18:30; 31:36). This anger can *be against* someone (1 Chr 13:10). *Charah* connotes *burning* with anxiety or *being agitated* (Ps 37:1). People *burn* with zeal when *competing* or *excelling* (Jer 12:5; 22:15). Once *charah* appears as *diligently* to modify another verb (Neh 3:20). *Charah* in Scripture most often refers to God who *is angry* at human sins. *Charon* (41x) occurs 34 times with *'ap* as *burning anger* (Num 25:4). *Charon* suggests *wrath* (Ezek 7:12), *burning* (Ps 58:9), *anger*, *fury*, and *burning wrath*. *Choriy* (6x) with *'ap* suggests *outburst of* (*fierce, burning*) *anger* (Deut 29:24; Isa 7:4; Lam 2:3).

The Journey

KADESH-BARNEA TO THE PLAINS OF MOAB

Numbers–Deuteronomy Timeline

1600–1525 BC

AARON
1529–1409?

1530
The Hittites destroy Babylon.

1528
Pharaoh orders that all newborn Hebrew males be thrown into the Nile.

1525
Ahmose I, first pharaoh of Egypt's Eighteenth Dynasty, expels the Hyksos from Egypt.

1525
Amenhotep I becomes pharaoh of Egypt.

1506
Thutmose I becomes pharaoh of Egypt.

1500
The Hittites develop iron technology.

1500–1450 BC

MOSES
1526–1406

1500
Glass bottles are first used in Egypt.

1500
Egyptians develop effective pharmaceutical compounds.

1500
Evidence of gold hammered into foil in South America.

1487
Moses flees Egypt.

1479–1457
Hatshepsut, female pharaoh in Egypt

1469
In the first well-documented battle in history, Pharaoh Thutmose III defeats an alliance of enemies at Megiddo.

1450–1445 BC

JOSHUA
1490?–1380?

1450
Thutmose III erects numerous obelisks in Egypt. The shadow of the obelisk was used to calculate time, seasons, and solstices.

1446
Passover is instituted.

1446
The exodus and defeat of Pharaoh at the Red Sea

1446
The Ten Commandments are given at Mount Sinai.

1445
The tabernacle is built and dedicated.

1445
Exploration of Canaan by 12 spies

1445–1375 BC

1445
Events in Leviticus

1445–1407
Events in Numbers

1406
Events in Deuteronomy

1406–1380?
Events in Joshua, including the miraculous crossing of the Jordan River

1400
The Egyptians develop a water clock.

Adversaries along the Journey

AMALEKITES

Descendants of Amalek, the grandson of Esau (Gen 36:12), this nomadic tribe inhabited the desolate wasteland of the northeast Sinai Peninsula and the Negev. They were the first to attack Israel after the exodus (Num 24:20). Israel won the initial battle (Exod 17:8–16) but later was driven back into the Sinai wilderness by a coalition of Amalekites and Canaanites (Num 14:39–45). Thereafter the Amalekites waged a barbaric guerrilla war against Israel (Deut 25:17–19). Fighting continued after Israel settled in Canaan. Because of their atrocities, God commanded Saul to exterminate the Amalekites (1 Sam 15:2–3). Saul disobeyed and the Amalekites were not defeated completely until late in the eighth century BC (1 Chr 4:43).

AMORITES

People who occupied part of the promised land and often fought Israel. Their most influential king was Hammurabi (1792–1750 BC). Sihon and Og, two Amorite kings, resisted the Israelites' march to Canaan as they approached east of the Jordan (Num 21:21–35), but after the Israelite victory here, Gad, Reuben and half of Manasseh settled in the conquered area. These two early victories over the Amorites foreshadowed continued success against other Amorites to the west and were often remembered in both history (Deut 3:8; Josh 12:2; Judg 11:19) and poetry (Num 21:27–30; Pss 135:10–12; 136:17–22).

EDOMITES

The Israelites regarded the Edomites as close relatives, even more closely related to them than the Ammonites or Moabites. Specifically, they identified the Ammonites and Moabites as descendants of Lot, Abraham's nephew, but the Edomites as descendants of Esau, Jacob's brother (Gen 19:30–36; 36). Thus Edom occasionally is referred to as a "brother" to Israel (Amos 1:11–12). Edomites seem not to have been barred from worship in the Jerusalem temple with the same strictness as the Ammonites and Moabites (Deut 23:3–8). Yet, as is often the case with personal relations, the closest relative can be a bitter enemy. According to the biblical writers, enmity between Israel and Edom began with Jacob and Esau (when the former stole the latter's birthright) and was exacerbated at the time of the Israelite exodus from Egypt (when the Edomites refused the Israelites passage through their land).

MIDIANITES

Personal and clan name meaning "strife." Midian was the son of Abraham by his concubine Keturah (Gen 25:2). Abraham sent him and his brothers away to the east, leading to the association of the Midianites with the "people of the east" (Judg 6:3). Midianites took Joseph to Egypt (Gen 37:28,36). Their main homeland seems to be east of the Jordan and south of Edom. The people of Israel had both good and bad relationships with the Midianites. When Moses fled from Pharaoh, he went east to Midian (Exod 2:15). Here he met Jethro (also called Reuel), the priest of Midian, and married his daughter. During the wandering in the wilderness, Reuel's descendant Hobab served as a guide for the Israelites (Num 10:29–32). The Midianites are associated with the Moabites in seducing Israel into immorality and pagan worship at Baal-peor (Num 25:1–18). For this reason God commanded Moses to execute a war of vengeance against them (Num 31:3; cp. Josh 13:21).

MOABITES

Personal and national name and monument the nation left behind. The narrow strip of cultivable land directly east of the Dead Sea was known in biblical times as Moab. According to Numbers 21:25–30, sometime before the appearance of the Israelites in the region, the Amorites had taken it from Moab. In Numbers 22, Balak, the king of Moab, sent for Balaam the prophet to pronounce a curse on the Israelites. Balaam, however, spoke no curse, and Balak was denied a military victory over Israel. Then the Amorites lost it to the Israelites, and Moses assigned it to the tribe of Reuben (Josh 13:15–23). According to Judges 11:13, Amon claimed the land belonged to them, even though they apparently had never occupied it. Moab finally reconquered the area, probably in the mid-ninth century BC (2 Kgs 3; Isa 15–16; Jer 48).

Complaints in the Wilderness

REFERENCE	COMPLAINT	BY WHOM	AGAINST WHOM
Exodus 5	Pharaoh increased the Israelite struggles because of Moses.	The Israelites; Moses	Moses and Aaron; Pharaoh and God
Exodus 14:11–12	Taking them out of Egypt to supposedly die in the wilderness	The Israelites	Moses and God
Exodus 15:22	Bitter water	The Israelites	Moses and God
Exodus 16:1–4	Hunger	The Israelites	Moses
Exodus 17:1–4	Thirst	The Israelites	Moses
Exodus 32	Impatience	The Israelites and Aaron	Moses on mountain
Numbers 11:1–34	Hardships and food	The Israelites	God
Numbers 12:1–12	Challenging Moses's prophetic authority and his marriage to a Cushite woman	Miriam and Aaron	Moses
Numbers 13:26–33; 14:6–9	Doubts in their ability to defeat the promised land inhabitants and take over the land	All the Israelite scouts except for Caleb and Joshua	Moses, Aaron, God
Numbers 13:30–14:3	Rejections of the promised land	The Israelites	Moses, Aaron, God
Numbers 14:1–10	Demanding a new leader to guide them back to Egypt	The Israelites	Moses and Aaron
Numbers 14:10–12,22,37	Refusal to enter the promised land	The Israelites, except for Caleb and Joshua	God
Numbers 16:1–50	Rejection of priestly authority—believing the entire community of Israelites were holy	Korah, Dathan and Abiram, and On, along with 250 prominent Israelite men	Moses and Aaron
Numbers 20:1–13	Lack of water	The Israelites	Moses
Numbers 21:4–5	The final complaint—that God had led them to die in the wilderness with no bread, water, and "wretched food"	The Israelites	God and Moses

KEY VERSE

"Listen to what I say: If there is a prophet among you from the Lord, I make myself known to him in a vision; I speak with him in a dream. Not so with my servant Moses; he is faithful in all my household. I speak with him directly, openly, and not in riddles; he sees the form of the Lord. So why were you not afraid to speak against my servant Moses?"

NUMBERS 12:6–8

KEY VERSE

These were the ones registered by Moses and the priest Eleazar when they registered the Israelites on the plains of Moab by the Jordan across from Jericho. But among them there was not one of those who had been registered by Moses and the priest Aaron when they registered the Israelites in the Wilderness of Sinai. For the LORD had said to them that they would all die in the wilderness. None of them was left except Caleb son of Jephunneh and Joshua son of Nun.

NUMBERS 26:63–65

Deuteronomy

Genre | **HISTORICAL NARRATIVE, LAW**

The book of Deuteronomy is a collection of exhortations from Moses recounting Israel's history with God and the laws and statutes they were to follow to live under his rule in the promised land.

INTRODUCTION

AUTHOR The book itself asserts that Moses is the principal source and author for the material (1:1), as do subsequent OT texts (Josh 1:7–8; 1 Kgs 2:3; Ezra 3:2) and NT texts (Matt 19:7; Acts 3:22; Rom 10:19). Structural similarities between Deuteronomy and Near Eastern treaty texts from the second millennium BC support the unity and antiquity of the book.

BACKGROUND Because of their rebellious spirit, the Israelites were forced to wander in the desert for 40 years (2:7) until at last they arrived in Moab, just opposite Jericho (32:49). It was there that Moses put pen to parchment to compose this farewell treatise (31:9,24).

MESSAGE AND PURPOSE Though the initial covenant between the Lord and Israel was made at Sinai, the generation that received it had largely died out in the 38 years since that event. Now the younger generation needed to affirm their commitment to the covenant (4:1–8). The purpose of Deuteronomy is to provide guidelines for the younger covenant community to enable them to live obediently before God and to carry out his intentions for them.

SUMMARY The title of this book of the Pentateuch, Deuteronomy, comes from the Septuagint (the Greek translation of the Old Testament) and means "second law" or "repetition of the law." The phrase is actually a mistranslation of 17:18, which reads "a copy of this instruction." It is still a fitting title since much of the book contains repetitions of the laws found in Exodus, Leviticus, and Numbers.

STRUCTURE The style of the book of Deuteronomy appears as a series of repetitious, reminiscent, and even irregular exhortations, which is fitting for a collection of Moses's sermons preparing the people for their move into the promised land. The book of Deuteronomy could be considered the constitution for the nation of Israel once it was established in the promised land.

Outline

I. **First Address of Moses (1:1–4:49)**
   A. Preface and historical introduction (1:1–5)
   B. Review of Israel's history (1:6–4:49)

II. **Second Address of Moses (5:1–26:19)**
   A. A series of exhortations (5:1–11:32)
   B. A series of laws and statutes (12:1–21:23)
   C. A series of laws for Israel's social life (22:1–26:19)

III. **Third Address of Moses (27:1–30:20)**
   A. Provision for future renewal of the covenant (27:1–26)
   B. Covenant blessings and curses (28:1–29:15)
   C. Final exhortation to obedience (29:16–30:20)

IV. **Final Days of Moses (31:1–34:12)**
   A. Designation of Moses's successor (31:1–30)
   B. Song of Moses (32:1–52)
   C. Moses's final blessing of Israel (33:1–29)
   D. Death and burial of Moses (34:1–12)

WORD STUDY

beriyth

Hebrew pronunciation:
[beh REETH]

CSB translation:
covenant

Uses in Deuteronomy: 27
Uses in the OT: 287

Focus passage:
Deuteronomy 4:13,23,31

Beriyth probably relates to an Akkadian word pointing to *covenants* (Gen 6:18) as bonds, a fundamental implication being obligation. *Beriyth* also denotes *treaty* (Josh 9:15) or *agreement* (Isa 33:8). People confirmed *covenants* by oath (Gen 21:22–27); *word, testimony, counsel, agreement,* and *law* are associated terms. *Covenants* initiated relationships implying love, friendship, loyalty, goodness, peace, and brotherhood. People entered covenants by "cutting" (making) them, originally cutting apart animals (Gen 15:9–10; Jer 34:18). "Cut a *covenant*" appears as *form an alliance* (Ps 83:5) or *made a covenant* (Isa 28:15). Other ceremonies were sacrifices (Exod 24:3–8), meals (Gen 26:26–31), sharing salt (Lev 2:13), and shaking hands (Ezek 17:18). *Covenants* were between men, with God, and figuratively with animals (Hos 2:18). God dealt with mankind through two important kinds of *covenant*, an obligatory one modeled after suzerain-vassal *treaties* (e.g., Mosaic) and a promissory one comparable to royal grants (e.g., Davidic).

'elohiym

Hebrew pronunciation:
[eh loh HEEM]

CSB translation:
God, gods

Uses in Deuteronomy: 374
Uses in the OT: 2,602

Focus passage:
Deuteronomy 5:2,6–7, 9,11–12,14

'Elohiym occurs about a third as often as *Yahweh* and ten times more than *'el*. *'Elohiym* and *'el* seem related; *'elohiym* could be an expanded plural of *'el* or the plural of another root that merged with *'el*. Both words probably connote power. *'Eloah* (58x), another name for God, also seems related and synonymous. *'Elohiym* is evidently a plural connoting majesty when describing God; its modifiers are usually singular. *'Elohiym* alone indicates *God* but occurs 891 times in the phrase *Lord God*. It appears in titles like *God of my salvation* (Ps 18:46). In many contexts, *'elohiym* denotes *god* (40x, Isa 37:38) and *gods* (203x, Exod 20:3). It sometimes refers to their images (Exod 20:23). *'Elohiym* designates *judges* acting in God's name (Exod 21:6), *heavenly beings* (Ps 138:1), and *spirit form* (1 Sam 28:13). "Fire of *'elohiym*" appears as *divine fire* (2 Kgs 1:12) and *God's fire* (Job 1:16).

shamar

Hebrew pronunciation:
[shah MAR]

CSB translation:
keep, watch, guard

Uses in Deuteronomy: 73
Uses in the OT: 469

Focus passage:
Deuteronomy 27:1

Shamar means *keep* (Gen 17:9), *maintain, tend, preserve, continue,* or *guarantee*. It is *watch, observe* (Ezek 43:11), *take note,* or *notice*. It denotes *stand watch, guard* (Gen 3:24), *restrain, safeguard, protect, watch over, care for* (Exod 22:10), *take care of, look after, be in charge of,* or *be responsible for*. People *do, obey, carry out* (Josh 22:3), *fulfill,* or *perform* duties. *Shamar* means *besiege* (2 Sam 11:16), *avoid* (Ps 17:4), or *preserve* (2 Sam 22:44). One *is devoted to* or *cherishes* (Jonah 2:8). Participles signify *watchman, guardian, keeper, spy* (Judg 1:24), or *sentry*. Passive participles indicate *secured* (2 Sam 23:5) or *saved*. Passive-reflexive verbs convey *make/be sure* (Gen 24:6), *pay attention* (Exod 23:13), *calm down,* and *be careful, on guard,* or *kept safe* (Ps 37:28). With other verbs *shamar* implies *carefully* or *exactly* (Num 23:12). People *spare* life, *follow* instruction, *uphold* justice, *remain* faithful, *harbor* rage, and *accept* rebuke.

KEY VERSE

"Indeed, ask about the earlier days that preceded you, from the day God created mankind on the earth and from one end of the heavens to the other: Has anything like this great event ever happened, or has anything like it been heard of? Has a people heard God's voice speaking from the fire as you have, and lived? Or has a god attempted to go and take a nation as his own out of another nation, by trials, signs, wonders, and war, by a strong hand and an outstretched arm, by great terrors, as the LORD your God did for you in Egypt before your eyes? You were shown these things so that you would know that the LORD is God; there is no other besides him. He let you hear his voice from heaven to instruct you. He showed you his great fire on earth, and you heard his words from the fire. Because he loved your ancestors, he chose their descendants after them and brought you out of Egypt by his presence and great power, to drive out before you nations greater and stronger than you and to bring you in and give you their land as an inheritance, as is now taking place. Today, recognize and keep in mind that the LORD is God in heaven above and on earth below; there is no other. Keep his statutes and commands, which I am giving you today, so that you and your children after you may prosper and so that you may live long in the land the LORD your God is giving you for all time."

DEUTERONOMY 4:32–40

KEY VERSE

Moses summoned all Israel and said to them, "Israel, listen to the statutes and ordinances I am proclaiming as you hear them today. Learn and follow them carefully. The **Lord** our God made a covenant with us at Horeb. He did not make this covenant with our ancestors, but with all of us who are alive here today. The **Lord** spoke to you face to face from the fire on the mountain."

DEUTERONOMY 5:1–4

KEY VERSE

"This is the command—the statutes and ordinances—the LORD your God has commanded me to teach you, so that you may follow them in the land you are about to enter and possess. Do this so that you may fear the LORD your God all the days of your life by keeping all his statutes and commands I am giving you, your son, and your grandson, and so that you may have a long life. Listen, Israel, and be careful to follow them, so that you may prosper and multiply greatly, because the LORD, the God of your ancestors, has promised you a land flowing with milk and honey. Listen, Israel: The LORD our God, the LORD is one. Love the LORD your God with all your heart, with all your soul, and with all your strength. These words that I am giving you today are to be in your heart."

DEUTERONOMY 6:1–6

Jesus Quotes Deuteronomy

THEME	DEUTERONOMY	JESUS IN THE GOSPELS
Worshipping the True God	*Deuteronomy 4:35*	*Mark 12:32*
The Ten Commandments	*Deuteronomy 5:16–20*	*Matthew 5:21,27–28; 15:4; 19:18–19; Mark 10:19; Luke 18:20*
The Greatest Command	*Deuteronomy 6:4–5*	*Matthew 22:37,38; Mark 12:29–30; Luke 10:27*
Remembering God through Obedience	*Deuteronomy 6:13*	*Matthew 4:10; Luke 4:8*
Don't Test God	*Deuteronomy 6:16*	*Matthew 4:7; Luke 4:12*
Remember the Lord	*Deuteronomy 8:3*	*Matthew 4:4; Luke 4:4*
Festivals and Customs	*Deuteronomy 16:16–17*	*Luke 2:42*
Restoring a Brother	*Deuteronomy 17:6*	*Matthew 18:16*
Witnesses in Court	*Deuteronomy 19:15*	*Matthew 18:16; John 8:17*
The Property of Others	*Deuteronomy 22:4*	*Matthew 12:11–12*
Keeping Vows	*Deuteronomy 19:15*	*Matthew 5:33–34*
Marriage and Divorce	*Deuteronomy 24:1*	*Matthew 5:31; 19:4–9; Mark 10:4–9*

Covenant Pattern

LAW CODES AND COVENANTS (SECOND MILLENNIUM BC)[2]		
LAW CODE		**COVENANT**
TITLE	Identifies superior partner.	**TITLE** *(Exod 20:2a; Deut 5:6a)*
PROLOGUE	Shows how the superior partner has cared for the subordinate one in the past, thereby inspiring gratitude and obedience within the subordinate partner.	**PROLOGUE** *(Exod 20:2b; Deut 5:6b [cp. Deut 1–3])*
LAWS	Lists the laws given by the superior partner, which are to be obeyed by the subordinate partner. Partner has cared for the subordinate one in the past, thereby inspiring gratitude and obedience within the subordinate partner.	**STIPULATIONS/LAWS** *(Exod 20:3–17; Deut 5:17–21 [cp. Deut 12–26])*
	Provides for the preservation of the text in the temple of the subordinate partner.	**DEPOSITIONS READINGS** *(Exod 25:21; 32:15; 40:20; Deut 10:5; 31:10–12 [cp. Exod 24:7; Josh 8:30–35])*
	Witnessed and guaranteed by the gods of both partners.	**WITNESSES** *(Deut 4:26; 30:19–20; 31:28)*
BLESSINGS AND CURSES	Pronounces curses on those who disobey and blessings on those who obey.	**BLESSINGS AND CURSES** *(Deut 27:11–28:68)*
	Ratified by an oath and a ceremony, and sanctions are pronounced against any person who breaks the covenantal relationship.	**OATH CEREMONY SANCTIONS** *(Exod 24:3–8 [cp. Gen 15:17–21; Jer 34:17–20; Matt 27:22–25])*

KEY QUOTE

In the concluding statement about Moses, that "there never has arisen a prophet like Moses, whom God knew face to face" (34:10), there is the implication that many prophets have come and gone, patterned after the Mosaic model in fulfillment of Deuteronomy 18. Yet no-one has risen to his stature. This text signals the end not only of an historical epoch but of the literary document of the Torah [or Law]. Conveniently, it not only brings closure to this text but prepares the way for the next section of the canon, the Prophets, which details the exploits of many of these individuals. Moses' incomparability and the new title given to him, "servant of Yahweh," prefigure another unique prophetic servant who also died "outside the land" for his people.

STEPHEN G. DEMPSTER[3]

Joshua

Genre | **HISTORICAL NARRATIVE**

The book of Joshua describes the Israelites' military conquest of the promised land of Canaan and the division of the land into tribal allotments.

INTRODUCTION

AUTHOR The author of the book of Joshua is not identified in the Bible and otherwise remains anonymous. If Joshua himself did not originally compose the book that bears his name, then it may be presumed that someone who knew him and his exploits recorded the work. There are numerous references throughout Joshua that suggest a final formation of the book after his lifetime (4:9; 5:9; 6:25; 7:26; 8:28–29; 10:27; 13:13; 14:14; 15:63; 16:10; 22:17; 23:8).

BACKGROUND The accounts in the book of Joshua occur in the period immediately after Moses's death. This was a new generation, not the one that had left Egypt. The story of Joshua is thus set when the nation of Israel first appeared in the land west of the Jordan River—the land that would bear their name.

MESSAGE AND PURPOSE Chapter 1 establishes Joshua as a divinely appointed leader and as the successor to Moses. God addressed Joshua directly, promising both the land that he promised to Moses (Deut 34:4) and his divine presence (Josh 1:3–5). Joshua's military leadership recurs throughout the first 12 chapters of the book. Its theological dimensions raise questions about the extermination of all people from the land. Joshua's allocation of the land in chapters 13–21 continued the process already begun by Moses in Transjordan. Insofar as God was giving this land to his people as an inheritance, the tribal allotments take on a covenantal character.

SUMMARY The book of Joshua is named for the most famous member of the Israelites in the generation after the death of Moses. The book describes the history of the generation that crossed the Jordan River and entered the promised land of Canaan. Their battles and faithfulness have a place among the greatest stories of faith in the Old Testament. Joshua led the people to defeat the adversaries who opposed God's people. He then oversaw the division of the land into the tribal allotments. Finally, Joshua renewed the covenant between the people and God.

STRUCTURE The book of Joshua should be seen as a land grant, similar to the land grants and suzerain treaties of the ancient Near East. The suzerain, who was Israel's God, gave to his people the land that they were meant to receive. There are three major parts to the structure of the land grant: (1) a review of the history and events leading up to the gift of the land, (2) the allotment of the territories to the tribes and families of Israel, and (3) a renewal of the covenant.

Outline

I. Preparation for the Land (1:1–5:12)
- A. Joshua assumes leadership (1:1–18)
- B. Rahab's faith (2:1–24)
- C. Across the Jordan River (3:1–4:24)
- D. Circumcision and Passover (5:1–12)

II. Victories in the Land (5:13–12:24)
- A. Success against Jericho (5:13–6:27)
- B. Failure of Achan (7:1–26)
- C. Success against Ai (8:1–29)
- D. Covenant renewal (8:30–35)
- E. Failure of Israel and Gibeon (9:1–27)
- F. Victories in the land (10:1–12:24)

III. Allotment of the Land (13:1–21:45)
- A. Remaining lands (13:1–7)
- B. Transjordan's allotment (13:8–14:5)
- C. Judah's allotment (14:6–15:63)
- D. Joseph's allotment (16:1–17:18)
- E. Mapping the remaining land (18:1–10)
- F. Tribal allotments (18:11–19:51)
- G. Cities of refuge (20:1–9)
- H. Cities of the Levites (21:1–42)
- I. God's promises fulfilled (21:43–45)

IV. Worship of God (22:1–24:33)
- A. Transjordan and the altar of controversy (22:1–34)
- B. Joshua's farewell address (23:1–16)
- C. Israel's covenant at Shechem (24:1–28)
- D. Joshua and his generation die (24:29–33)

WORD STUDY

nuach

Hebrew pronunciation: [NEW ahkh]

CSB translation: rest

Uses in Joshua: 9
Uses in the OT: 140

Focus passage: Joshua 1:13,15

Nuach means *rest* (Exod 23:12) or *come to rest* (Gen 8:4). Locusts *settle* (Exod 10:14). Rest from enemies means *gaining relief from them* (Esth 9:16). *Nuach* connotes *wait* (1 Sam 25:9), *reside* (Prov 14:33), *remain* (Ps 125:3), *abide* (Eccl 7:9), or *be calm* (Isa 14:7). Causally, *nuach* signifies *give rest* or *comfort* (Josh 1:13; Prov 29:17). *Nuach* describes *settling* people (Josh 6:23). It means *leave* something (Gen 19:16) or, with a preposition, *leave alone* (Exod 32:10). It suggests *place* (Gen 2:15), *set down* (Josh 4:3), *store* (Deut 14:28), or *deposit* (Num 19:9). One *lets* hands *slip* or *rest* (Eccl 7:18; 11:6). *Letting rest* conveys *allowing* (Ps 105:14) or *tolerating* (Esth 3:8). With objects like wrath or spirit, *nuach* denotes *vent* (Ezek 5:13), *satisfy* (Ezek 16:42), or *pacify* (Zech 6:8). Guards are *stationed* (2 Chr 1:14). The infinitive indicates *relief* (Neh 9:28).

charam

Hebrew pronunciation: [khah RAM]

CSB translation: set apart to destruction, devote, completely destroy

Uses in Joshua: 14
Uses in the OT: 50

Focus passage: Joshua 10:1,28,39–40

Charam, closely associated with God, negatively implies judicial punishment that *sets* people or things *apart for destruction* (Isa 34:2). It means *completely destroy* (Num 21:2) or *annihilate* (Dan 11:44). The context was usually warfare, but such punishment might overtake an individual (Exod 22:20). Positively, Israelites could *permanently set* possessions *apart* to the Lord as holy (Lev 27:28). They *set apart* their plunder for the Lord (Mic 4:13). The passive may connote *forfeit* (Ezra 10:8). *Cherem* (29x) occurs three times with *charam* (Lev 27:28,29; Josh 6:18). *Cherem* involves *what is set apart for destruction* (Lev 27:29). Both people (Josh 6:18) and *things* (Josh 7:13) can be *set apart*. *Cherem* signifies *total destruction* (Isa 43:28), *curse of destruction* (Zech 14:11), or *curse* (Mal 4:6). It also indicates things, animals, or people *permanently dedicated* (Num 18:14) or *set apart* (Lev 27:28) to God as holy. These things became the priests' property (Ezek 44:29).

chalaq

Hebrew pronunciation: [khah LAK]

CSB translation: divide, share, apportion

Uses in Joshua: 7
Uses in the OT: 55

Focus passage: Joshua 18:2,5,10

Chalaq, a homonym of *chalaq* meaning "be smooth," denotes *divide* (Gen 49:27) or *share* (Prov 17:2). It signifies *endow* (Job 39:17), *appoint* (2 Chr 23:18), *be a partner* (Prov 29:24), or *provide* (Deut 4:19). Intensives imply *divide up* (Joel 3:2), *disperse* (Gen 49:7), *allot* (Mic 2:4), *apportion* (Job 21:17), *establish* (Neh 9:22), or *distribute* (Josh 18:10). People *allot* (*give, claim*) *as a portion* (Isa 34:17; Jer 37:12). *Cheleq* (66x) means *portion* (Gen 31:14), *section*, or *share*. It represents *fate* (Isa 17:14), *lot* (Job 20:29), or *reward* (Eccl 2:10). It is *plot of land* (2 Kgs 9:10), *allotted land* (Mic 2:4), *land*, or *field* (Hos 5:7). It connotes *association* (Ps 50:18) and *what one knows* (Job 32:17). *Machaloqet* (42x) is *division* (Neh 11:36), *allotment, portion,* and *tour of duty*. *Chelqah* (23x) indicates *field* and *portion* (Deut 33:21), *section, plot, piece,* or *parcel* of land. *Chaluqqah* means *division* (2 Chr 35:5).

Seeing Jesus in the Promised Land

THE LORD | *The Lord of All the Earth (Josh 3:11,13)*	**JESUS CHRIST IS LORD** | *The Confession of Every Tongue (Phil 2:9–11)*
JOSHUA Entrusted Himself to God's Exaltation *(Josh 3:7)*	**JESUS** Entrusted Himself to God's Vindication *(1 Pet 2:23)*
JOSHUA (HEBREW) Name Means "The LORD Is Salvation"	**JESUS (GREEK)** Salvation Is Found in No Other Name *(Acts 4:12)*
JOSHUA Led His People into a Temporary Rest *(Josh 11:23)*	**JESUS** Leads His People into an Eternal Rest *(Heb 3–4)*
RAHAB Saved by Faith *(Josh 2; 6; Heb 11:31)*	**JESUS** The Author and Perfecter of Our Faith *(Heb 12:2)*
THE JUDGES Saved the People While Still Alive *(Judg 2:18)*	**JESUS** Saves His People Forever, Being Raised from the Dead *(Rom 8)*
GIDEON'S ARMY OF 300 God's Glory through Weakness *(Judg 7:2)*	**PREACH CHRIST CRUCIFIED** God's Power and Wisdom *(1 Cor 1:24)*
SAMSON'S DEATH Vengeance upon His Idolatrous Enemies *(Judg 16:28)*	**JESUS'S DEATH** Salvation for His Enemies Who Believe *(Rom 5:8–10)*
BOAZ A Kinsman Redeemer, Even for a Moabitess *(Ruth 2:20; 4:1–12)*	**JESUS** The Redeemer Who Gave Himself for All People *(Titus 2:11–14)*
RUTH Great-Grandmother of David *(Ruth 4:17)*	**JESUS** The Son of David, the Messiah *(Matt 1)*
SAMUEL A Prophet to Whom God Revealed Himself by His Word *(1 Sam 3:21)*	**JESUS** In These Last Days, God Has Spoken to Us by His Son *(Heb 1:2)*
OLD TESTAMENT	**NEW TESTAMENT**

The Conquest of the Promised Land

JOSHUA

The Promise of Land

By faith, we all walk as foreigners and temporary residents on the earth, holding on to the promise of a better place—a heavenly one, wherein God dwells (Heb 11:13–16).

THE CREATION

God created *the heavens and the earth* in six days and *rested* from all his work on the seventh day. God planted a garden in Eden with the *tree of life* and a *river* to water the garden. Adam and Eve were placed in the garden to work it and watch over it (Gen 1–2).

A FALLEN WORLD

OLD TESTAMENT

Adam and Eve listened to the serpent's deception and disobeyed God. Their punishment was death and *exile* from the garden. The ground was *cursed*, impacting humanity's work and provision (Gen 3).

NEW TESTAMENT

All of creation, which has been bound by the *curse*, is awaiting its restoration with the revelation of God's children, heirs of God and coheirs with Christ. *We are to eagerly wait for that day with patience and hope* (Rom 8:19–25).

THE PROMISED LAND

The Lord called Abram to leave his land and go to a land he would show him (Canaan), a promised land for his descendants, an *inheritance* from which to bless the nations. Through Abram, all the peoples on earth would be blessed (Gen 12:1–3; 13:14–17; 15:18–20; 17:8). But fulfillment of this promise would not come for more than 400 years, so the patriarchs were to live as *foreigners* until then (Gen 15:13–16).

By faith, Abraham lived as a *foreigner* in the land of promise because he was looking forward to the *city* that has foundations, whose architect and builder is God. He desired a better place—a heavenly one, full of God's *presence*. *We, too, are to live by faith and set aside every weight and sin and run with endurance the race set before us, keeping our eyes on Jesus* (Heb 11:10,13–16; 12:1–2).

The Lord raised up Moses to lead his people out of slavery in Egypt and back to the promised land. The Lord would be their God and be *present* with them; he would give them *rest* in the land (Exod 33:14). But with the exception of Joshua and Caleb, the generation that came out of Egypt did not obey to take possession of the land; therefore, God said they would not enter the land, and they died in the wilderness (Num 13–14).

The generation that came out of Egypt under Moses heard the Lord's voice, saw his works, yet still rebelled against him when he commanded them to enter and possess the promised land. They sinned and disobeyed in unbelief, so God swore they would not enter his *rest*. *We have received the good news of God's rest just as they did, only we should believe in Jesus so that we may enter into it, and we must believe "today"* (Heb 3:7–4:7).

After 40 years in the wilderness, Joshua succeeded Moses and led the people into the land to take possession of it as the Lord had commanded. They conquered the land, but not all of it, and received their *inheritance*, portions of the land distributed to the tribes of Israel. And the Lord gave them *rest* from all the enemies around them (Josh 23:1). Not one of God's good promises had failed (Josh 23:14–16). But the Israelites soon disobeyed and worshipped other gods (Judges).

The *rest* God gave the Israelites in the promised land through the leadership of Joshua was temporary and but a shadow of a greater *rest*. There is a *rest* to come for God's people in which we, too, will *rest* from our works, just as God did from his on the seventh day. *We must make every effort to enter into that rest, obeying in faith* (Heb 4:8–11).

A FALLEN WORLD

OLD TESTAMENT

The Lord raised up King David, a man after his own heart, to lead his people. He completed the task of taking possession of the promised land. His son King Solomon was a "man of *rest*" who built the *temple* for the Lord in *Jerusalem* (1 Chr 22:9–10). The Lord gave them *rest*, and again, not one of God's good promises had failed (1 Kgs 8:56). But the king and the people soon disobeyed and worshipped other gods (1 Kgs 11).

Eventually the people were *exiled* from the land for their disobedience, just as the Lord had promised. But after 70 years of *exile*, the people returned to the Lord and were given permission to return to the land, also as the Lord had promised. The *temple* was rebuilt, the wall around *Jerusalem* was rebuilt, and the covenant was renewed (Ezra–Nehemiah). Still, there was no king and no kingdom; the people were subject to another nation while they awaited the Messiah and the restoration of the kingdom.

NEW TESTAMENT

Jesus is the son of David, the Messiah (Matt 1:1), whose kingdom is the kingdom of heaven (Matt 4:17). His kingdom is *inherited* by those who are righteous from all nations, those who obey the King (Matt 25:31–40). He is greater than the *temple* and he is the Lord of the Sabbath (Matt 12:6,8). Jesus calls the weary and burdened to himself because he will give them *rest*, for he is gentle and humble in heart. *We must come to Jesus, take up his yoke, and learn from him so we may find rest for ourselves* (Matt 11:28–30).

Christians are sojourners, *foreigners*, temporary residents, and *exiles* in this world (1 Pet 1:1,17; 2:11). Jesus has gone to prepare a place for his followers and will come back for them, that where he is, they may be also—and he is the way into the Father's *presence* (John 14:1–6). He suffered outside *Jerusalem* to save us from sin, so we must go outside the camp to join him in his disgrace because we don't have an enduring *city* here, but we look forward to the one to come (Heb 13:12–14). *Through Jesus, we must honor our Father by our actions and praise him with our lips* (1 Pet 1:17; Heb 13:15).

THE NEW CREATION

With the second coming of Jesus, *a new heaven and a new earth* will arise, and the *new Jerusalem* will come down out of heaven from God, and God's dwelling will be with humanity. There will be no *temple* in it, for the Lord God the Almighty and the Lamb are its *temple*. The *river* of living water will flow from the throne of God and of the Lamb, and the *tree of life* will be on both sides of the *river*, and there will no longer be any *curse*. God's people will serve him and will reign forever and ever (Rev 21–22).

KEY VERSE

"Therefore, fear the LORD and worship him in sincerity and truth. Get rid of the gods your ancestors worshiped beyond the Euphrates River and in Egypt, and worship the LORD. But if it doesn't please you to worship the LORD, choose for yourselves today: Which will you worship—the gods your ancestors worshiped beyond the Euphrates River or the gods of the Amorites in whose land you are living? As for me and my family, we will worship the LORD."

JOSHUA 24:14–15

Joshua's Life

THE BOOK OF EXODUS

- Born a slave in Egypt, then redeemed along with the Israelites (Exod 5–15)
- Chosen by Moses to lead defensive attack against Amalek (Exod 17)
- Moses's assistant
  - *On Mount Sinai when Moses received the law (Exod 24:13)*
  - *Stayed in the tent of meeting (Exod 33:11)*

THE BOOKS OF NUMBERS/DEUTERONOMY

- Chosen as one of the spies to scout out Canaan, the promised land (Num 13:8,16)
  - *Moses renamed him from Hoshea ("Salvation") to Joshua ("The Lord is salvation") (Num 13:16)*
- Joshua and Caleb alone gave a positive, faithful report of the land (Num 13–14)
- Joshua and Caleb alone from their generation were promised to enter the land (Num 14:30)
- Chosen by the Lord to succeed Moses (Num 27:12–22; Deut 31)
  - *Encouraged to be strong and courageous (Deut 31:7,23)*
- Chosen by the Lord to help distribute the land to the tribes (Num 34:16–29)
- Moses died; Joshua assumed leadership (Deut 34)

THE BOOK OF JOSHUA

- Reaffirmed by the Lord as the leader to succeed Moses (Josh 1)
  - *Encouraged to be strong and courageous (Josh 1:6,7,9,18)*
- Led the Israelites across the Jordan River on dry ground (Josh 3–4)
- Officiated over a covenant renewal in circumcision and Passover (Josh 5)
- Obeyed the Lord's instructions for conquering Jericho (Josh 6)
- Army defeated at Ai because of Achan's sin; Achan judged (Josh 7)
- Obeyed the Lord's instructions for conquering Ai (Josh 8)
- Fulfilled blessings and curses ceremony at Mount Gerizim and Mount Ebal (Josh 8:30–35)
- Made an ill-advised covenant with the Gibeonites without seeking the Lord's counsel (Josh 9)
- Conquered southern cities of the promised land (Josh 10)
- Conquered northern cities of the promised land (Josh 11)
  - *The land had rest from war (Josh 11:23)*
- Released the two and a half tribes to return to their homes on the east side of the Jordan River (Josh 13)
- Distributed the promised land to the remaining nine and a half tribes (Josh 14–21)
- Officiated over a final covenant renewal with all the Israelites (Josh 23–24)
- Died at the age of 110 (Josh 24:29)

Joshua's Cities of Conquest

CITY	SCRIPTURE	OCCUPANTS	COMMENTS
Gilgal	4:19–5:15	Unoccupied?	No battle; became worship center
Jericho	6:1–27	Canaanites	Rahab spared; oldest walled city; Achan sinned
Ai	7:1–8:29	Amorites	Israel defeated because of Achan's sin; Ai means "ruin"
Gibeon; Chephirah; Beeroth; Kiriath-jearim	9:1–10:27	Hivites; patriarchs	Entered covenant with Israel to be servants at worship place
Jerusalem	10:1–27	Jebusites	Part of coalition Joshua defeated but city not conquered
Hebron	10:1–27,36–37	Amorites, but in patriarchal times Hethites; also home of Anakim (11:21)	Coalition partner whose city was destroyed; patriarchal city (Gen 13:18); given to Caleb (14:9–13); city of refuge (20:7)
Jarmuth	10:1–27	Amorites	Coalition partner
Lachish	10:1–27,31–33	Amorites	Coalition partner whose city was destroyed
Eglon	10:1–27,34–35	Amorites	Coalition partner whose city was destroyed
Makkedah	10:16–17,28	?	Scene of battle with coalition
Libnah	10:29–30	?	Levitical city (21:13)
Gezer	10:33	Canaanites	Old, large city whose king Joshua defeated; city not occupied (Judg 1:29); Levitical city (21:21)
Debir	10:38–39	Amorites; home of Anakim (11:21)	Captured by Joshua and Othniel (15:15–17); Levitical city (21:15); name of king of Eglon (10:3)
Hazor	11:1–15	Canaanites	Largest city in Canaan; ancient history; head of northern coalition; destroyed by Joshua
Madon	11:1	?	Northern coalition partner Joshua defeated; Greek Septuagint calls it Meron; compare Waters of Merom
Shimron	11:1	?	Has various spellings in mss; appears in ancient Egyptian sources
Achshaph	11:1	?	Means "place of sorcery"; mentioned in ancient Egyptian sources

CITY	SCRIPTURE	OCCUPANTS	COMMENTS
Geder	12:13	?	Mystery city unknown elsewhere; sometimes seen as scribe's notation for city of longer name
Hormah	12:14	?	Southern border city (Num 14:45); defeated by Simeon and Judah (Judg 1:1,17)
Arad	12:14	Canaanites	Defeated by Moses (Num 21:1–3) and named Hormah; occupied by Kenites (Judg 1:16–17)
Adullam	12:15	?	Patriarchal ties (Gen 38)
Bethel	12:16	?	Strong patriarchal ties (Gen 12:28,35); means "house of God"; associated with Ai (7:2); house of Joseph defeated it (Judg 1:22–25)
Tappuah	12:17	?	Border city between Ephraim and Manasseh (16:8; 17:7–8)
Hepher	12:17	?	Name of a clan in Manasseh (17:2; cp. Num 26:28–37)
Aphek	12:18	?	In ancient Egyptian sources (cp. 1 Sam 4:1)
Lasharon	12:18	?	Unusual Hebrew construction; means "of Sharon"; may modify Aphek
Taanach	12:21	Canaanites	In ancient Egyptian sources; Levitical city (21:25); Manasseh could not occupy it (Judg 1:27)
Megiddo	12:21	Canaanites	Major ancient city guarding military pass; in Egyptian sources; Manasseh could not occupy it (Judg 1:27)
Kedesh	12:22	?	City of refuge (20:7); Levitical city (21:32); home of Barak (Judg 4:6)
Jokneam	12:22	?	Also spelled Jokmeam; Levitical city (21:34); in Egyptian sources
Dor	12:23; cp. 11:2	Associated with sea peoples	Manasseh could not occupy it (17:11–13; Judg 1:27); in Egyptian records
Goiim in Gilgal	12:23	Name means "nations"	Compare Genesis 14:1; uncertain scribal reading in text; appears to be in Galilee
Tirzah	12:24	Canaanites	Ancient city; became capital of Israel (1 Kgs 14:17); see Song 6:4

Judges

Genre | **HISTORICAL NARRATIVE**

The book of Judges presents the downward spiral of Israel morally and spiritually once they lived inside the land of Canaan and became like the Canaanites themselves.

INTRODUCTION

AUTHOR No author is named in the book of Judges, nor is any indication given of the writer or writers who are responsible for it. The three divisions of the book are on a different footing regarding the sources from which they are drawn. The main portion of the book, comprising the narratives of the judges, appears to be based on oral or written traditions of a local observer.

BACKGROUND We cannot ascertain exactly when the book of Judges was composed. The period of the Israelite judges lay between the conquest of the promised land under Joshua and the rise of the monarchy with Saul and David. The events described are thus to be dated from the early fourteenth century BC to the latter part of the eleventh century BC, a period of around 350 years. This was a time of social and religious anarchy, characterized by the repeated refrain "In those days there was no king in Israel; everyone did whatever seemed right to him" (17:6; 18:1; 19:1; 21:25).

MESSAGE AND PURPOSE The book of Judges chronicles the moral and spiritual descent of Israel from the relative high point at the beginning of the book through a series of downward spirals to the depths of degradation in chapters 17–21. Though God raised up a sequence of deliverers—the judges—they were unable to reverse this trend and some even became part of the problem. By the end of the book, Israel had become as pagan and defiled as the Canaanites they had displaced. If this trend continued, it would be only a matter of time before the land would vomit them out, as it had the Canaanites before them (Lev 18:28).

SUMMARY The book of Judges is the second of the Historical Books in the Old Testament (Joshua–Esther). In the Hebrew Bible, these books are called the Former Prophets; the theological and spiritual concerns found in the Pentateuch and the Prophets take precedence over the mere records of historical facts. The book derives its name from the Hebrew designation of the principal characters, *shophetim* (2:16), which could also be translated as "governors." These judges were the Lord's agents of deliverance. The Lord is both the central character and the hero of Judges.

STRUCTURE The book falls into three parts. The prologue (1:1–3:6) deals with the failure of the second generation to press on with the conquest of Canaan. This is followed by a sixfold cycle of sin and salvation (3:7–16:31), which forms the core of the book, structured around the six major judges with six minor judges interspersed. Finally, there is an appendix (chaps. 17–21) that shows the full effects of total depravity let loose upon the people. This structure demonstrates not only the repetition of patterns of sin and judgment but also regression.

Outline

I. Prologue (1:1–3:6)
   A. Israel's failure to possess the land (1:1–36)
   B. The pattern of sin, judgment, and restoration (2:1–3:6)

II. The Judges (3:7–16:31)
   A. Othniel (3:7–11)
   B. Ehud (3:12–30)
   C. Shamgar (3:31)
   D. Deborah and Barak (4:1–5:31)
   E. Gideon and Abimelech (6:1–9:57)
   F. Tola and Jair (10:1–5)
   G. Jephthah (10:6–12:7)
   H. Ibzan, Elon, and Abdon (12:8–15)
   I. Samson (13:1–16:31)

III. Epilogue (17:1–21:25)
   A. The religious degeneration of Israel (17:1–18:31)
   B. The moral degeneration of Israel (19:1–21:25)

WORD STUDY

za'aq

Hebrew pronunciation: [zah AK]

CSB translation: cry out, summon

Uses in Judges: 13
Uses in the OT: 74

Focus passage: Judges 6:6–7,34–35

Za'aq means *cry out* (Exod 2:23), *cry, call* (Judg 12:2), or *scream* (1 Sam 28:12). It may involve *weeping* (2 Sam 13:19). Armies and gatherings are *summoned* (Josh 8:16) or *mustered* (Judg 18:22). They *rally* (Judg 6:34) or *assemble* (1 Sam 14:20). "Cry out and say" signifies *issue a decree* (Jonah 3:7). *Za'aq* denotes *make appeal* (2 Sam 19:28). *Ze'aqah* (18x) means *cry* (Isa 15:5), *outcry* (Gen 18:20), *crying, shout* (Eccl 9:17), and *lamentation* (Esth 9:31). *Tza'aq* (55x) sounds like *za'aq* and denotes *cry out* (Gen 4:10). Soldiers are *summoned* (1 Sam 13:4), *called, called out,* or *called together* (Judg 10:17). People *cry loudly* (Isa 33:7), *call out* (Deut 26:7), and *appeal* (2 Kgs 8:3). *Tse'aqah* (21x) means *cry, outcry, crying out,* and *wailing* (Exod 12:30). The verbs often describe prayer, imply distress, occur alongside "wail," take their related nouns as objects, and appear together (Ps 107:6,13,19,28).

mal'ak

Hebrew pronunciation: [mal AHKH]

CSB translation: angel, messenger

Uses in Judges: 31
Uses in the OT: 213

Focus passage: Judges 13:3,6,9,13,15–18, 20–21

Mal'ak refers to divine and human *messengers. Mal'ak* can mean *angel* and *messenger* in the same verse (2 Kgs 1:3). When indicating a divine manifestation, the phrase "*mal'ak* of the LORD" (58x) is translated *angel of the LORD* (40x, Exod 3:2) or *him* (2x). Otherwise the words (14x) imply a regular *angel* (1 Kgs 19:7). "*Mal'ak* of God" (Judg 13:9) is synonymous with "*mal'ak* of the LORD" (Judg 13:3). It identifies God (Gen 31:11) as one known to Israel (Judg 13:6). It also indicates ordinary *angels* (1 Sam 29:9). *Mal'ak* describes God elsewhere according to context (Gen 48:16). It can also describe prophets (Hag 1:13), priests (Mal 2:7), and ordinary messengers (1 Sam 23:27). It can mean *envoy* (2 Sam 5:11) or *ambassador* (Ezek 17:15). *Mal'ak* can denote *agents* (1 Sam 19:11), as well as simply *messengers* (Josh 6:17). Winds and divine judgments are figuratively called *messengers* (Pss 78:49; 104:4).

The Canaanite Gods[4]

NAME OF DEITY	TITLE OR POSITION	RANK
El	"Father of the gods"	First tier of pantheon
Baal	Storm-god	Second tier of pantheon (sometimes first tier)
Anath	Goddess of love and war	Second tier of pantheon
Mot	God of death and underworld	Second tier of pantheon
Dagon	Baal's father/god of agriculture	Second tier of pantheon
Other deities	Servants to higher gods	Third tier of pantheon

In the ancient world, people typically believed in a pantheon (or hierarchical community) of deities, and this was the case with the Canaanites as well. The first tier was reserved for the most powerful and authoritative gods (e.g., El and in some cases Baal) and the third tier for the more subservient spiritual beings. While the Bible does not affirm everything the Canaanites might have believed about a particular god to be true, it does not deny the existence of sinister spiritual beings that wrongly receive worship from human beings (see Deut 32:15–17; 1 Cor 10:18–22). The biblical authors consistently present Yahweh, the God of Israel, as the one eternal and transcendent Creator who made all things and who possesses no actual rivals (Isa 44:6–8; 1 Cor 8:4–6), but both the OT and NT teach that a plurality of spiritual beings, good and evil, exist and exercise influence on the world (1 Kgs 22:19–23; Eph 6:11–12; Col 1:15–16; Heb 1:5–14).

In coming to occupy the Canaanite lands, the Israelites would not only face physical warfare but also be tempted to worship gods other than Yahweh (Deut 6:14–15; Jer 35:15). Such background reveals the relevance of the first of the Ten Commandments: "Do not have other gods *besides* me" (Exod 20:3, emphasis added). God forbade the Israelites from conceiving of other deities as existing on his level, as if Yahweh belonged somewhere among the Canaanite pantheon of gods.

Joshua–Ruth Timeline

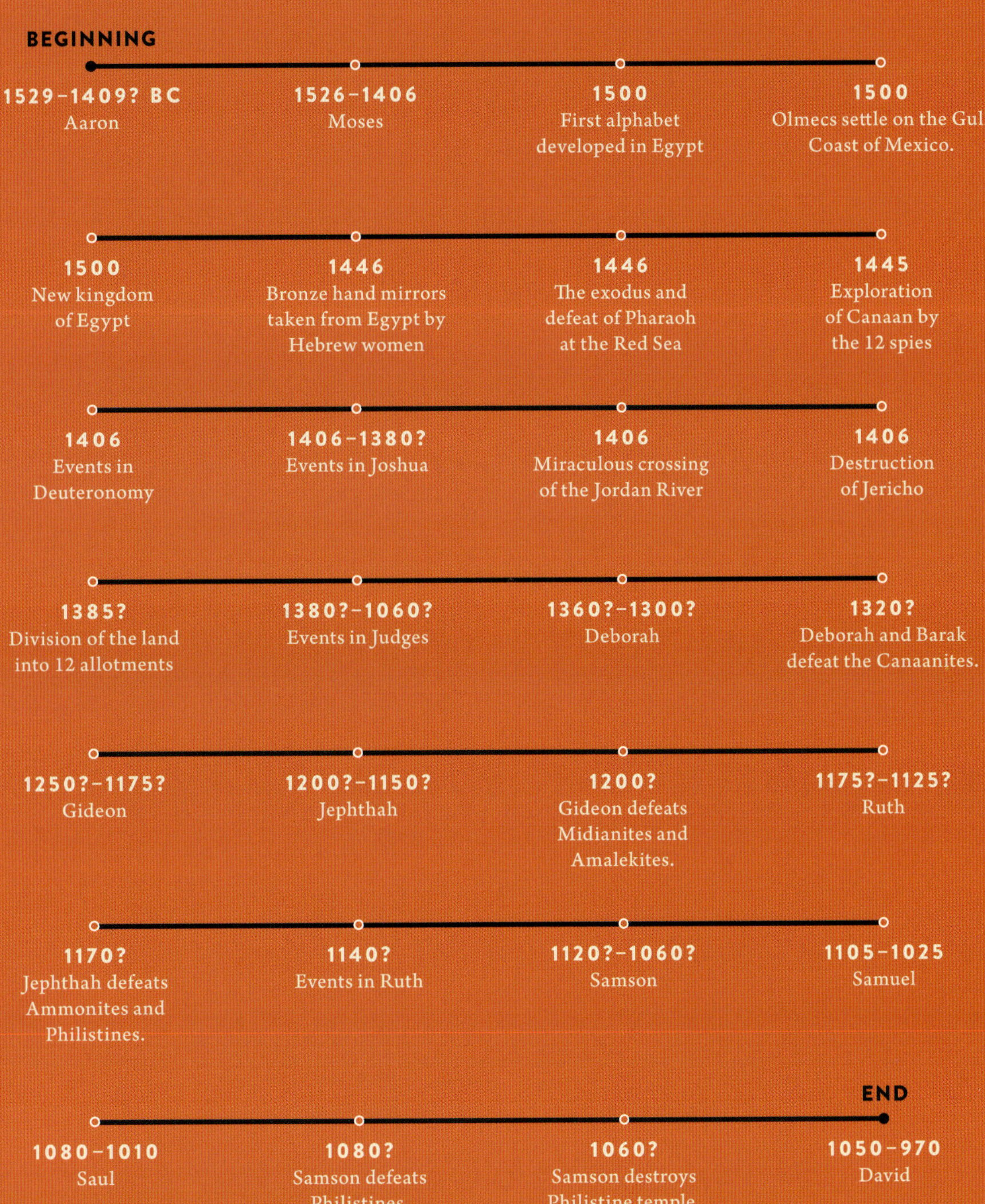

The Judges

NAME	REFERENCE	SIN & JUDGMENT	DELIVERANCE & LEGACY
Othniel	Judges 1:12–13; 3:7–11	The Israelites did what was evil in the Lord's sight; Cushan-rishathaim, king of Mesopotamia, ruled over them 8 years *(Judg 3:7–8)*	Israel cried out to the Lord, and he raised up **Othniel** as a deliverer—the Spirit of the Lord came on him, and he judged Israel; 40 years of peace *(3:9–11)*
Ehud	Judges 3:12–30	The Israelites again did what was evil in the Lord's sight; Eglon, king of Moab, ruled over them 18 years *(3:12–14)*	Israel cried out to the Lord, and he raised up **Ehud**, a left-handed Benjaminite, as a deliverer; 80 years of peace *(3:15–30)*
Shamgar	Judges 3:31		**Shamgar**, son of Anath (likely a non-Israelite), delivered Israel from the Philistines, killing 600 Philistines with a cattle prod *(3:31)*
Deborah	Judges 4–5	The Israelites again did what was evil in the Lord's sight; Jabin, king of Canaan, and Sisera, the commander of his forces, oppressed them 20 years *(4:1–3)*	Israel cried out to the Lord; **Deborah**, a woman, was judging Israel at that time, and she summoned Barak to fight for them; he was hesitant, so Deborah went with him; in the end, Jael, not Barak, killed Sisera; 40 years of peace *(4:3–5:31)*
Gideon	Judges 6–8	The Israelites did what was evil in the Lord's sight; Midian oppressed them 7 years *(6:1–6)*	Israel cried out to the Lord, and he sent a prophet; then the Lord sent fearful **Gideon** to deliver them, leading 300 men to victory against 135,000 Midianites; 40 years of peace, though he crafted an ephod, which became an idol for the people and his household *(6:7–8:35)*
Tola	Judges 10:1–2		**Tola** arose to deliver Israel; he judged Israel 23 years
Jair	Judges 10:3–5		**Jair** judged Israel 22 years
Jephthah	Judges 11:1–12:7	The Israelites again did what was evil in the Lord's sight; the Philistines and the Ammonites oppressed them 18 years *(10:6–9)*	Israel cried out to the Lord, but he said they should cry out to the other gods they had chosen, so they got rid of their idols; the Spirit of the Lord came on **Jephthah**, the son of a prostitute, to fight for them; in keeping a foolish vow, he sacrificed his daughter; he judged Israel 6 years *(10:10–12:7)*
Ibzan	Judges 12:8–10		**Ibzan** judged Israel 7 years
Elon	Judges 12:11–12		**Elon** judged Israel 10 years
Abdon	Judges 12:13–15		**Abdon** judged Israel 8 years
Samson	Judges 13–16	The Israelites again did what was evil in the Lord's sight; the Philistines were over them 40 years (13:1)	The Lord raised up **Samson** to deliver Israel; though a Nazirite from birth, he often disregarded his vows, and he desired Philistine women; the Spirit of the Lord directed him numerous times until his hair was cut, the Lord left him, and he was captured; he was a more effective judge in his death, collapsing a building on himself and numerous Philistines, than he was in his life; he judged Israel 20 years (13:2–16:31)

The Judges of Israel

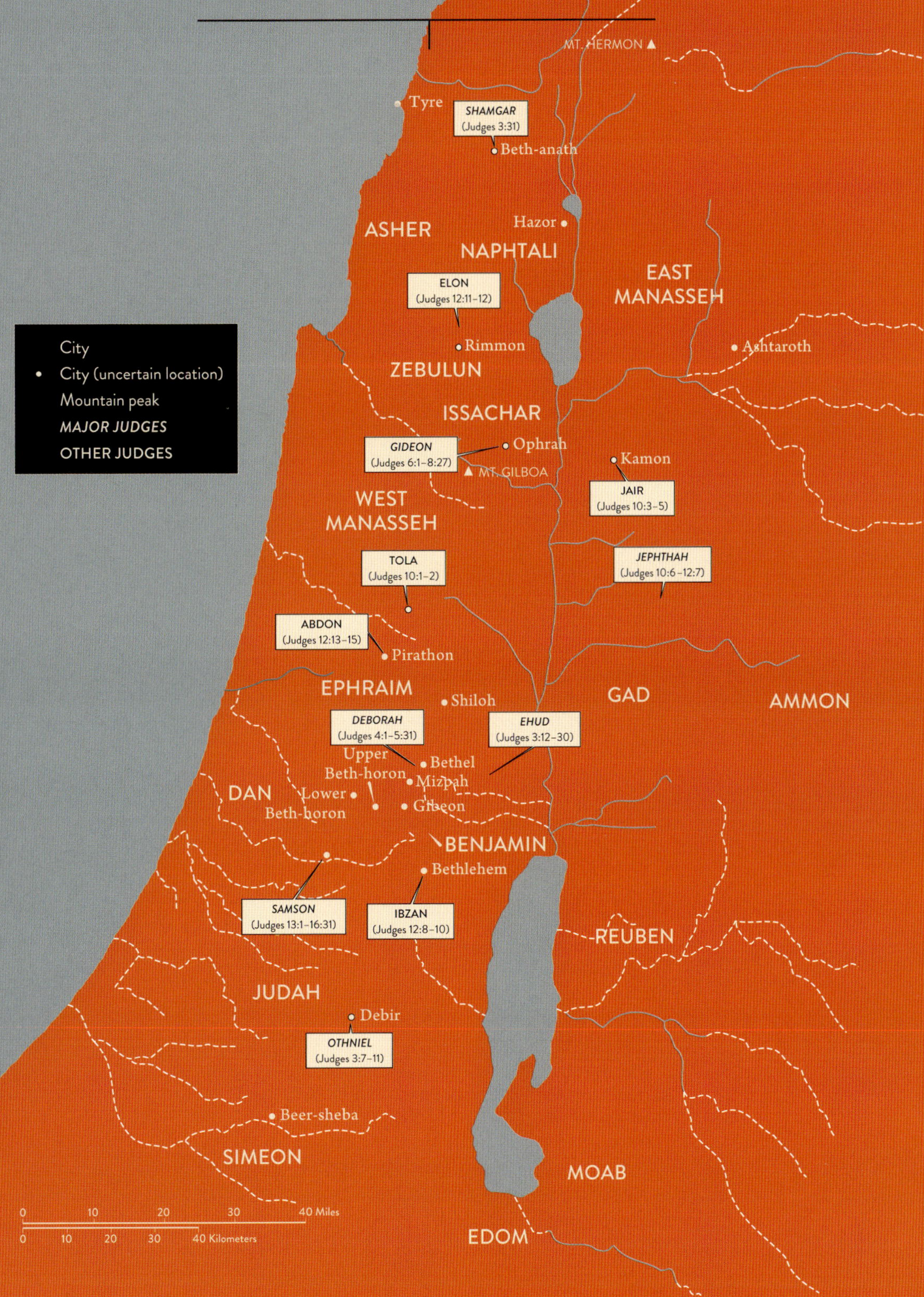

JUDGES

The Oppressors of Israel

THE OPPRESSOR	HISTORY IN JOSHUA, JUDGES, AND RUTH	ISRAEL'S DELIVERER
Mesopotamia	A Mesopotamian king subdued Israel for a time during the period of the judges *(Judg 3:8)*.	**Othniel**
The Moabites	The story of Ehud and Eglon illustrates conflict *(Judg 3:15–24)*, while the Israelites and Moabites in the book of Ruth illustrate peaceful relations *(Ruth 4:18–22)*.	**Ehud**
The Ammonites	The Ammonites made claim to all the territory in Moab as far south as the Arnon *(Judg 11:13)*, while the book of Joshua makes the same claim for Israel *(13:15–28)*.	**Ehud, Jephthah, Ibzan, Elon, Abdon**
The Amalekites	The atrocities of the descendants of Esau *(Gen 36:12)* against Israel caused God to command Saul to exterminate the Amalekites *(1 Sam 15:2–3)*.	**Ehud**
The Canaanites	Located between the Mediterranean Sea and the Jordan River; biblical evidence is scant for any type of concerted Canaanite aggression against the Israelites. The book of Joshua *(see 9:1–2; 10:1–5)* indicates that in emergency situations the independent city-state kings formed defense coalitions, but no one had power to unite all Canaan against Israel. In Judges *(see chaps. 4–5)*, Deborah is depicted as having fought against the Canaanites. However, the Canaanites and Israelites gradually melded together, a phenomenon essentially completed by the end of David's rule.	**Deborah and Barak**
The Midianites	In the time of the judges, the Midianites along with the Amalekites began to raid Israel using camels to strike swiftly over great distances. Gideon drove them out and killed their leaders *(see Judg 6–8)*.	**Gideon, Tola, Jair**
The Philistines	The most dramatic phase of Philistine history began in the period of the judges, when the Philistines were the principal enemy of and the major political threat to Israel. This threat is first seen in the stories of Samson *(see Judg 13–16)*. The threat intensified as the Philistines encroached on the territory of the tribe of Dan, ultimately forcing Dan to move north *(see Judg 18:11,29)*.	**Samson**

Mighty Acts of God in Early Israel

Stopped the Jordan River

Joshua 3:9–17

Destroyed Jericho's wall

Joshua 6:15–21

Stopped time for a day

Joshua 10:1–15

Threw a Canaanite army into confusion

Judges 4:12–16

Gave the sign of the fleece to Gideon twice

Judges 6:33–40

Sustained Samson with flowing water from a rock

Judges 15:19

Strengthened Samson again to bring down a Philistine temple barehanded

Judges 16:26–30

Ruth

Genre | **HISTORICAL NARRATIVE**

The book of Ruth recounts the unexpected way that God extended the family line of a widow named Naomi through Ruth, who was an ancestor of David and Jesus.

INTRODUCTION

AUTHOR The Talmud attributes the authorship of Ruth to Samuel, but the book itself offers no hint of the identity of its author. We can only speculate about who might have written the book of Ruth, and its provenance and date must be deduced from the internal evidence—language and style, historical allusions, and themes. The family records at the end and the explanation of archaic customs require a date during or later than the reign of King David (1011–971 BC).

BACKGROUND The book of Ruth is set "during the time of the judges" (1:1), a period of social and religious disorder when "everyone did whatever seemed right to him" (Judg 17:6). Historically, this era bridged the time between the conquest of the land under Joshua and the rise of King David, whose family records form the conclusion of the book.

MESSAGE AND PURPOSE The family records of David at the end of the book show that the Lord worked through this story to provide for his people's need of a king. The book of Ruth demonstrates how the Lord shows his covenant faithfulness to his undeserving people, often in surprising ways. In the course of the narrative, each of the main characters proved to be a person of extraordinary courage and covenant love (Hb. *chesed*; "loving-kindness, faithfulness, loyalty"). The key word in the book is "kindness" (1:8; 2:20; 3:10).

SUMMARY The book of Ruth gets its name from one of its principal characters, a Moabite woman named Ruth who was the ancestor of David and Jesus. After reading the book of Judges, which paints a dark and depressing picture of Israel, the reader is relieved to encounter Ruth. Although the book is relatively short, it is rich in examples of kindness, faith, and patience. It is one of the five scrolls that was to be read during the Jewish festivals, in particular the Festival of Weeks.

STRUCTURE The book of Ruth is a delightful short story with a classical plot that moves from crisis to complication to resolution. The narrator draws the reader into the minds of the characters (successively Naomi, Ruth, and Boaz), inviting us to identify with their personal anxieties and joys and in the end to celebrate the movement from emptiness and frustration to fulfillment and joy.

Outline

I. Scene 1: Moab (1:1–22)
- A. Elimelech's departure (1:1–5)
- B. Naomi's despair (1:6–13)
- C. Ruth's decision (1:14–22)

II. Scene 2: Fields of Bethlehem (2:1–23)
- A. Ruth meets Boaz (2:1–14)
- B. Boaz provides for Ruth and Naomi (2:15–23)

III. Scene 3: Boaz's Threshing Floor (3:1–18)
- A. Boaz's desire to marry Ruth (3:1–11)
- B. Marriage delayed (3:12–18)

IV. Scene 4: City of Bethlehem (4:1–22)
- A. Boaz marries Ruth (4:1–12)
- B. Ruth gives birth to Obed (4:13–15)
- C. Naomi is blessed with a new family (4:16)
- D. Ruth is an ancestor of David (4:17–22)

WORD STUDY

menuchah

Hebrew pronunciation:
[meh noo KHAH]

CSB translation:
rest, security

Uses in Ruth: 1
Uses in the OT: 21

Focus passage:
Ruth 1:9

Menuchah, from *nuach* (*rest*), denotes *rest* (Jer 45:3). Often *menuchah* signifies *resting place* as a dwelling place: a homestead (Isa 32:18), campsite (Num 10:33), temple (1 Chr 28:2), tribal inheritance (Gen 49:15), or nation (Mic 2:10). *Menuchah* connotes resting place (Isa 66:1). *Menuchah* indicates *rest* from enemies (1 Chr 22:9), *relief* from anxiety (2 Sam 14:17), or *rest* (Ruth 1:9). It functions adjectivally as *quiet* (Ps 23:2) or adverbially as *easily* (Judg 20:43). A *quartermaster* is a "master of *rest,*" supplying troops with physical necessities (Jer 51:59). *Menuchah* describes Canaan as a restful home for Israel (Deut 12:9).

ga'al

Hebrew pronunciation:
[gah AHL]

CSB translation:
redeem, avenge

Uses in Ruth: 22
Uses in the OT: 104

Focus passage:
Ruth 4:1,3–4,6,8,14

Ga'al occurs only in biblically related usage. The original sense may have been "restore, repair." Once *ga'al* implies *reclaim* (Job 3:5). Four times each it is parallel with *padah* ("ransom," Jer 31:11) or *yasha'* ("save," Ps 106:10). A legal duty to *redeem* fell on relatives (Lev 25:49), and participles connote *relative* (Num 5:8) or *kinsman* (1 Kgs 16:11). Land, houses, livestock, and people could be *redeemed* from another's possession by payment (Lev 25:25; 27:28). *Avengers* of blood were relatives responsible to slay murderers of family members (Num 35:19,21). God is the *Redeemer* (Isa 49:26), rescuing people from slavery (Exod 6:6), transgressions (Isa 44:22), harm (Gen 48:16), enemies (Ps 107:2), captivity (Isa 43:14), and death (Hos 13:14). *Ga'al* with *ge'ullah* (14x) suggests *take the right of redemption* (Ruth 4:6).

Women in Jesus's Lineage

ABRAHAM
ISAAC
JACOB
JUDAH — TAMAR
PEREZ
HEZRON
ARAM
AMMINADAB
NAHSHON
SALMON — RAHAB
BOAZ — RUTH
OBED
JESSE
KING DAVID — BATHSHEBA
KING SOLOMON
JOSEPH* — MARY
JESUS CHRIST — (FROM MATT 1:1–6,16)

TAMAR

Not to be confused with David's daughter in 2 Samuel 13, this Tamar was the daughter-in-law of Judah and wife of his eldest son, Er (Gen 38:6). Er was "evil in the LORD's sight" (v. 7) and died before fathering a child with Tamar, and so Judah charged Er's brother Onan with the responsibility of bearing a child in Er's name. Onan refused to "produce offspring for his brother" (v. 9), which was "evil in the LORD's sight" (v. 10), and so he died as well. After Judah consigned Tamar to widowhood, she would later deceive him to become pregnant (vv. 12–19). She gave birth to twins, Perez and Zerah (vv. 27–30). Judah, Tamar, Perez, and Zerah are each mentioned in Jesus's genealogy (Matt 1:3).

RAHAB

A prostitute in Jericho. Having received knowledge of what God had done for the Israelites in Egypt and in the wilderness, she believed that God would give the land to the Israelites, so she protected Joshua's spies from the king's officials and asked for mercy for her and her family, which she received (Josh 2:1–24; 6:15–25). The New Testament points to Rahab as an example of faith and obedience (Heb 11:31; Jas 2:25–26).

RUTH

A Moabitess. She was widowed by the death of her Israelite husband, Mahlon, but instead of returning to her people, in faith she traveled to Israel with her mother-in-law, Naomi, pledging loyalty to her, her people, and her God until death (Ruth 1:16–17). She worked hard to provide for both herself and Naomi, and she received the favor of **Boaz**, her family redeemer who would later marry her.

BATHSHEBA

Wife of Uriah the Hethite (2 Sam 11:3), Bathsheba is known from the notorious account of King David's act of adultery. Focusing on David's fixation with her and his conniving attempts to cover his sin, the narrative presents David as blameworthy for the events that unfold. After David slept with her, Bathsheba became pregnant. Following a failed attempt to cover up his involvement with the pregnancy, David enacted a scheme that would result in Uriah's death on the battlefield (11:14–17). David married Bathsheba, who bore him a son who died as a result of David's egregious sin (12:11–20). Bathsheba went on to bear David's son Solomon, eventually playing a vital role in his becoming king (1 Kgs 1:11–2:19).

MARY

Famously the mother of Jesus, Mary was a young woman and virgin who lived in Nazareth and a relative of Elizabeth, mother of John the Baptist (Luke 1:5,26). She became the wife of Joseph after receiving word that she would give birth to Jesus, Son of the Most High and Son of David, through supernatural means (vv. 31–35). Despite Mary's unprecedented pregnancy, Joseph agreed to go forward with the marriage after learning from an angel in a dream that the child's conception came as a result of the Holy Spirit's work (Matt 1:18–25). Matthew presented the supernatural-virgin conception in Mary as a fulfillment of Isaiah 7:14.

*Though his conception as a human came in an unusual, supernatural manner (Matt 1:20), Jesus's lineage from David through Joseph was nonetheless legal and legitimate because Joseph was seen as his adoptive father (see Luke 1:27; 2:4; 3:23ff; 4:22; John 1:45; 6:42). Note also how Matthew differentiated between how others in this line were "fathered," while he described Joseph as "the husband of Mary, who gave birth to Jesus" (Matt 1:16), indicating Jesus's extraordinary origins.

1–2 Samuel

Genre | **HISTORICAL NARRATIVE**

The books of 1–2 Samuel narrate a transition in Israel's history from theocracy to monarchy, focusing primarily on the downfall of Saul's kingship and the establishment of David's kingship.

INTRODUCTION

AUTHOR

Early tradition suggests 1 and 2 Samuel were originally one book. Some scholars believe Samuel was largely responsible for the material up to 1 Samuel 25 and that the prophets Nathan and Gad gave significant input to the rest (based on 1 Chr 29:29). This proposal, however, must remain speculative because the books name no authors. The reference to "kings of Judah" places the writing of 1–2 Samuel well after the kingdom divided (1 Sam 27:6).

BACKGROUND

After Israel's conquest of the land during the days of Joshua, Israel entered a time of apostasy. The book of Judges describes recurrences of a cycle with predictable phases of idolatry, oppression, deliverance, and repentance. The book of 1 Samuel picks up the historical record toward the end of those stormy days.

MESSAGE AND PURPOSE

The books of 1 and 2 Samuel describe God's relationship with his covenant people and his faithful response to the terms of that covenant. The Lord also established a special covenant with David, a covenant that ultimately found its fulfillment in the Lord Jesus Christ. The books of 1 and 2 Samuel describe Israel's transition from a loosely organized tribal league under God (a theocracy) to a centralized leadership under a king who answered to God (a monarchy). Samuel's life and ministry greatly shaped this period of restructuring as he consistently pointed people back to God.

SUMMARY

The books of 1 and 2 Samuel highlight a significant transition time in Israel's history. As 1 Samuel begins, Israel is a loosely organized tribal league living under poor spiritual leadership. God's plan for his people nonetheless continued as he raised up Samuel to guide Israel's transition from a theocracy to a monarchy. Saul's kingship constitutes the remainder of 1 Samuel, while David's kingship is largely the focus of 2 Samuel.

STRUCTURE

The first seven chapters of 1 Samuel describe Samuel's birth, call, and initial ministry among the Israelites. Chapter 8 is a major turning point as the people ask for a king to rule them "the same as all the other nations have" (1 Sam 8:5). Chapters 9–12 then describe Saul's selection—at God's direction, yet not his perfect will for the time (1 Sam 12:16–18). First Samuel 13–31 describes Saul's victories and failures. Second Samuel 1–4 describes the struggle for Israel's throne that began with Saul's death. Second Samuel 5–24 presents highlights of David's reign, most notably God's promise to establish the throne of David's kingdom forever (2 Sam 7:1–29).

Outlines

1 SAMUEL

I. **Samuel's Ministry (1:1–12:25)**
   A. Samuel's birth and call (1:1–3:21)
   B. The ark narrative (4:1–7:17)
   C. The people ask for a king (8:1–12:25)

II. **Saul's Reign (13:1–31:13)**
   A. Saul's battles with the Philistines (13:1–14:52)
   B. Saul's failure against the Amalekites (15:1–35)
   C. David's selection as Saul's successor (16:1–23)
   D. David's victory over Goliath (17:1–58)
   E. David's struggles with Saul (18:1–26:25)
   F. Saul's reign ends (27:1–31:13)

2 SAMUEL

I. **David's Activities after Saul's Death (1:1–4:12)**
   A. David grieves for Saul and Jonathan (1:1–27)
   B. David in Hebron as king of Judah (2:1–4:12)

II. **David as King of Judah and Israel (5:1–15:6)**
   A. David's military successes (5:1–10:19)
   B. David's great sin and its consequences (11:1–13:39)
   C. David's problems with his son Absalom (14:1–15:6)

III. **Absalom's Rebellion and David's Final Days as King (15:7–24:25)**
   A. Insurrection and death of Absalom (15:7–19:8)
   B. David returns to Jerusalem as king (19:9–20:26)
   C. Events of David's latter days (21:1–24:25)

WORD STUDY

nacham

Hebrew pronunciation:
[nah KHAHM]

CSB translation:
relent, comfort, repent

Uses in 1 Samuel: 4
Uses in the OT: 108

Focus passage:
1 Samuel 15:11,29,35

Nacham means *change one's mind* (Exod 13:17). God *regrets* (Gen 6:6) or *relents* (1 Chr 21:15). Sinners feel *regret* (Jer 31:19). One *takes* words *back* (Ps 110:4). *Nacham* often entails reaching a positive condition; one *finishes mourning* (Gen 38:12), *is moved to pity* (Judg 2:18), or *is satisfied* (Isa 57:6). *Nacham* implies *having* (Judg 21:6) or *showing* (Jer 15:6) *compassion*. Intensive forms denote *console* (2 Sam 10:2), *comfort* (Gen 37:35), or *bring relief* (Gen 5:29). Intensive participles suggest *comforters* (Ps 69:20) or *men with condolences* (2 Sam 10:3). Reflexive-passive verbs signify *console oneself* (Gen 27:42), *find comfort* (Ps 119:52), *be appeased* (Ezek 5:13), or *have compassion* (Deut 32:36). God sometimes does not *change his mind* (Num 23:19). *Tanchum* (5x) encompasses *comfort* (Ps 94:19) and *consoling* (Jer 16:7). *Nichumiym* (3x) involves *compassion* (Hos 11:8) and *comfort* (Zech 1:13). *Nechamah* (2x, Job 6:10) is *comfort*. *Nocham* means *compassion* (Hos 13:14).

meshiyach

Hebrew pronunciation:
[meh SHEE akh]

CSB translation:
anointed

Uses in 2 Samuel: 5
Uses in the OT: 38

Focus passage:
2 Samuel 1:14,16

Meshiyach, from *mashach* (*anoint*, 70x), describes somebody *anointed* to serve God, usually kings (1 Sam 10:1), prophets (1 Kgs 19:16), or priests (Exod 28:41). *Meshiyach* figuratively designates patriarchs as specially chosen (Ps 105:15). Cyrus is *God's anointed* because of his role in delivering Israel from Babylonian captivity (Isa 45:1). All priests were anointed (Exod 29:21), but the specially anointed high priest was called *the anointed priest* (Lev 4:3). The king of Israel is often called *the* LORD*'s anointed* (2 Sam 1:14). After David, *meshiyach* indicates Davidic kings (Ps 18:50). *Meshiyach* identifies God's *Anointed One*, Christ, in Psalm 2:2, according to Acts 4:26. *Meshiyach* is translated *Anointed One* in Daniel 9:25–26. *Mashach* also means *pour oil* (Gen 31:13), *coat* (Exod 29:2), *oil* (Isa 21:5), *paint* (Jer 22:14), or *anoint oneself* (Amos 6:6). *Mishchah* (21x, Exod 25:6) and *moshchah* (2x, Exod 40:15) mean *anointing*, and *mimshach* suggests *anointed* (Ezek 28:14).

bayith

Hebrew pronunciation:
[BA yith]

CSB translation:
house, temple, palace, family

Uses in 2 Samuel: 125
Uses in the OT: 2,287

Focus passage:
2 Samuel 7:1–2,5–7,11,13, 16,18–19

The root, basically meaning *house*, occurs in other Semitic languages; in the OT ***bayith*** refers to various containers. The *building* (1 Chr 29:4) is a *palace* (Exod 7:23), *shrine* (Judg 17:5), or *home* (Gen 43:26). A "*house* of weapons," "slaves," "wine," or "women" is, respectively, *armory* (Isa 39:2), *place of slavery* (Exod 13:3), *banquet hall* (Song 2:4), or *harem* (Esth 2:3). *Bayith* suggests *cell, pen, tomb, quarters, haven, estate*, or *shelter*. It can indicate *holders* (Exod 25:27) or *bottles* (Isa 3:20), a *prison* (Gen 40:14), or a spider's *web* (Job 8:14). *Bayith* also designates the inhabitants or members of a house: *people* (Neh 4:16), *household* (Gen 7:1), or *family* (Gen 35:2). It signifies dynasties (1 Sam 2:35) or ones *fathers' families* (Num 1:2). In certain phrases *bayith* indicates what is *inside* (Gen 6:14), *behind* (Exod 26:33), or *inward* (2 Sam 5:9). Transliterated *Beth*, it forms part of place names.

1–2 Samuel Timeline

1200 BC

SAMSON 1120?–1060?

SAMUEL 1105?–1025?

1200 The Olmec civilization flourishes in Central America, establishing a foundation for subsequent civilizations in the Americas.

1200–1000 The process of iron smelting is developed in Armenia.

1184 The city of Troy falls to the Greeks after a 10-year siege.

1170 World's first recorded labor strike, Thebes, Egypt

1140? Events in Ruth

1100 BC

SAUL 1080?–1010
DAVID 1050?–970

1114–976 Botanical gardens developed by Assyrians during the reign of Tiglath-pileser I

1105?–1010 Events in 1 Samuel

1105 Chou-pei, one of China's early mathematical works

1050 Saul anointed as king

1000 Iron technology advances throughout India.

1000 The Chinese store ice for use in refrigeration.

1000 Oats are cultivated in central Europe.

1000 BC

BATHSHEBA 1025?–960?

1085–945 Egyptian 21st Dynasty

1010 David becomes king of Judah.

1003 David becomes king over all Israel.

1000? David conquers Jerusalem.

1000? David moves the ark to Jerusalem.

SOLOMON 990?–931
REHOBOAM 971–913

1010–970 Events in 2 Samuel

1010–970 Events in 1 Chronicles

975? Absalom's revolt

970 Solomon becomes king.

966 Solomon begins construction of the temple in Jerusalem.

959 The temple dedicated

950 Ascendancy of Neo-Assyrian Empire

900 BC

JEROBOAM 971?–909

931? The kingdom divides.

931–722 Israel: the northern kingdom

931–586 Judah: the southern kingdom

900 Celts migrate across Europe and begin to settle in Britain.

900 Etruscans emigrate from Lydia to Italy as a result of an extended famine.

Movement/Locations of the Ark

The origin of the ark goes back to Moses at Sinai. It was built after all the tabernacle specifications had been communicated and completed. Designed for mobility, the ark was about four feet long, two and a half feet wide with permanent poles for carrying, since only priestly (Levitical) personnel were allowed to carry it.

Joshua 3–6 The ark played a prominent role in the "holy war" narratives of the crossing of the Jordan and the conquest of Jericho.

Deuteronomy 11:26–32; 27:1–26; Joshua 8:30–35; Judges 20:26 After the conquest, it was variously located at Gilgal, Shechem, or Bethel, wherever Israel was gathered for worship.

1 Samuel 1:9; 3:3 The ark was permanently located in Shiloh Ⓐ, where a temple was built to house it.

1 Samuel 4 The ark was captured by the Philistines in the battle of Ebenezer.

1 Samuel 5:1–6:12 The adventures of the ark in the cities of Ashdod Ⓑ, Gath Ⓒ, and Ekron Ⓓ were told to magnify the strength and glory of God.

1 Samuel 6 The men of Beth-shemesh Ⓔ of Israel welcomed the return of the ark, until they violated its holiness by looking into it.

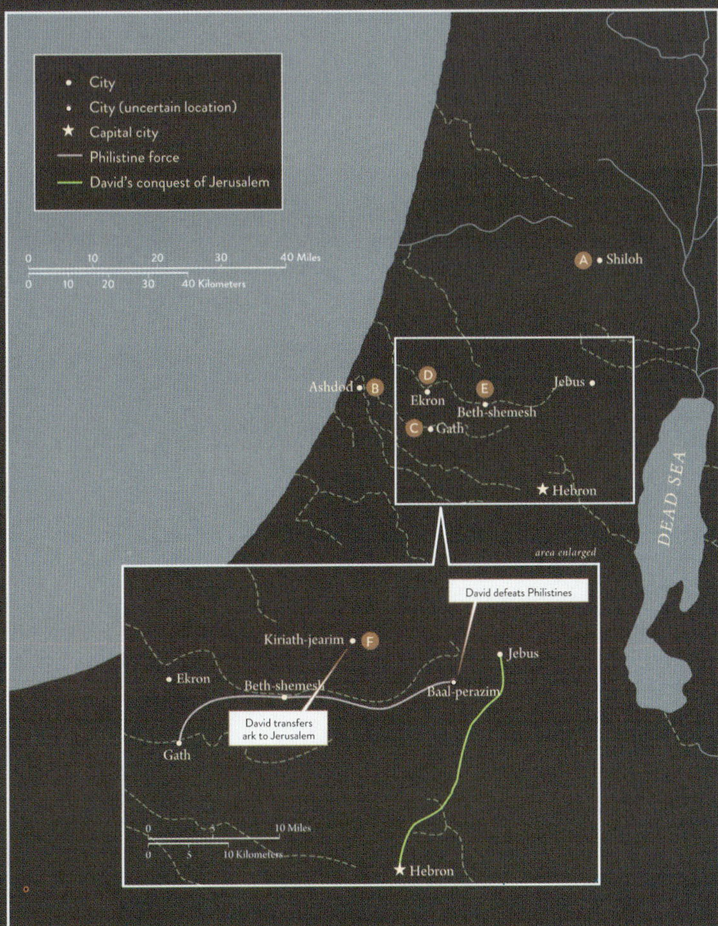

1 Samuel 7 Then the ark was carried to Kiriath-jearim Ⓕ, where it remained in neglect until David's time.

1 Samuel 6:21–7:2; 2 Samuel 6 David recovered the ark and moved it to his new capital and sanctuary in Jerusalem.

1 Kings 8; 2 Chronicles 5:1 Finally, Solomon built the temple, planned by David, to house the ark, which he then transported into the holy of holies.

King Saul vs. King David

KING SAUL	KING DAVID
Chosen by God and anointed by Samuel *(1 Sam 10:1,21)*	Chosen by God and anointed by Samuel *(1 Sam 16:12–13)*
Cowered when chosen to assume the throne *(1 Sam 10:22)*	Waited on God when chosen to assume the throne *(1 Sam 24)*
Man's king *(1 Sam 10:23–24)*	God's king *(2 Sam 7:8–16)*
Did not seek the Lord's favor and rejected his instruction *(1 Sam 13:12; 15:10–31)*	Sinned and then confessed what he had done was against the Lord *(2 Sam 11; 12:13; 24:10; Ps 25)*
Failed to meet God's standards for kingship *(1 Sam 15:23,35; 16:1)*	Maintained his focus on eternity despite his failures *(2 Sam 7:29)*
Lost God's peace *(1 Sam 16:14)*	Found God's peace *(Ps 4:8; 37:11)*
Fearful *(1 Sam 17:11)*	Brave *(2 Sam 17:1; 1 Chr 18)*
Sought the people's praise *(1 Sam 18:6–8)*	Sought to follow God's heart and build his kingdom *(1 Sam 13:14; 2 Sam 7; Acts 13:22; Ps 119:34)*
Filled with jealousy *(1 Sam 18:8)*	Filled with faith *(1 Sam 17:32–37)*
Unforgiving *(1 Sam 14:44; 18:9)*	Forgiving *(1 Sam 26)*
Determined to kill David *(1 Sam 18:10–12,17–27)*	Determined not to kill Saul *(1 Sam 24:21–22)* and even avenged Saul's death *(2 Sam 1)*
Hateful *(1 Sam 20:30–32; 22:11–29)*	Kind *(2 Sam 9)*

Prophets, Priests, and Kings

Prophets, priests, and kings led their covenant people at various times and in different ways. Of these three groups, the kings assumed the greatest leadership role due to the coercive nature of political power when aligned with military force, not to mention the people's voluntary submission in asking for a king. The priests performed religious duties related to the temple or other shrines. The individual prophets were active in inverse proportion to the righteous actions of the kings. When the kings sinned against the Lord by violating his covenant instruction, the prophets appeared to confront the kings and to pronounce judgment if repentance did not ensue.

THE PROPHETS

- Prophets were called by God to speak about the future. They received a word from God through various means—declarations from God, visions, dreams, and so forth. They were primarily spokespersons who called God's people to obedience by appealing to Israel's past and future.
- Prophets relayed God's message by word and deed. All prophets occasionally saw a miraculous fulfillment of God's word (Isa 38:8).
- Prophets conveyed the word of God by writing (Isa 8:11; Ezek 43:11).
- Prophets were to minister to their people, testing God's people's lives (Jer 6:27) and watching for moral compromise (Ezek 3:17). Particularly important was the role of intercessor (1 Kgs 13:6; 17:17–24; 2 Kgs 4:18–37; Isa 59:16; Jer 14:17–21; Amos 7:2).
- Moses was a prophetic prototype (Acts 3:21–24). Deborah predicted victory and identified the right time to attack during the conquest of the promised land (Judg 4:6–14). Samuel, who led Israel during its transition to monarchy, was a prophet, priest, and judge (1 Sam 3:20; 7:6,15).
- The prophets did more than predict the future; their messages called Israel to honor God. Their prophecies were not general principles but specific words corresponding to Israel's historical context.[5]

THE PRIESTS

- The priesthood originally held an important place in the covenant community since God designated his people as his "kingdom of priests" (Exod 19:6).
- The priests were responsible for maintaining the religious shrines, whether the tabernacle in the wilderness or the temple in Jerusalem.
- The priests also had to educate the covenant people in the instruction Moses received on Mount Sinai (called the Torah).
- Historically, the priesthood became an establishment answerable to the king.

THE KINGS

- From the time Samuel anointed Saul as their first king (1 Sam 10) until the time the Babylonians blinded Zedekiah, Judah's last king, and took him into exile (2 Kgs 25), the covenant people lived under a total of 43 different kings.
- Saul, David, and Solomon presided over a more-or-less unified kingdom. After Solomon's death, the kingdom divided in two with the northern tribes taking the name Israel and the tribe of Judah becoming the southern kingdom.
- Interestingly, both Israel and Judah had 20 kings each during the duration of their kingdoms. Israel lasted from Solomon's death around 930 BC until the fall of the capital city of Samaria in 722 BC. The kingdom of Judah survived for an additional 136 years.
- The most significant theological truth about the period of the kings is that only 9 of the 41 kings "did what was right in the LORD's sight" (1 Kgs 15:5).
- The most notable example of these good kings was David. He became the proverbial measuring stick by which all other kings were assessed.
- When the Lord informed Jeroboam he would be king of Israel, Ahijah the prophet commended him to do what was right "as [the Lord's] servant David did" (11:38). A short time later, the Lord spoke through Ahijah again, judging Jeroboam because of his sin and because he was "not like [the Lord's] servant David" (14:8).
- The remaining eight kings who did what was right in the Lord's eyes were Asa, Jehoshaphat, Joash, Amaziah, Uzziah, Jotham, Hezekiah, and Josiah. All these kings, like David, were from Judah. All the northern kings did evil in the Lord's eyes.[6]

Israel's Counterparts in 1 Samuel

PEOPLE	FATHER	LOCATION	BATTLE OF THRONES
Moab/ Moabites	Moab, the son of Lot and his oldest daughter	East of the Dead Sea	○ Saul took control of some Moabite cities *(1 Sam 14:47)*. ○ Conquered by David *(2 Sam 8:2)*.
Ammon/ Ammonites	Ben-ammi, son of Lot and his second daughter	Northeast of the Dead Sea	○ Saul defeated King Nahash at Jabesh-gilead *(1 Sam 11:1–11)*. ○ Saul took control of some Ammonite cities *(1 Sam 14:47)*. ○ David defeated King Hanun *(2 Sam 12:26–31)*.
Edom/ Edomites	Esau, son of Isaac	Southeast and south of the Dead Sea	○ Saul took control of some Edomite cities *(1 Sam 14:47)*. ○ David defeated the Edomites *(1 Chr 18:12–13)*.
Kings of Zobah		South of Syria	○ Saul fought against "the kings of Zobah" *(1 Sam 14:47)*. ○ David defeated them, along with the Ammonites *(2 Sam 10)*.
Philistia/ Philistines		Southwest part of Canaan	○ The Philistines defeated the Israelites and captured the ark of the covenant in the battle of Ebenezer *(1 Sam 4:1–18)*. ○ Saul "caused havoc" against the Philistines *(1 Sam 14:47; also see 7:5–11)*. ○ David defeated them *(2 Sam 5:17–25)*.
Amalek/ Amalekites	Amalek, son of Eliphaz, a son of Esau	Southwest of the Dead Sea	○ Saul failed to follow God's command to completely destroy Amalek *(1 Sam 15:1–9)*. ○ David defeated the Amalekites after they burned down their town of Ziklag and kidnapped their wives, sons, and daughters *(1 Sam 30)*.

David's Enemies

DAVID'S ENEMY	ENEMY'S THREAT	DAVID'S ACTION	GOD'S PROVISION
Lion/Bear	Carried off lambs from David's flock *(1 Sam 17:34)*	Killed lions and bears to protect his sheep *(1 Sam 17:35–36)*	The Lord rescued David from the paw of the lion and the bear *(1 Sam 17:37)*
Goliath, a Giant	Defied the armies of the living God *(1 Sam 17:8–10,26)*	Defeated Goliath with a sling and a stone; with no sword of his own, he struck him down and killed him *(1 Sam 17:48–51)*	The Lord handed Goliath over to David *(1 Sam 17:45–47)*
King Saul	Tried to kill David with his spear and his army *(1 Sam 18–26)*	Fled from Saul and twice restrained himself from killing Saul, the Lord's anointed *(1 Sam 24;26)*	The Lord delivered David from the hand of Saul *(2 Sam 12:7)*
The Philistines	Searched for King David to kill him *(2 Sam 5:17–18)*	Went to war with the Philistines and defeated them *(2 Sam 5:20–25)*	The Lord handed the Philistines over to David *(2 Sam 5:19,24)*
David, Himself	Sinned against the Lord by committing adultery and murder *(2 Sam 11)*	When confronted by the prophet Nathan, he confessed his sin and repented *(2 Sam 12:1–13)*	The Lord took away his sin; he would not die, though his son would and rebellion would come from his own family *(2 Sam 12:10–14)*
Absalom, David's Son	Rebelled against his father to kill him and take the throne *(2 Sam 15:1–14)*	Fled Jerusalem, entrusting himself to the Lord's favor or judgment *(2 Sam 15:25–26)*	The Lord brought about Absalom's ruin to restore David to the throne *(2 Sam 17:14)*

Giants in the Bible

Giants—or persons of unusual stature who often are reputed to possess great strength and power—can be divided into three classes.

NEPHILIM [NEF UH LIM]

The earliest biblical references to giants are to the Nephilim born to the "daughters of mankind" and the "sons of God" (Gen 6:1–4). Interpreters differ on the origin of these giants. Some understand the "sons of God" to be angelic beings who intermarried with human women (see Jude 6). Others view them as descendants of Seth who intermarried with the ungodly. Later descendants of the Nephilim were called "the descendants of Anak" (Num 13:33) or Anakim (Deut 2:11; 9:2). They inhabited the land of Canaan before Israel's conquest. Egyptian records testify to their presence as early as 2000 BC. Similar races of giants had also inhabited Moab (Deut 2:9–10) and Ammon (Deut 2:19–20).

REPHAIM [REF AY IM]

A second class of giants who inhabited pre-Israelite Palestine was the Rephaim. Their last survivor was Og, king of Bashan (Deut 3:11,13). A valley near Jerusalem (Josh 15:8; 18:16) and part of the wooded country in the tribal territory of Ephraim (Josh 17:15) retained their name.

INDIVIDUAL GIANTS

The Old Testament also records cases of individual giants. The well-known Goliath (1 Sam 17) was a Philistine champion. A family of giants from Gath were among the Philistine enemies slain by David and his followers (2 Sam 21:16–22; 1 Chr 20:4–8).

Samuel's Life

THE YOUNG MAN

- Miraculously born to Hannah and Elkanah (1 Sam 1:20)
- Weaned and given to the Lord, as Hannah had promised (1:23–28)

Grew up in the presence of the Lord (2:21)

Grew in stature and in favor with the Lord and men (2:26)

- Heard the word of the Lord for the first time (3:1–14)

Grew, and the Lord was with him; a confirmed prophet (3:19–4:1)

THE JUDGE

- Officiated over a covenant renewal for the people (7:2–6)
- Judged Israel throughout his life (7:15)

THE KINGMAKER

- Grew old and appointed his sons as judges, but they were wicked (8:1–3)
- Heard the Israelites' demand for a king like the nations and gave God's response (8:4–22)
- Anointed Saul as ruler over Israel (10:1)
- Led the ceremony publicly identifying Saul as king (10:17–25)
- Led the ceremony confirming Saul as king (11:14–15)
- Gave final public speech, transitioning from judges to kings (12:1–25)
  - *Called the people to covenant faithfulness*
  - *Promised to pray for and teach the people*
- Arrived to offer a sacrifice before a battle, but Saul had already offered it (13:10–12)
  - *Confronted Saul—his reign would now be temporary (13:13–14)*
- Gave command to destroy the Amalekites completely, but Saul disobeyed (15:1–9)
  - *Confronted Saul—the kingdom was now torn from him (15:12–31)*
- Killed King Agag of Amalek (15:32–33)
- Anointed David as king over Israel (16:1–13)
- Met with David to protect him from King Saul's pursuit (19:18)
- Died and was mourned by all Israel (25:1)
- Called up as a spirit by Saul through a medium (28:11–19)
  - *Foretold the kingdom would be given to David*
  - *Prophesied Saul's loss and death in battle with the Philistines*

PROPHET: Delivered the word of the Lord to the people, and everything he prophesied the Lord fulfilled (3:19–20)

PRIEST: Served in the tabernacle and offered sacrifices for the people (3:3; 7:17; 10:8)

JUDGE: Led the Israelites to obey the covenant and delivered the people from the Philistines (7:2–17)

Seeing Jesus in the Kingdom

THE LORD | *The King of Glory to Whom Belongs All the Earth (Ps 24)*	**THE SON OF MAN** | *The King of Glory over All the Nations (Matt 25:31–46)*
SAMUEL Grew in Stature and in Favor with the Lord and Men *(1 Sam 2:26)*	**JESUS** Grew in Wisdom and Stature and in Favor with God and Men *(Luke 2:52)*
SAUL Disobeyed God to Offer Sacrifices to Him *(1 Sam 15)*	**JESUS** Sacrificed Himself in Obedience to God *(Heb 10:5–10)*
DAVID Unimpressive Appearance, but God's Chosen King *(1 Sam 16:6–13)*	**JESUS** Unimpressive Appearance, but God's Righteous Servant *(Isa 52:13–53:12)*
DAVID Defeated Goliath in the Name of the Lord *(1 Sam 17:45)*	**JESUS** Saves Us from Sin in the Name of the Lord *(Matt 21:9; Rom 10:13)*
JONATHAN Risked His Life for His Friend David *(1 Sam 19:4–7; 20:27–34)*	**JESUS** Laid Down His Life for His Friends *(John 15:12–14)*
DAVID'S SON He Would Build a House for God's Name *(2 Sam 7:13)*	**THE SON OF DAVID** Jesus's Body Is the Sanctuary *(John 2:21)*
SOLOMON A Son to God, Disciplined for His Sin *(2 Sam 7:14; 1 Kgs 11)*	**THE SON OF GOD** Jesus Knew No Sin but Died for Ours *(1 Pet 2:21–25)*
WISDOM God-Given Insight for Living Well *(Prov 1:1–7)*	**CHRIST JESUS** God-Given Wisdom for Our Salvation *(1 Cor 1:30)*
THE TEMPLE A Place for God's Name *(1 Kgs 5:5)*	**THE TRUE TEMPLE** A Person—Jesus, the Son of God *(John 2:13–22)*
JOB Needed a Mediator between God and Men *(Job 16:18–22)*	**JESUS** The One Mediator between God and Men *(1 Tim 2:5)*
OLD TESTAMENT	**NEW TESTAMENT**

God's Covenants

ABRAHAMIC COVENANT (GEN 12:1–3)	DAVIDIC COVENANT (2 SAM 7:8–16)	JESUS
Land	Rest in the Land	**Eternal Rest:** Found in Christ *(Matt 11:28; Heb 3–4)*
Descendant(s)	Descendant(s) on the Throne	**Eternal King:** The Son of David, the Son of Abraham *(Matt 1:1; Luke 1:31–33)*
Blessing	Son on an Eternal Throne	**Eternal Kingdom:** Given All Authority in Heaven and on Earth *(Matt 28:18)*
	Son to Build the Temple	Built the Temple of His Resurrected Body *(John 2:19–22)* and the Temple of His Church *(Matt 16:18; 1 Cor 3:16–17)* for the Blessing of the Whole World

The King of Kings

SAUL "A head taller than anyone else" (1 Sam 9:2; 10:23–24)

Son of Kish, of the tribe of Benjamin

30 years old when he became king of Israel

Reigned for 42 years

Died along with his sons in a battle with the Philistines (1 Sam 31:1–13)

GOOD

- The Spirit of God took control of Saul and he prophesied (1 Sam 10:9–10)
- The Spirit of God took control of Saul and he defended the Israelites (11:6–11)
- Credited the Lord with the victory (11:13)
- Fought bravely and defeated the enemies of Israel (14:47–48)

EVIL

- Foolishly offered the burnt offering instead of waiting for Samuel (1 Sam 13:3–15)
  - His reign would not be permanent but given to another—to a man after God's own heart
- Disobeyed the command to completely destroy the Amalekites (15:7–31)
  - Rejected by the Lord as king, and the Spirit of the Lord left him
- Jealous of David and tried to kill him on multiple occasions (18:8–11; 19:9–10; 24:1–22; 26:1–25)
- Consulted a medium to seek guidance for a battle with the Philistines (28:1–25)

Saul exhibited pride, jealousy, and a resistance to submit to the Lord, even when confronted time and again with his sin. The kingdom was torn from him and given to one better than him because he rejected the word of the Lord.

DAVID "A man after [God's] own heart" (1 Sam 13:14; see 16:7,12)

Son of Jesse, of the tribe of Judah

30 years old when he became king of Israel

Reigned for 40 years

Died in a time of peace with rest from all his enemies (1 Kgs 2:10–11)

GOOD

- The Spirit of the Lord took control of David (1 Sam 16:13)
- Killed Goliath for the glory of the Lord (17:45–51)
- Victorious in battle against Israel's enemies (18:5)
- Spared Saul twice because he was the Lord's anointed, entrusting himself to the Lord's plan (24:1–22; 26:1–25)
- Desired to build God a temple for his name (2 Sam 7:1–7; 1 Kgs 8:18)
- Showed kindness to Mephibosheth, Jonathan's son (2 Sam 9:1–13)

EVIL

- Adultery with Bathsheba and the murder of her husband, Uriah (2 Sam 11:1–27)
- Ordered a census of his fighting men (24:1–10)

David was ruler over Israel and the shepherd of God's people. The Lord confirmed his covenant with David to build him a house and to establish his throne forever. His son after him would build God's temple, and God would treat him as a son, faithfully loved and disciplined when he did wrong. When David sinned and was confronted, he confessed his guilt and submitted himself to the discipline of the Lord.

SOLOMON "Solomon's wisdom" (1 Kgs 4:29–34 ; see 3:4–15)

Son of David, of the tribe of Judah

Reigned for 40 years

Died in a time of unrest from enemies the Lord raised up against him (1 Kgs 11:41–43)

GOOD

- Asked for wisdom from God to lead God's people (1 Kgs 3:4–15)
- Built God a temple for his name (5:1–6:38)
- Displayed his wisdom for the glory of God (4:29; 5:7; 10:1–9)

EVIL

- Had 700 wives and 300 concubines, who turned his heart to worship idols (1 Kgs 11:1–8)
  - The Lord disciplined him with enemies and took the majority of the kingdom from his son and gave it to his servant (11:9–40)

Solomon received the blessings of the Davidic covenant. His throne was firmly established in wisdom and justice, and he built the Lord's temple as God had said. The wisdom and prosperity of the king and his kingdom were a beacon of light to the nations of the greatness of Yahweh. However, he turned to worshipping idols, so the Lord disciplined him and tore the kingdom from his son, though he left him one tribe for the sake of God's promise to David.

JESUS

Son of David, son of Abraham (Matt 1:1)

All authority in heaven and on earth has been given to him (Matt 28:18)

No form, majesty, or beauty that we should desire him (Isa 53:2)

The Son of David and yet also David's Lord (Matt 22:41–45)

"Something greater than Solomon is here" (Luke 11:31)

Jesus is the true Son of God, the delight of his Father (Matt 3:17). Through perfect obedience to the Father, even unto death on a cross to save sinners (Phil 2:8), Jesus showed himself to be the true Son of David, the promised Messiah whose throne would have no end (Luke 1:30–33). He is the true shepherd who lays down his life for his sheep (John 10:11–18). He is the true temple through his resurrection from the dead (John 2:19–22). He is the King of kings and the Lord of lords (Rev 19:16).

1–2 Kings

Genre | **HISTORICAL NARRATIVE**

The books of 1–2 Kings narrate the history of Israel and Judah from the final days of King David until the time of the Assyrian exile (northern kingdom) and the Babylonian exile (southern kingdom).

INTRODUCTION

AUTHOR Scholars cannot identify the authors of any portions of these books. Traditional guesses such as Samuel and Jeremiah lack evidence, although a prominent worshipper of the Lord like Jeremiah would have been influential in the circles that produced these books. Since the books clearly incorporated many earlier documents, the complete authorship would include all writers who contributed to the source documents of this work. At some point, the Holy Spirit worked in the human authors to authenticate the inspired, inerrant books of 1 and 2 Kings.

BACKGROUND The history recorded in 1 and 2 Kings covers approximately 410 years. First Kings begins around 970 BC with the death of King David, and 2 Kings ends around 560 BC with the release of King Jehoiachin from prison. During this time, the nation of Israel split into two kingdoms (930 BC), and both kingdoms went into exile (Israel in 722 BC and Judah in 586 BC).

MESSAGE AND PURPOSE The theological perspective of 1 and 2 Kings is expressed in a number of themes: (1) the sinfulness of the kings and the nation, (2) the conflict between the demands of practical politics and the demands of faith, (3) the glory that God gave to the obedient covenant kings, (4) God's harshness in judgment on some occasions and leniency on others, and (5) the conflict between the worship of the Lord and the worship of other gods.

SUMMARY The titles of these books are certainly descriptive of their contents: the history of the kings and the kingdoms of Israel and Judah. First and Second Kings are part of the 12 Historical Books (Joshua–Esther) of the Old Testament. Originally, these two books were just one but were divided by the translators of the Septuagint (the Greek translation of the Old Testament; also called the LXX).

STRUCTURE The organizing principle of 1 and 2 Kings is not story or narrative. Kings is unique because its basic structural units are the formulaic royal records. Formal openers (1 Kgs 15:9–10) and closers (1 Kgs 15:23–24) usually identify the boundaries of these records. Then the writer could insert other types of literature before, between, and after the openers and closers: narratives, prayers, descriptions, and so on. But the most important element was the evaluation of the ruler's faithfulness to the covenant (1 Kgs 15:11–15). All these materials made up a history of covenant obedience or disobedience.

Outlines

1 KINGS

I. Final Days of King David (1:1–2:12)
- A. Adonijah tries to seize the throne (1:1–40)
- B. Solomon anointed as David's successor (1:41–53)
- C. David's charge to Solomon (2:1–12)

II. Solomon's Reign over the United Kingdom (2:13–11:43)
- A. Solomon deals with his opponents (2:13–46)
- B. Solomon's wisdom (3:1–28)
- C. Solomon's officials (4:1–19)
- D. Solomon's splendor (4:20–34)
- E. Solomon builds the Lord's temple (5:1–8:66)
- F. Solomon's fame and reputation (9:1–10:29)
- G. Solomon's sin and death (11:1–43)

III. The Divided Kingdoms of Judah and Israel (12:1–22:53)
- A. Judah's King Rehoboam (12:1–24)
- B. Israel's King Jeroboam (12:25–14:20)
- C. Judah's King Rehoboam (continued) (14:21–31)
- D. Judah's Abijam and Asa (15:1–24)
- E. Israel's Nadab and Baasha (15:25–16:7)
- F. Israel's Elah, Zimri, Tibni, and Omri (16:8–28)
- G. Israel's King Ahab and the prophet Elijah (16:29–22:40)
- H. Judah's King Jehoshaphat (22:41–50)
- I. Israel's King Ahaziah (22:51–53)

2 KINGS

I. The Divided Kingdom: From Israel's Ahaziah to the Fall of Israel (1:1–17:41)
- A. Ahaziah and the prophet Elijah (1:1–18)
- B. Elijah succeeded by Elisha (2:1–25)
- C. Israel's King Joram (3:1–27)
- D. Elisha's ministry of miracles (4:1–8:15)
- E. Judah's King Jehoram (8:16–24)
- F. Judah's King Ahaziah (8:25–29)
- G. Israel's King Jehu and the prophet Elisha (9:1–10:36)
- H. Queen Athaliah (11:1–16)
- I. Three good kings: Joash, Amaziah, and Azariah (11:17–15:7)
- J. Five bad kings: Zechariah, Shallum, Menahem, Pekahiah, and Pekah (15:8–31)
- K. Jotham (15:32–38)
- L. Ahaz (16:1–20)
- M. Hoshea and God's indictment against Israel (17:1–41)

II. The Kingdom of Judah: From King Hezekiah to the Captivity (18:1–25:30)
- A. Revival under Hezekiah and apostasy (18:1–21:26)
- B. Revival under Josiah and apostasy (22:1–25:7)
- C. Jerusalem falls to the Babylonians (25:8–30)

WORD STUDY

shama'

Hebrew pronunciation:
[sha MAH]

CSB translation:
hear, listen, obey

Uses in 1 Kings: 60
Uses in the OT: 1,165

Focus passage:
1 Kings 10:1,6–8,24

Shama' denotes *hearing* (Gen 3:8) or *listening* (Gen 3:17). *Listening* may imply *agreeing* (1 Sam 30:24) or *discerning* (2 Sam 14:17). God's hearing may involve *being a witness* (Judg 11:10). *Shama'* suggests *responding* to evidence (Exod 4:8). "Listen to my voice" is an idiom for *obey me* (Exod 4:1). The imperative *shema'* calls people to *listen* and obey (Deut 6:4). News can *reach* (Gen 45:16). Intensive forms imply *carefully obeying* (Deut 11:13) or *paying close attention* (Job 21:2). A "*hearing* ear" is *receptive* (Prov 25:12). Passively, *shama'* suggests *resound* (Jer 6:7) or *become public knowledge* (Esth 2:8); something is *reported* (Neh 6:6), *overheard* (1 Sam 17:31), or *heeded* (Eccl 9:16). *Shama'* in causative forms means *proclaim* (Isa 48:20), *summon* (1 Sam 23:8), *tell* (Isa 41:22), or *reveal* (1 Sam 9:27). It can mean *sing, sound, predict, announce*, or *pronounce*. Permissively, it is *allow to be heard, let experience*, or *enable to hear*.

shemen

Hebrew pronunciation:
[SHEH men]

CSB translation:
oil, olive oil, perfume, rich

Uses in 2 Kings: 7
Uses in the OT: 193

Focus passage:
2 Kings 4:2,6–7

Shemen denotes *oil* (Gen 28:18), particularly *olive oil* (Deut 33:24) used in lamps (Exod 27:20), foods (Exod 29:2), and holy anointing oil (Exod 30:24–25). *Shemen* describes "wood" as *olive wood* (1 Kgs 6:23). "Son of shemen" is translated *very fertile* (Isa 5:1). *Shemen* denotes something *large* (Isa 10:27). It suggests *rich* (Isa 28:1) or *choice* (Isa 25:6). Emaciated is literally "grows lean of fat" (Ps 109:24). *Shemen* signifies *perfume* (Song 1:3). The adjective *shamen* (10x) means *fat* (Ezek 34:16), *rich* (Gen 49:20), *fertile* (Num 13:20), *stout* (Judg 3:29), or *plentiful* (Isa 30:23). The verb *shamen* (5x) denotes *become fat* (Deut 32:15). The causative indicates *become prosperous* (Neh 9:25); it describes *dulling minds* (Isa 6:10). *Mishman* (4x) suggests *well-fed* (Isa 10:16), *rich part* (Dan 11:24), *healthy* (Isa 17:4), or *fit* (Ps 78:31). *Shaman* (2x) means *richness* (Gen 27:28); *'ashman*, healthy (Isa 59:10); and *mashmanniym*, what is *rich* (Neh 8:10).

shakav

Hebrew pronunciation:
[shah KAV]

CSB translation:
lie down, sleep, rest

Uses in 2 Kings: 19
Uses in the OT: 212

Focus passage:
2 Kings 15:7,22,38

Shakav means *lie* (Job 21:26) or *lie down* (Judg 5:27). *Shakav* occurs (4x) with *yashen* ("sleep," Ps 3:5), and *shakav* sometimes means *sleep* (Exod 22:27). People *stretch out* (Jonah 1:5), *go to bed* (Gen 19:4), or *stay in bed* (Prov 6:9). Someone ill *is laid up* (2 Kgs 9:16). Felled trees *are laid low* (Isa 14:8). *Shakav* connotes sex as *sleep* with (Gen 19:32; Exod 22:16), *have sex* (Deut 22:22), or *have sexual relations/intercourse* (Exod 22:19). When sex is forced, *shakav* denotes *rape* (Gen 34:2). *Shakav* signifies *rest* (Prov 6:10); minds *rest* (Eccl 2:23). *Lie down/rest with one's fathers* involves dying (Gen 47:30; Deut 31:16). Causative verbs indicate *laying* someone *out* (2 Chr 16:14), *enabling to rest* (Hos 2:18), or *making lie down* (2 Sam 8:2). One *lays* or *puts* babies somewhere (1 Kgs 3:20). People *are laid to rest* (Ezek 32:19). Someone *tilts* jars (Job 38:37).

Kingdoms of Israel and Judah

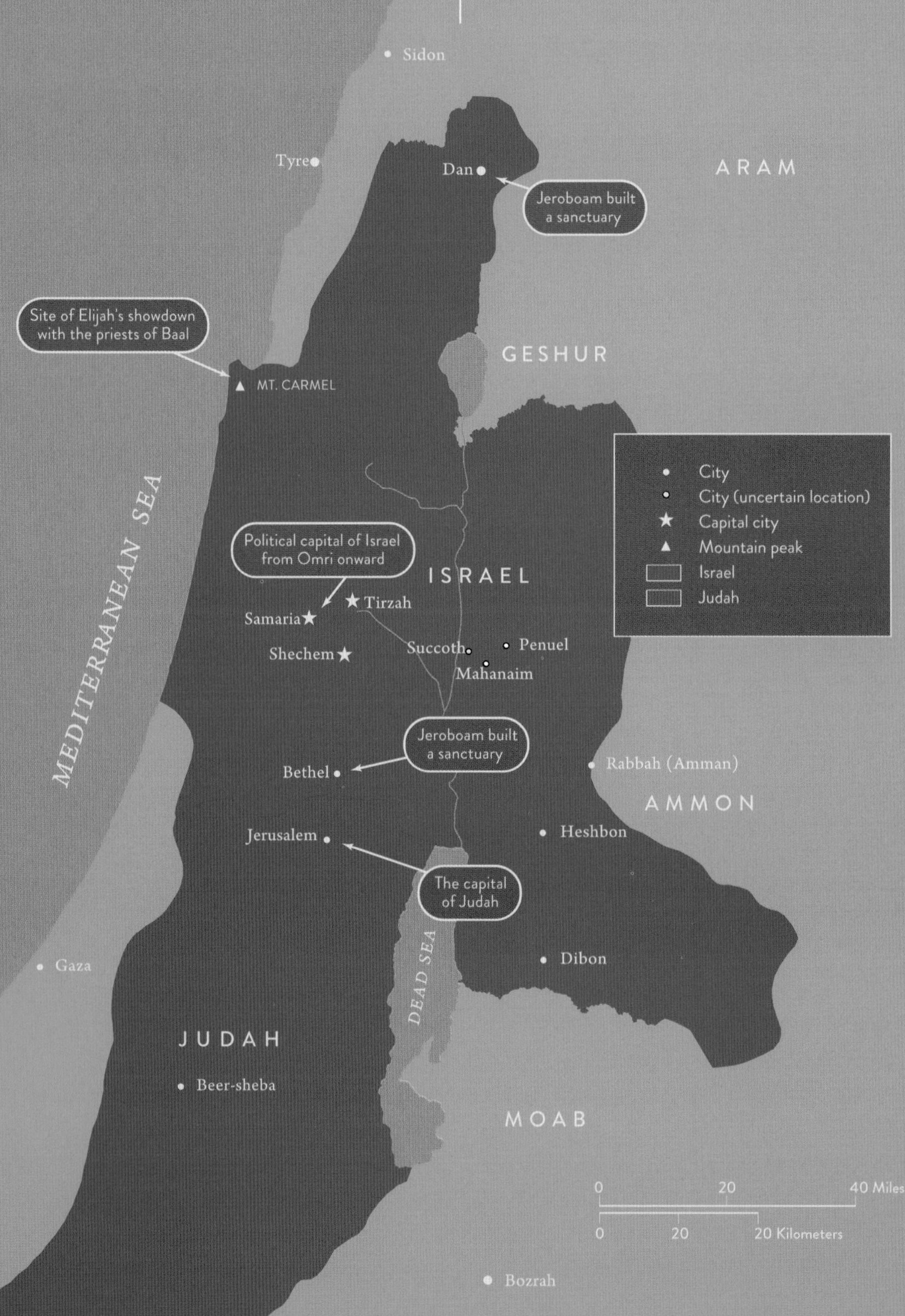

1–2 Kings Timeline

1000 BC

DAVID 1010–970
SOLOMON 970–931

1010
David becomes king of Judah.

1003
David becomes king over all Israel.

1000?
David conquers Jerusalem.

970
Solomon becomes king.

966
Temple construction begins.

959
Temple of Solomon is dedicated.

931
Kingdom divides: Rehoboam, king of southern kingdom; Jeroboam I, king of northern kingdom

900 BC

REHOBOAM 931–913
JEROBOAM 931–909

897
First temple reform under Asa

880
Omri makes Samaria his capital.

862–852
Elijah's ministry

857
Ben-hadad attacks Samaria.

850?–798?
Elisha's ministry

836–796?
Joel's ministry

812
Second temple reform under Joash

800 BC

AHAB 874–853
JOASH 835–796

783–746
Events in Amos

750–722?
Events in Hosea

750–686
Events in Micah

745–732
Tiglath-pileser's invasions of Israel

742–700
Isaiah's ministry

735?
Syro-Ephraimite War; Aram and Israel invade Judah

600 BC

HEZEKIAH 715–686
JOSIAH 640–609

722
Samaria falls; northern kingdom taken into exile by Assyrians

715
Third temple reform under Hezekiah

701
Sennacherib's invasion of Judah

627–586?
Jeremiah's ministry

622
Fourth temple reform under Josiah

609
Josiah killed in battle by Pharaoh Neco

605, 597, 586
Nebuchadnezzar's three invasions of Judah

586
Temple of Solomon destroyed

Kings of the Divided Kingdom

JUDAH	YEARS OF REIGN	ISRAEL	YEARS OF REIGN
Rehoboam (1 Kgs 12:1–24; 14:21–31)	931–913	Jeroboam I (1 Kgs 11:26–40; 12:1–14:20)	931–909
Abijam/Abijah (1 Kgs 15:1–8)	913–911	Nadab (1 Kgs 15:25–32)	909–908
Asa (1 Kgs 15:9–24)	911–871	Baasha (1 Kgs 15:27–16:7)	908–886
		Elah (1 Kgs 16:8–14)	886–885
		Zimri (1 Kgs 16:9–20)	885
Jehoshaphat (1 Kgs 22:41–50)	870–848	Tibni (1 Kgs 16:21–22)	885–880
		Omri (1 Kgs 16:16–17,21–28)	885–874
		Ahab (1 Kgs 16:29–17:1; 18:1–19:3; 20:1–22:40)	874–853
		Ahaziah (1 Kgs 22:51–53; 2 Kgs 1:1–18)	853–852
Jehoram/Joram (2 Kgs 8:16–24)	848–841	Joram/Jehoram (2 Kgs 3:1–27; "king of Israel" in 6:8–7:20; 9:14–26)	852–841
Ahaziah (2 Kgs 8:25–29; 9:21–28)	841	Jehu (2 Kgs 9:1–10:36)	841–814
Athaliah (2 Kgs 11:1–20)	841–835		
Joash/Jehoash (2 Kgs 12:1–21)	835–796	Jehoahaz (2 Kgs 13:1–9)	814–798
Amaziah (2 Kgs 14:1–22)	796–767	Joash/Jehoash (2 Kgs 13:10–25; 14:8–16)	798–782
Azariah/Uzziah (2 Kgs 15:1–7)	767–739	Jeroboam II (2 Kgs 14:23–29)	782–753
		Zechariah (2 Kgs 15:8–12)	753–752
		Shallum (2 Kgs 15:10,13–16)	752
Jotham (2 Kgs 15:32–38)	750–732	Menahem (2 Kgs 15:14–22)	752–742
		Pekahiah (2 Kgs 15:23–26)	742–740
Ahaz (2 Kgs 16:1–20)	735–715	Pekah (2 Kgs 15:25,27–31)	740–732
		Hoshea (2 Kgs 15:30; 17:1–6)	732–722
		Fall of Samaria (2 Kgs 17:6ff)	722
Hezekiah (2 Kgs 18:1–20:21)	715–696		
Manasseh (2 Kgs 21:1–18)	696–642		
Amon (2 Kgs 21:19–26)	642–640		
Josiah (2 Kgs 22:1–23:30)	640–609		
Jehoahaz (2 Kgs 23:31–34)	609		
Jehoiakim (2 Kgs 23:35–24:7)	609–597		
Jehoiachin/Jeconiah (2 Kgs 24:8–17; 25:27–30)	597		
Zedekiah (2 Kgs 24:18–20)	597–586		
Destruction of Jerusalem and the temple (2 Kgs 25:1–21)	586		

Foreign Gods in the Times of the Kings

NAME	SCRIPTURE	DESCRIPTION
Milcom	1 Kings 11; 2 Kings 23	Ammonite god
Ashtoreth	1 Kings 11; 2 Kings 23	Canaanite goddess
Chemosh	1 Kings 11; 2 Kings 23	Moabite war god
Molech/Moloch	2 Kings 23	Ammonite god
Rimmon/Ramman/Rammon	2 Kings 5	Babylonian/Syrian storm-god
Ashima	2 Kings 17	Samaritan moon goddess
Nergal/Meshlamthea	2 Kings 17	Cuth/Assyrian/Babylonian war and underworld god
Succoth-Benoth/ Zarpanitu/Zerpanitum	2 Kings 17	Babylonian fertility goddess
Adrammelech and Anammelech	2 Kings 17	Sepharvite gods
Nibhaz and Tartak	2 Kings 17	Avvite gods
Nisroch	2 Kings 19	Assyrian god
Baal/Baalim	1 Kings 9; 16; 18; 19; 22 2 Kings 1; 3; 4; 10; 11; 17; 21; 23	Canaanite god[s] of fertility, vegetation, and storms

The Temple

	BEARS GOD'S NAME	HOSTS GOD'S PRESENCE	FOR GOD'S MISSION
THE TEMPLE	Solomon built the temple for the name of Yahweh, the God of Israel *(1 Kgs 5:5; 8:20)*.	The glory of the Lord filled the temple, a place built for God's dwelling forever *(1 Kgs 8:10–13)*.	A place for foreigners to seek the Lord that all the peoples of the earth may know Yahweh alone is God *(1 Kgs 8:41–43,60)*.
JESUS	The Word who was with God and who was God became flesh and dwelled among us, the Son of God *(John 1:1,14)*.	He came in glory as the one and only Son from the Father, full of grace and truth, and he has revealed the Father to us (John 1:14,18).	Jesus referred to the sanctuary of his body when speaking of his sacrificial death and resurrection three days later *(John 2:19–22)*.
THE CHURCH	The church belongs to Jesus, the Christ, the Son of the living God; whatever we do, in word or deed, should be done in the name of the Lord Jesus *(Matt 16:16–19; Col 3:17)*.	We are the sanctuary of the living God, called to be holy in his presence as he dwells among us through the Holy Spirit *(1 Cor 3:16; 2 Cor 6:16–18)*.	As the Father sent the Son, so we are sent on his mission, having received his Holy Spirit *(John 20:21–23)*.

Seeing Jesus in the Divided Kingdom

THE LORD | *High and Lifted Up; His Glory Fills the Whole Earth (Isa 6)*	**JESUS** | *Isaiah Saw Jesus's Glory and Spoke of Him (John 12:37–41)*
ELIJAH THE PROPHET Encountered God in a Still, Small Voice on Mount Horeb *(1 Kgs 19)*	**GOD'S SON** Revealed His Glory with Elijah and Moses at the Transfiguration *(Matt 17:1–5)*
NAAMAN THE SYRIAN Healed of Leprosy; Praised the God in Israel *(2 Kgs 5:14–15)*	**JESUS THE SAVIOR** Healed Leprosy by His Touch; He Is God in Israel *(Luke 5:12–15)*
THE SUFFERING SERVANT Rejected by Men; Wounded for Our Healing *(Isa 52:13–53:12)*	**THE SUFFERING CHRIST** Reviled by Men; Bore Our Sins on the Tree *(1 Pet 2:21–25)*
HEZEKIAH Prayed for God's Glory in the Saving of His People from Assyria *(2 Kgs 19)*	**JESUS** Prayed for God's Glory in the Saving of People from Their Sin *(John 17)*
HOSEA Pursued His Adulterous Wife; Bought Her Back from Slavery for Purity *(Hos 3)*	**JESUS** Gave Himself for His Church to Make Her Holy and Blameless *(Eph 5:25–27)*
JONAH In the Belly of a Great Fish Three Days and Nights *(Jonah 1:17)*	**THE BETTER JONAH** In the Heart of the Earth Three Days and Nights *(Matt 12:39–41)*
JOEL Prophesied of God's Spirit Poured Out on Those Who Call on Yahweh *(Joel 2:28–32)*	**JESUS** Pours Out His Spirit on All Who Call on Him to Be Saved *(Acts 2; Rom 10)*
JEREMIAH Prophesied of a New Covenant for the Forgiveness of Sin *(Jer 31:31–34)*	**JESUS** Shed His Blood to Establish the Covenant for the Forgiveness of Sin *(Matt 26:28)*
THE KINGS OF JUDAH Sinned, Calling the Davidic Covenant into Question *(2 Kgs 24:19–20)*	**THE SON OF DAVID** God Remained Faithful to His Covenant with David *(Matt 1:1–17)*
EZEKIEL Prophesied of a Resurrection for God's People, a Restoration to the Land *(Ezek 37)*	**JESUS** The Resurrection and the Life for All Who Believe in Him *(John 11:25–26)*

The Divided Kingdom

The LORD said, "I have made a covenant with my chosen one; I have sworn an oath to David my servant: 'I will establish your offspring forever and build up your throne for all generations'" (Ps 89:3–4).

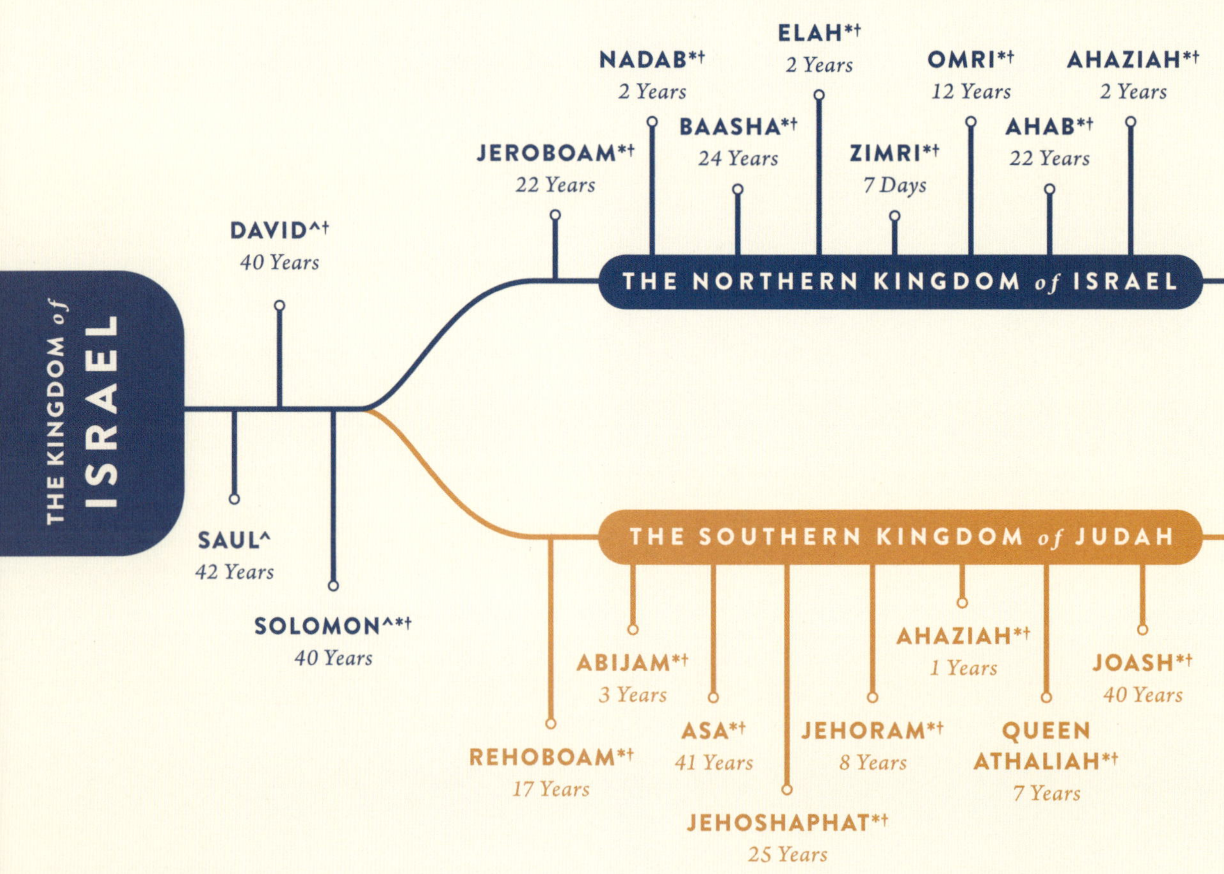

IN THE BIBLE

- ^ 1–2 SAMUEL
- * 1–2 KINGS
- † 1–2 CHRONICLES

ISRAEL
CONQUERED BY
ASSYRIA
722 BC

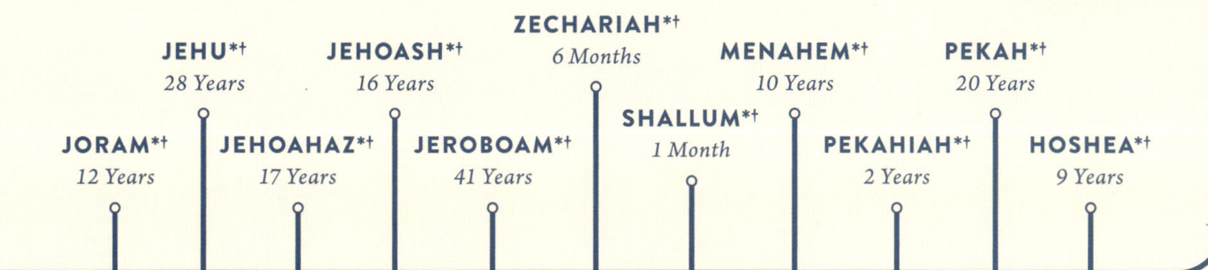

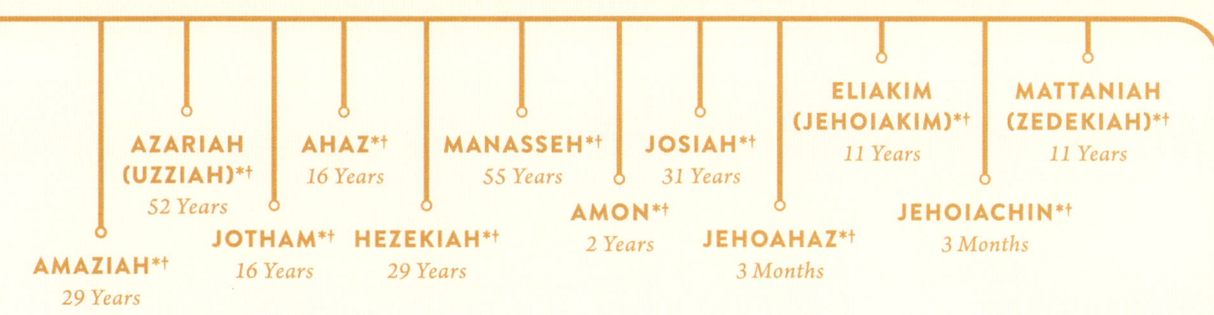

JUDAH
CONQUERED BY
BABYLON
586 BC

Elijah and Elisha

ELIJAH ("YAHWEH IS MY GOD")	ELISHA ("GOD SAVES")
Prophesied no rain in the land as God's judgment for Ahab's and Israel's idolatry *(1 Kgs 17:1)* **An example of a righteous man's effective prayer (*Jas 5:17–18*)**	Called as Elijah's successor *(1 Kgs 19:19–21)* **Elisha's response serves as an example of discipleship (*Luke 9:61–62*)**
Provided food for a Gentile widow and raised her son from the dead *(1 Kgs 17:8–24)* **A characteristic of Jesus's ministry among Gentiles (*Luke 4:23–26*)**	Witnessed Elijah's departure and received his mantle; parted the Jordan River to cross on dry ground *(2 Kgs 2:11–15)*
Faced off against 450 prophets of Baal and executed them; prayed for end of the famine *(1 Kgs 18)*	Gave instructions to a widow of a prophet to pour oil into empty jars in order to pay her debt and provide for her family *(2 Kgs 4:1–7)*
Fled from Jezebel and experienced the Lord at Horeb in a still, small voice; told to anoint successors for Aram, Israel, and himself *(1 Kgs 19)*	Rewarded the Shunammite woman with a son for her hospitality; later raised her son from the dead *(2 Kgs 4:8–37)* **Jesus raised people from the dead (*Luke 7:11–17; John 11*)**
Called Elisha as his successor *(1 Kgs 19:19–21)*	Multiplied bread for the people to eat and had some left over *(2 Kings 4:42–44)* **Jesus fed 5,000 from bread and fish and had some left over (*John 6:1–14*)**
Confronted Ahab over Naboth's vineyard and prophesied judgment on his house *(1 Kgs 21:17–29)*	Healed Naaman, a Gentile, of leprosy *(2 Kgs 5:1–19)* **A characteristic of Jesus's ministry among Gentiles; he also healed those with skin diseases (*Luke 4:23–27; 5:12–14*)**
Confronted Ahaziah for inquiring of a foreign god; called fire from heaven to destroy Ahaziah's men sent to arrest him *(2 Kgs 1)* **An example not followed by Jesus (*Luke 9:51–55*)**	Defeated the Arameans sent to capture him, being surrounded by horses and chariots of fire; Arameans blinded and led to the king of Israel *(2 Kgs 6:8–23)*
Parted the Jordan River with his mantle to cross on dry ground, and then taken into heaven in a whirlwind by a chariot and horses of fire *(2 Kgs 2:8–11)*	Anointed Hazael as king over Aram and Jehu as king over Israel, fulfilling the Lord's word to Elijah at Horeb *(2 Kgs 8:7–15; 9:1–10)*
Appeared along with Moses at the transfiguration of Christ *(Luke 9:28–36)* **Elijah was foretold to come again as a forerunner of the Messiah; this prophecy was fulfilled in John the Baptist (*Mal 4:5–6; Matt 17:10–13; Luke 1:16–17*)**	Died and was buried; later, a dead Israelite was thrown into Elisha's tomb—he touched Elisha's bones, was revived, and stood up *(2 Kgs 13:20–21)*

Connections

LOOKING BACKWARD		LOOKING FORWARD
MOSES	**ELIJAH**	**JOHN THE BAPTIST**
• Led Israel out of slavery toward, but not into, the promised land (*Exodus–Deuteronomy)* • Led Israel on dry ground through the Red Sea *(Exod 14)* • Spoke with the Lord on Mount Horeb *(Exod 20–24)* • Died outside the promised land *(Deut 34)*	• Started to lead the people out of their idolatry and worship of Baal *(1 Kgs 18)* • Jezebel sought his life for his stand against Baal *(1 Kgs 19:1–3)* • Spoke with the Lord on Mount Horeb *(1 Kgs 19)* • Walked through the Jordan River on dry ground *(2 Kgs 2:6–8)* • Taken from the earth while outside the promised land *(2 Kgs 2:9–12)*	• Started baptizing Jews for repentance in preparation for the kingdom of heaven *(Matt 3:1–6)* • A "voice of one crying out in the wilderness"; the "Elijah" to precede the Messiah *(Matt 3:3; 11:7–15; Luke 1:17)* • Executed at the request of Herod's wife for his stand against their unlawful marriage *(Matt 14:1–12)*

LOOKING BACKWARD		LOOKING FORWARD
JOSHUA	**ELISHA**	**JESUS THE MESSIAH**
• Name means "Yahweh Is Salvation" • Succeeded Moses • Led Israel on dry ground through the Jordan River into the promised land *(Josh 3–4)* • Led Israel in conquering the promised land *(Josh 5–11)*	• Name means "My God Is Salvation" • Succeeded Elijah • Walked through the Jordan River on dry ground *(2 Kgs 2:13–14)* • Ministry led to the destruction of Baalism in Israel *(2 Kgs 10:18–27)*	• Name means "Yahweh Is Salvation" • Supersedes all • Baptized in the Jordan River in identification with Israel *(Matt 3:13–17; Luke 3:21–22)* • Ministry led to victory over sin and death for all who believe *(1 Cor 15:57; 1 John 5:4–5)*

Solomon's Wisdom

WISDOM LITERATURE	STYLE	PURPOSE	NEW TESTAMENT REFERENCES	POINTS TO JESUS
Proverbs	A few extended wisdom poems, but largely consists of unrelated proverbs strung together—proverbs are general rules, not absolute promises	Gives positive and negative principles for successful living in the world God has created, chiefly the need to "fear . . . the LORD" *(Prov 1:7)*	• Hebrews 12:5–7 *(Prov 3:11–12)* • James 4:6 *(Prov 3:34)* • 1 Peter 4:8 *(Prov 10:12)* • Romans 12:20 *(Prov 25:21–22)*	All the treasures of wisdom and knowledge are found in Jesus Christ, who created all things and holds all things together *(Col 1:15–17; 2:3)*
Ecclesiastes	A mixture of poetry and prose; overtly pessimistic about life "under the sun," or apart from God	Answers the question "What is the meaning of life?" and the answer is "Fear God and keep his commands" *(Eccl 12:13)*	Luke 12:15–21—Jesus's parable of a rich fool echoes Ecclesiastes; we should be rich toward God, not store up treasure for ourselves	To fear God is to know him and the One he has sent—Jesus *(John 17:3)*; we are to obey him and teach others to do the same *(Matt 28:18–20)*
Song of Solomon, or Song of Songs	A song composed entirely of Hebrew poetry, featuring a bride, a groom, and a chorus of friends	Answers the question "Should a husband and wife enjoy the sexual dimension of their relationship?" and the answer is yes	—	This ideal romance, as with every marriage, is a picture of the greater relationship between Christ and his bride, the church *(Eph 5:22–33)*

Comparison: Kings and Chronicles

Kings	Chronicles
1 Kings 1:1–4:34	2 Chronicles 1:1–17
1 Kings 5:1–8:66	2 Chronicles 2:1–7:10
1 Kings 9:1–11:43	2 Chronicles 7:11–9:31
1 Kings 12:1–14:31	2 Chronicles 10:1–12:16
1 Kings 15:1–16:28	2 Chronicles 13:1–16:14
1 Kings 16:29–18:46	
1 Kings 19:1–22:53	2 Chronicles 17:1–20:37
2 Kings 1:1–5:27	
2 Kings 6:1–10:36	2 Chronicles 21:1–22:9
2 Kings 11:1–16:20	2 Chronicles 22:10–28:27
2 Kings 17:1–41	
2 Kings 18:1–21:26	2 Chronicles 29:1–33:25
2 Kings 22:1–25:30	2 Chronicles 34:1–36:23

1–2 Chronicles

Genre | **HISTORICAL NARRATIVE**

With a focus on the Davidic line of kings and the people's worship, 1–2 Chronicles emphasize Judah's historical identity within the purposes of God.

INTRODUCTION

AUTHOR An ancient tradition ascribes the authorship of Chronicles to Ezra. The author must have lived sometime after the return of the Jews to Israel from the Babylonian exile. He also had a strong interest in the reimplementation of the law and the temple, and he must have had access to historical records.

BACKGROUND The books of 1 and 2 Chronicles include extensive genealogies from the time of Adam and take the reader up to the period of the nation's exile and restoration. First Chronicles gives us the genealogies and focuses on the reign of King David. Second Chronicles focuses on all the kings who followed David up to the exile and restoration. It covers the same time period as 1 and 2 Kings, but 2 Chronicles focuses exclusively on the kings of Judah.

MESSAGE AND PURPOSE Having resettled in Jerusalem after the exile, the people needed to reconnect with their identity as the people of God. Chronicles met this purpose by reminding them of their heritage and by directing them back to God's presence in their midst as symbolized by the temple. The important ideas that 1 and 2 Chronicles emphasize are (1) a direct connection to God's people in the past, (2) the continuity of the line of David on the throne of Judah, (3) the centrality of the temple and its rituals in focusing on God, (4) the importance of music in worshipping God, (5) the invincibility of God's people when they obey him, and (6) the inevitability of punishment when God's people disobey him.

SUMMARY The word Chronicles in Hebrew has the meaning of an ongoing account, almost like a journal or diary or minutes taken at a meeting. They are the first and second books of a four-book series that includes Ezra and Nehemiah. Together these four books provide a priestly history of Israel from the time of Adam to the rebuilding of the house of God and the walls of Jerusalem. At one time the book of Chronicles was probably one single scroll, which was divided later for convenience by those who translated the Old Testament into Greek (the Septuagint, also called the LXX).

STRUCTURE The Hebrew Bible divides its books into three categories: the Law, the Prophets, and the Writings. In this arrangement, the books of Samuel and Kings are counted among the Prophets, whereas Chronicles belongs to the Writings. This classification may be partially due to the fact that Chronicles repeats information, such as the genealogies of Genesis and the histories of the kings of Judah, from the books of Samuel and Kings. Still the Chronicler uses this repeated content to support his own point, and he also adds a lot of information that we find in Chronicles alone. He limits his discussion of the various kings almost entirely to those of Judah, the southern kingdom.

Outlines

1 CHRONICLES

I. The Genealogies (1:1–9:44)
- A. Genealogies of the human race (1:1–54)
- B. Genealogies of the 12 tribes (2:1–9:44)

II. The Reign of David (10:1–29:30)
- A. Fall of Saul's house and rise of David (10:1–14:17)
- B. Removal of the ark to Jerusalem (15:1–16:43)
- C. David's desire to build God a house (17:1–27)
- D. David's victories over Israel's enemies (18:1–21:30)
- E. David's preparations for building the temple (22:1–19)
- F. Arrangements for the service of the Levites (23:1–26:32)
- G. David's final days (27:1–29:30)

2 CHRONICLES

I. The Reign of Solomon (1:1–9:31)
- A. Solomon builds the temple (1:1–7:22)
- B. The glory of Solomon's kingdom (8:1–9:31)

II. The Reigns of Solomon's Successors (10:1–36:23)
- A. Rehoboam (10:1–12:16)
- B. Abijah (13:1–22)
- C. Asa (14:1–16:14)
- D. Jehoshaphat (17:1–20:37)
- E. Jehoram (21:1–20)
- F. Ahaziah and Athaliah (22:1–12)
- G. Joash (23:1–24:27)
- H. Amaziah (25:1–28)
- I. Uzziah (26:1–23)
- J. Jotham (27:1–9)
- K. Ahaz (28:1–27)
- L. Hezekiah (29:1–32:33)
- M. Manasseh (33:1–20)
- N. Amon (33:21–25)
- O. Josiah (34:1–35:27)
- P. Last kings of Judah (36:1–23)

WORD STUDY

shem

Hebrew pronunciation:
[SHAIM]

CSB translation:
name

Uses in 2 Chronicles: 45
Uses in the OT: 864

Focus passage:
2 Chronicles 6:5–10,20, 24,26,32–34

This root in various languages suggests a *distinguishing mark*. ***Shem*** was associated with *being, character,* and *public standing*. *Names* bore meanings (Exod 2:10,22), and changed *names* connoted changed characters (Gen 32:28). "Call the *name*" often appears as *name* (Gen 3:20) or *call* (Jer 20:3). One called by someone's *name* belonged to him (Isa 4:1). God's *name* is synonymous with God (Ps 75:1); God's *name* dwells in his temple (Deut 16:2). Walking (Mic 4:5) or living (Ps 69:36) in his *name* is living as he instructs. "Calling on his *name*" is prayer (Ps 116:4) or worship (Gen 12:8). One acts in his *name* (Deut 18:5,22). *Shem* denotes *reputation* (Josh 9:9). "*Name* of the day" signifies *today's date* (Ezek 24:2). One acts on someone's *behalf* (1 Sam 25:9). *Shem* functions as *fame* (Zeph 3:20), *prominent* (Num 16:2), or *notorious* (Ezek 23:10). *Infamous* is "unclean of *name*" (Ezek 22:5).

pillel

Hebrew pronunciation:
[pil LAIL]

CSB translation:
pray, intercede

Uses in 2 Chronicles: 14
Uses in the OT: 84

Focus passage:
2 Chronicles 6:19–21,24, 26,32–34

This root does not occur in other languages as "pray." The intensive means *expect* (Gen 48:11), *help* (Ezek 16:52), and *intervene* (Ps 106:30). It is *intercede* when occurring with a reflexive (1 Sam 2:25). The reflexive normally means *pray* (Gen 20:7) and takes prepositions meaning "to" (Num 11:2), "for" (Job 42:8), "on behalf of" (Jer 42:2), or "about" (Isa 37:21). Once it denotes *confess* (Isa 45:14). Nine times it occurs with the related noun *tepillah* (*prayer*, 77x). *Paliyl* (3x) implies *judicial assessment* (Exod 21:22), *conceding* (Deut 32:31), or *deserving punishment* (Job 31:11). *Peliylah* is a judgment or *decision* (Isa 16:3). *Peliyliy* (Job 31:28) suggests something *deserving* judicial *punishment*. *Peliyliyyah* (Isa 28:7) is a court *judgment*. **Pillel** can mean *interpose*. The reflexive would involve interposing oneself in *prayer*, or *interceding*. Some authorities posit *pillel* and *paliyl* as homonyms, but 1 Samuel 2:25 seems evidence against that distinction.

ma'al

Hebrew pronunciation:
[mah AHL]

CSB translation:
be unfaithful,
act unfaithfully

Uses in 2 Chronicles: 92
Uses in the OT: 36

Focus passage:
2 Chronicles 28:19,22

The history of ***ma'al*** is uncertain. It indicates *being unfaithful* (Neh 1:8), primarily toward God. But husbands and wives *acted unfaithfully* by committing adultery (Num 5:6). *Ma'al* describes individuals *breaking faith* (Deut 32:51) with God. In 20 verses the verb occurs alongside the noun *ma'al* (29x), both together translated as *be unfaithful* (Num 5:12), *commit treachery* (Josh 22:16), *commit unfaithfulness* (Ezek 39:26), or *show disloyalty* (Dan 9:7). The noun alone is *unfaithfulness* (Ezra 9:4) or *treachery* (Josh 22:22), and once *deceptive* (Job 21:34). Like adultery, *ma'al* implies grave sin. Saul died for it (1 Chr 10:13), and Moses and Aaron could not enter Canaan (Deut 32:51). *Ma'al* characterizes kings like Ahaz (2 Chr 28:19) and Manasseh (2 Chr 33:19). It brought exile to the northern (2 Chr 30:7) and southern (1 Chr 9:1) kingdoms. *Unfaithfulness* and disgrace summarize Israel's sin (Ezek 39:26).

Kings during the Neo-Babylonian and Persian Periods

	KING	SCRIPTURE	SIGNIFICANCE
NEO-BABYLONIAN EMPIRE (625–539 BC)	**Josiah**	2 Kings 23; 2 Chronicles 35	Killed by Pharaoh Neco at Megiddo
	Jehoahaz	2 Kings 23	Josiah's son, placed on the throne for a brief period
	Jehoiakim (Eliakim)	2 Kings 23:34; 24:1	Jehoahaz's brother, placed on the throne by the Egyptians
	Jehoiachin	2 Kings 24:12–15	Surrendered Jerusalem and was taken captive to Babylon along with many chief officials and treasures from the temple
	Zedekiah	2 Kings 24:17–20; 25:7	Son of Josiah; rebellion led to the temple's destruction
	Nebuchadnezzar II	2 Kings; 2 Chronicles; Jeremiah; Ezekiel; and Daniel 4:30	Marked by military victories, elaborate building projects (temples and shrines to pagan gods); had roads paved with bricks, fortified walls, and canals that could be flooded to protect the city from attack
	Evil-merodach	2 Kings 25:27–30; Jeremiah 52:31–34	Responsible for releasing Jehoiachin from prison, setting him above the other kings, and permitting him to eat at the king's table
	Nabonidus		Reign marked the end of the Neo-Babylonian Empire
	Cyrus the Great, ruler of Persia	Ezra 1:7–11 ; Isaiah 13:17–22; Jeremiah 29:4–10	In the first year of his rule, decreed that the Jews could return to the Judean territory and rebuild the temple.
THE PERSIAN EMPIRE (539–331 BC)	**Darius**	Daniel 6:1–28; 9:1–20	Cyrus initially delegated the rule of Babylon to Darius. When Daniel was placed in the lions' den and received the prophecy of the 70 weeks, Darius may simply have been a lesser leader under Cyrus.
	Cambyses		Conquered Egypt but was unsuccessful in subduing Ethiopia
	Darius Hystaspis		When Haggai and Zechariah encouraged rebuilding of the temple
	Xerxes (likely King Ahasuerus)	(Esther); Ezra 4:6	Suppressed a revolt in Egypt and abolished the kingdom of Babylon; murdered in 465 BC
	Artaxerxes I (Longimanus)	Ezra 7:11–26; Nehemiah 1:1–2:11; 5:14	Weak ruler; under his reign, Ezra obtained the needed treasure for the temple of God and Nehemiah was appointed as governor over Judah
	Xerxes II		Murdered by his half-brother less than two months into his rule
	Artaxerxes II		Son of King Darius II; younger brother rebelled against him. The rebellion was put down, but the damage lingered.
	Artaxerxes III		Spirited but cruel ruler who was murdered in 338 BC. The last three kings to rule the Persian Empire were either murdered or killed in battle. Alexander the Great entered into the territory in 334 BC. In less than three years, the Persian Empire fell.

Asking the Right Questions

THEOLOGICAL CONTRIBUTIONS OF EZRA–NEHEMIAH AND 1–2 CHRONICLES

QUESTION	ANSWER	THEOLOGICAL SIGNIFICANCE
How does Ezra begin?	"In the first year of King Cyrus of Persia, in order to fulfill the word of the LORD spoken through Jeremiah, the LORD roused the spirit of King Cyrus to issue a proclamation throughout his entire kingdom and to put it in writing . . ." (see Ezra 1:1–3)	By revisiting Cyrus's decree for the Jewish people to return to the promised land and rebuild the temple (c. 538 BC), the perspective of these books—Ezra–Nehemiah and 1–2 Chronicles—shows that Israel still awaits a true return from exile despite already being in their homeland when this account would have been written. In the traditional Jewish arrangement of the Hebrew Scriptures (commonly known as the TaNaK*), 1–2 Chronicles was typically placed at the end of canonical books. So, with these being the final words of the TaNaK, the biblical author reflects a hope and longing for a greater, future deliverance from exile.
How does 2 Chronicles end?	"In the first year of King Cyrus of Persia, in order to fulfill the word of the LORD spoken through Jeremiah, the LORD roused the spirit of King Cyrus of Persia to issue a proclamation throughout his entire kingdom and also to put it in writing . . ." (see 2 Chron 36:22–23)	

QUESTION	ANSWER	THEOLOGICAL SIGNIFICANCE
What is Ezra about?	Rebuilding of the Jerusalem temple (emphasis on the law, holiness, and worship)	Both books highlight the shortcoming of the return to the land with the men's religious compromise in marrying foreign women and the need for continued reforms (see Ezra 9–10; Neh 13). Thus, while God's people were out of physical exile, spiritual and moral "exile" were still an ongoing problem.
What is Nehemiah about?	Rebuilding of the city walls (emphasis on repopulation and security in the land along with the law, holiness, and worship)	

QUESTION	ANSWER	THEOLOGICAL SIGNIFICANCE
How does the TaNaK (the Jewish arrangement of the OT) end?	With 1–2 Chronicles containing emphases on the purity of worship and the Davidic lineage among the kings of Judah, the ending of the TaNaK renarrates the exile and the initial decree to return to the land (see above).	The placing of Chronicles last in the arrangement of the TaNaK on this intentional note indicates a messianic anticipation, a hope for a new and better David who will rule the people, purify and reform the worship of the Lord, and once for all bring an end to both physical and spiritual exile.
How does the New Testament begin?	"An account of the genealogy of Jesus Christ, the Son of David, the Son of Abraham . . ." (see Matt 1:1–17)	Along with the other NT authors, Matthew sees Jesus, God's Son and the Messiah, as the climax and conclusion to the Old Testament story left open by the narrator of 1–2 Chronicles. The genealogy is Matthew's literary way of presenting Jesus as (1) the true seed of Abraham, (2) the true Son of David, and (3) the true solution to exile.

TaNaK is an acronym that refers to a traditional Jewish arrangement of what Christians call the Old Testament. Historically the Jewish community arranged these 24 books according to a threefold division: the Law (Torah), the Prophets (Nevi'im), and the Writings (Ketuvim). By taking the first letter of each section and supplying a vowel, "TaNaK" became the shorthand, conventional way of referring to the whole of the Hebrew Scriptures. Though the TaNaK and the 39 books of the Old Testament consist of the same content, this traditional Jewish arrangement typically organizes the canon into 24 books by treating 1–2 Samuel, 1–2 Kings, Ezra–Nehemiah, and 1–2 Chronicles as single books along with the books of the Minor Prophets being treated as one collective work known as "The Twelve."

Ezra–Nehemiah

Genre | **HISTORICAL NARRATIVE**

Ezra–Nehemiah narrates the Israelites' return to the promised land from exile, framed around the rebuilding of the temple and the restoration of the walls of Jerusalem.

INTRODUCTION

AUTHOR The books of Ezra and Nehemiah are anonymous. Ancient Jewish sources usually credit Ezra as the author of Ezra–Nehemiah. More likely Ezra–Nehemiah was written by the "Chronicler," the person (or persons) responsible for 1 and 2 Chronicles. Not only is Ezra–Nehemiah linked to Chronicles at its introduction (Ezra 1:1–2 = 2 Chr 36:22–23), but it also shares many similarities in language, terminology, themes, and perspective.

BACKGROUND It is probably safe to assume that Ezra–Nehemiah was written soon after the conclusion of Nehemiah's ministry. Most likely the book was written no later than 400 BC. The two events in which Ezra and Nehemiah were together were significant. In Nehemiah 8, the context is the reading of the law to the people, while in Nehemiah 12 the two joyous processions walking around the city walls in the dedication ceremony include Ezra (Neh 12:36) and Nehemiah (Neh 12:38).

MESSAGE AND PURPOSE Ezra continues where 2 Chronicles left off. While it provides us with key historical insights, it is rich in messages for God's people. The events in Ezra–Nehemiah connect the Israelites with the preexilic community. The returning exiles experienced a new exodus and remained a part of God's redemptive plan. God even used pagan leaders like Cyrus and Artaxerxes to restore his people.

SUMMARY The books of Ezra and Nehemiah bear the names of the key person in each of the books. Until the third century AD, though, the books of Ezra and Nehemiah were regarded as a single book. Each contains material found in the other, and they complete each other. The separation of the book in the Christian community took place through the influence of the Vulgate, the Latin translation prepared by Jerome, who, following Origen before him, separated Ezra–Nehemiah into two distinct books. In the Jewish community, Ezra and Nehemiah were not separated into two distinct books until the fifteenth-century printing of the Hebrew Bible. In the Hebrew Bible, Ezra–Nehemiah is part of the third division of the canon, called the Writings (Hb. *ketuvim*).

STRUCTURE Ezra–Nehemiah is similar to Samuel and Kings, and especially Chronicles, in that many sources were utilized in its composition. These include two major types of sources. Much of Ezra–Nehemiah consists of material from the Ezra Memoir and the Nehemiah Memoir. For a community attempting to reestablish itself after the disaster of 586 BC and the subsequent exile to Babylon, this material was crucial in reordering their life as a community.

Outlines

EZRA

I. **Return from Exile (1:1–6:22)**
   A. The decree of Cyrus (1:1–11)
   B. Exiles who returned (2:1–70)
   C. Restoration of worship (3:1–13)
   D. Opposition (4:1–24)
   E. Rebuilding the temple (5:1–6:22)

II. **Reform through Ezra (7:1–10:44)**
   A. Ezra's arrival (7:1–10)
   B. Artaxerxes's letter (7:11–28)
   C. Returnees with Ezra (8:1–14)
   D. Search for Levites (8:15–20)
   E. Preparing to return (8:21–30)
   F. Arrival in Jerusalem (8:31–36)
   G. Sin and confession (9:1–10:44)

NEHEMIAH

I. **Rebuilding the Walls (1:1–6:19)**
   A. Jerusalem's plight and Nehemiah's prayer (1:1–11)
   B. Nehemiah's mission (2:1–10)
   C. Surveying the walls (2:11–20)
   D. Rebuilding begun (3:1–32)
   E. Opposition and oppression (4:1–6:19)

II. **Restoration of the Community (7:1–13:31)**
   A. Repopulating Jerusalem (7:1–73a)
   B. The covenant renewed (7:73b–10:39)
   C. Repopulating Jerusalem (continued) (11:1–21)
   D. Essential records (11:22–36)
   E. Temple personnel (12:1–26)
   F. Dedication of the wall (12:27–47)
   G. Nehemiah's further reforms (13:1–31)

WORD STUDY

yasad

Hebrew pronunciation:
[yah SAD]

CSB translation:
lay a foundation, establish, destine

Uses in Ezra: 4
Uses in the OT: 41

Focus passage:
Ezra 3:6,10–12

Yasad describes *laying the foundation* of buildings (Zech 4:9), cities (Josh 6:26), or the earth (Isa 51:13). It means *lay* (Isa 28:16), *found* (Ps 89:11), *establish* (Ps 78:69), or *build up* (2 Chr 31:7). *Yasad* signifies *destine* (Isa 23:13), *appoint* (1 Chr 9:22), or *order* (Esth 1:8). Verbal forms imply *foundation* as an act (Ezra 3:12), a material (1 Kgs 6:37), or a measurement (2 Chr 3:3). Passive forms connote *set* (Song 5:15) and *sure* (Isa 28:16). *Yesod* (20x) means *base* (Exod 29:12), *foundation* (Ezek 13:14), *foot* (Hab 3:13), *security* (Prov 10:25), or *restoration* (2 Chr 24:27). *Mosad* (8x) and *mosadah* (5x) refer to building *foundations* (Isa 58:12) and to *foundations* of mountains (Deut 32:22), earth, and heaven (2 Sam 22:8). *Musadah* (2x) means *appointment* (Isa 30:32) or *foundation*. *Musad* (2x, Isa 28:16), *massad* (1 Kgs 7:9), and *yesudah* (Ps 87:1) denote something *founded*. *Yesud* signifies *beginning* (Ezra 7:9).

tsom

Hebrew pronunciation:
[TSOAM]

CSB translation:
fast

Uses in Ezra: 1
Uses in the OT: 26

Focus passage:
Ezra 8:21

The noun ***tsom*** means *fast*, as does the verb *tsum* (21x, Ezra 8:23). *Fasting* was associated with grieving and often included wearing sackcloth and confessing sins (Neh 9:1–2). David *fasted* for defeated Israel (1 Sam 31:13) partly because defeat signaled prior national sin (Deut 28:25). *Fasting* marked recognition of sin and attended the forsaking of idols (1 Sam 7:2–6). People also *fasted* to plead with God for some request (Esth 4:16), humbling themselves to pursue his mercy (1 Kgs 21:27–29), protection (Ezra 8:21), or healing (Ps 35:13). Yet others might scorn these people (Ps 69:10). Self-humbling anticipated divine responsiveness to petitions, but *fasting* was needed to further his purposes (Isa 58:4–6), being done for him (Zech 7:5). God's refusal to respond signaled judgment (Jer 14:12). God (Joel 2:12) and kings (2 Chr 20:3) called for *fast* days, and recurring official *fast* days followed the exile (Zech 8:19).

nokri

Hebrew pronunciation:
[nok REE]

CSB translation:
foreign

Uses in Ezra: 7
Uses in the OT: 46

Focus passage:
Ezra 10:2,10–11,14, 17–18,44

Nokri, from *nakar* (*recognize, be foreign*), is synonymous with *zar* (*strange*). The words occur together as nouns or adjectives (11x); *nokri* implies *foreigners* (Obad 11), *wayward woman* (Prov 2:16; 23:27), or *stranger* (Prov 27:2), where *zar* is, respectively, "strange," "strangers," "forbidden," and "another." *Nokri* connotes *outsider* (Gen 31:15). It usually indicates *foreigners* (Ruth 2:10), such as Moabite, Edomite, and Hittite women whom Israelites improperly married (1 Kgs 11:1; Ezra 10:2). Some *foreigners* worshipped God (2 Chr 6:32), but most were idolaters (1 Kgs 11:8). They could be charged interest (Deut 23:20) and remained debtors after the year of remission (Deut 15:3). Related *nekar* (*foreignness*) occurs (36x) as *foreigners*, literally "sons of *foreignness*." *Foreigners* could not celebrate Passover (Exod 12:43). *Nekar* as *foreign* had negative connotations (Neh 13:30), especially in the phrase *foreign gods* (2 Chr 33:15). *Nekar* suggests *pagan* (2 Chr 14:3).

The Second Exodus

"The days are coming"—the LORD's declaration—"when it will no longer be said, 'As the LORD lives who brought the Israelites from the land of Egypt,' but, 'As the LORD lives, who brought and led the descendants of the house of Israel from the land of the north and from all the other countries where I had banished them.' They will dwell once more in their own land" (Jer 23:7–8).

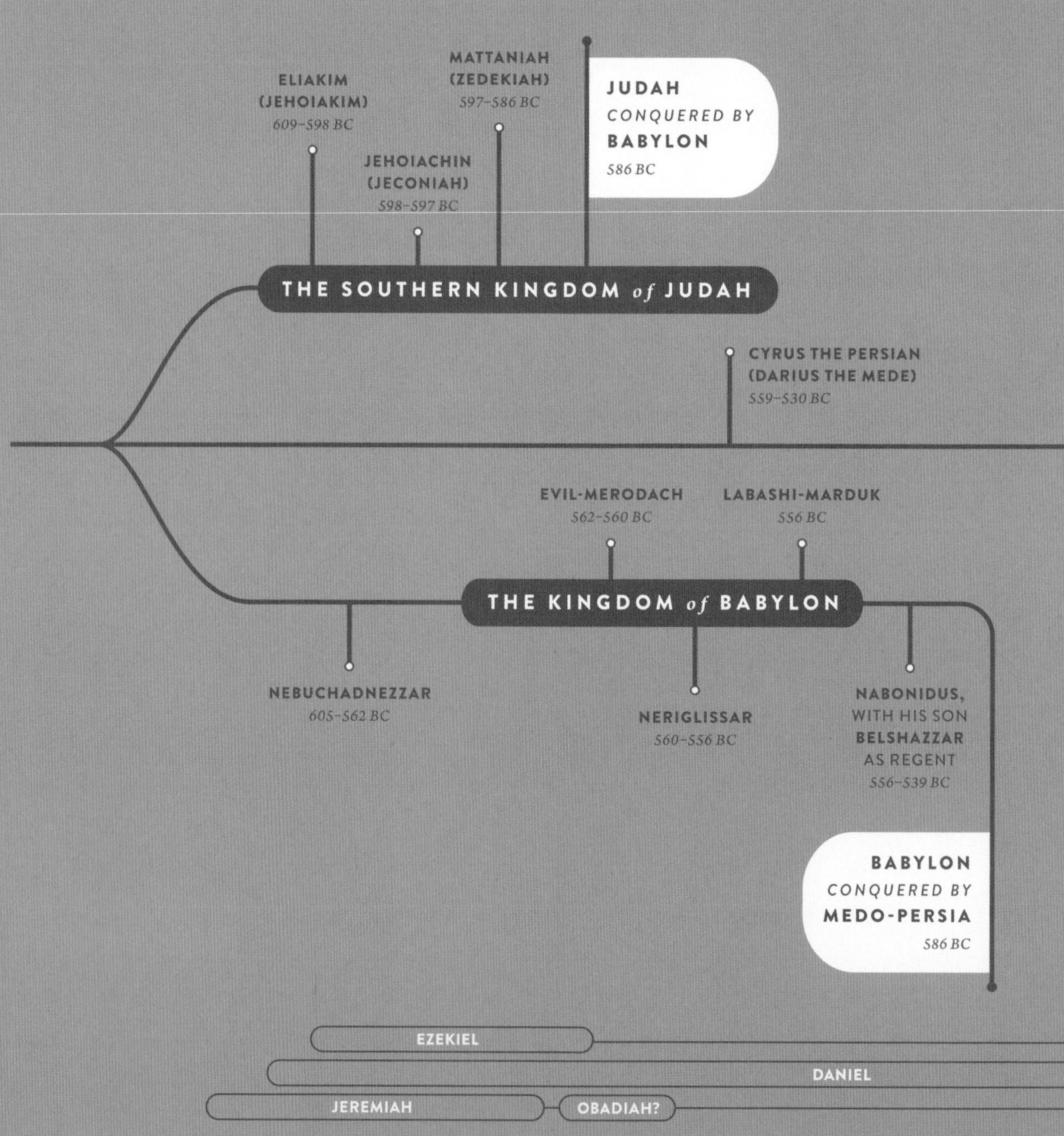

REBUILDING THE TEMPLE AND JERUSALEM

YEAR	EVENT	SCRIPTURE
538 BC	Cyrus's decree	Ezra 1:1–4
537 BC	Altar rebuilt	Ezra 3:2–3
536 BC	Temple reconstruction began	Ezra 3:8–9
536 BC	Dedication for temple foundation	Ezra 3:10–13
536–520 BC	Opposition to rebuilding the temple	Ezra 4:1–5,24
520 BC	Temple rebuilding resumed	Ezra 5:1–2
515 BC	Temple completed and dedicated	Ezra 6:14–18
458 BC	Ezra arrived in Jerusalem	Ezra 7:8–10
445 BC	Nehemiah arrived in Jerusalem	Nehemiah 2:11
445 BC	Wall around Jerusalem rebuilt	Nehemiah 6:15
445 BC	Ezra publicly read the law	Nehemiah 8:1–12

For the sin of God's people of chasing after other gods and forsaking the one true God who brought them out of Egypt and settled them in the promised land, Jeremiah prophesied a 70-year exile in the land of Babylon. Reflecting on this prophecy and praying for its fulfillment, Daniel received understanding from God that "seventy weeks" (or seventy sevens) were decreed before the full restoration of God's people and city and the end of rebellion and sin. Cyrus's decree, and subsequent ones from other kings, began the second exodus, the return of the Jews from exile in Babylon. Yet Ezra and Nehemiah both recognized their continued slavery even after returning to the land of Judah. Only Jesus the Messiah—cut off for the sin of his people and given the authority to rule a kingdom of those from every people, nation, and language—can end this exile and lead his people out of slavery to sin and death and into the promised land of eternal life in the kingdom of God.

THE KINGDOM *of* MEDO-PERSIA

DARIUS
521–486 BC

XERXES (AHASUERUS)
486–465 BC

ARTAXERXES
465–423 BC

CAMBYSES
530–522 BC

MALACHI?

ZECHARIAH

HAGGAI

Esther

Genre | **HISTORICAL NARRATIVE**

God spares the Jewish people from potential annihilation through unlikely figures and events.

INTRODUCTION

AUTHOR As with most Old Testament books, the author of the book is unknown. In the Jewish Talmud it is suggested that the members of the Great Synagogue wrote the book. However, it is hard to imagine this prestigious group of religious scholars writing a book that mentions the Persian king 190 times but never mentions God. Many early writers, Jewish as well as Christian, suggested Mordecai as the author.

BACKGROUND The story of Esther is rooted in the historical situation of King Xerxes (Ahasuerus), who ruled as king of Persia from 486 to 465 BC. The book gives every indication of being a historical narrative.

MESSAGE AND PURPOSE The principal message of the book of Esther called all Jews to celebrate Purim. The purposes of Esther can be distinguished into two types: those purposes that pertain to the original audience of the book during the Persian period and the broader, theological purposes that transcend the book's original readers. It is unlikely the lack of any mention of God in the book is accidental. It leaves the reader to ponder the work of God, evident but unseen, in the unfolding story of deliverance and redemption. This is fitting since Jews in exile would be tempted to find lack of evidence for God's overt presence to be evidence for his actual absence. The book of Esther counters this notion, depicting God's providence as ruling even the events of foreign lands during the Jews' exile.

SUMMARY Esther is a unique book. Although the book does not mention God, his presence is implied due to Mordecai's allusion to divine providence (4:14). At times the book seems rather secular; historically, this has contributed to questions regarding its place in the canon of the synagogue and the church. Esther is tightly connected with specific historical events, yet it is also a piece of literature, a narrative with all the literary features necessary to make it a great story. It is a book in which its purposes are not always explicitly stated but are derived from the story as a whole.

STRUCTURE The book of Esther is written in a form of late biblical Hebrew common to the postexilic era and found in other biblical books of that time, such as Chronicles, Ezra–Nehemiah, and Daniel. Like Ezra–Nehemiah, Esther shows the growing influence of Aramaic in its grammar and vocabulary, as well as the presence of many Persian words.

Outline

I. **A Replacement Queen (1:1–2:20)**
   A. Vashti angers the king (1:1–12)
   B. The king's decree (1:13–22)
   C. Search for a new queen (2:1–14)
   D. Esther becomes queen (2:15–20)

II. **A Dangerous Threat (2:21–3:15)**
   A. Mordecai saves the king (2:21–23)
   B. Haman's plan to kill the Jews (3:1–15)

III. **Esther's Daring Decision (4:1–5:14)**
   A. Mordecai's appeal to Esther (4:1–17)
   B. Esther approaches the king (5:1–14)

IV. **The Great Reversal (6:1–10:3)**
   A. Mordecai honored by the king (6:1–14)
   B. Haman is executed (7:1–10)
   C. Esther intervenes for the Jews (8:1–17)
   D. Victories of the Jews (9:1–32)
   E. Mordecai remembered (10:1–3)

WORD STUDY

betulah

Hebrew pronunciation:
[beh too LAH]

CSB translation:
young woman, virgin

Uses in Esther: 4
Uses in the OT: 50

Focus passage:
Esther 2:2–3,17,19

Betulah designates *young woman,* for *betulah* is paired with *bachur,* which implies *fit young man* (2 Chr 36:17). A *betulah* was normally unmarried (Lev 21:14) and was expected to be a *virgin* because Israelite sexual law put a penalty on premarital sex (Deut 22:23–29). *Betulah* may not have had to entail virginity, for this fact is sometimes added after the word (Gen 24:16). Occasionally *betulah* must signify *virgin* (Esth 2:2; Ezek 44:22). Tamar probably tore her dress, one worn by *virgins,* to mark her grief at losing this status (2 Sam 13:18–19). *Betulah* can encompass an *engaged woman* (Joel 1:8). Harem *virgins* are still called *betulah* after spending a night with the king (Esth 2:17), and a *betulah* can be ravished (Isa 23:12). Whether *betulah* is *virgin* or *young woman* depends on what Scripture emphasizes. The stress can be on *youth* and stage in life (Ezek 9:6) or on *virginity* (Deut 22:19).

chatham

Hebrew pronunciation:
[khah THAHM]

CSB translation:
seal

Uses in Esther: 4
Uses in the OT: 27

Focus passage:
Esther 8:8,10

Chatham is a West Semitic word apparently borrowed from an Egyptian term dating to the Old Kingdom (2700–2160 BC). *Chatham* means *seal* (Deut 32:34). God *seals off* stars from shining (Job 9:7); springs can be *sealed* (Song 4:12). *Chatham* denotes *seal up* as confirming (Dan 9:24) or closing for preservation (Dan 12:4,9). The intensive describes *locking* oneself indoors (Job 24:16); the causative concerns *retaining* bodily discharges (Lev 15:3). *Chotham* (14x) denotes *signet ring* (Gen 38:18) or *seal* (Exod 28:11). Balls of clay (Job 38:14) imprinted by personal seals secured documents, containers (Job 14:17), and doors (Dan 6:17), thus preventing tampering. Seals were used in contracts (Jer 32:10) and binding agreements (Neh 9:38). They were marks of authority (1 Kgs 21:8), making royal edicts irrevocable (Esth 8:8). *Signet rings* were valuable (Hag 2:23), carefully engraved (Exod 28:11), and sometimes worn on a cord (Gen 38:18) over the heart (Song 8:6).

No Matter the Cost

BIBLICAL CHARACTER(S)	THE THREAT	DEATH-DEFYING FAITH	THE RESULT
Shadrach, Meshach, and Abednego	Worship the king's statue or be thrown into the fiery furnace *(see Dan 3:13–15)*	"God can rescue us, but even if he doesn't, we won't worship your statue" *(see Dan 3:16–18)*	Thrown into the furnace, but God rescued them from the fire *(Dan 3:19–29; see Heb 11:34)*
Daniel	For a 30-day period, pray only to the king or be thrown into the lions' den *(Dan 6:6–9)*	Prayed to God as he had always done *(Dan 6:10)*	Thrown into the lions' den, but God rescued him from the lions' mouths *(Dan 6:16–23; see Heb 11:33)*
Esther	Approach the king unbidden in order to rescue her people from destruction, but doing so risked the death penalty *(Esth 4:8–11)*	Believing she might be in her position "for such a time as this," she fasted and prayed for three days and then approached the king *(Esth 4:14–17)*	She won the approval of the king and was able to thwart the destruction of her people *(Esth 5–9)*
Zerubbabel, Jeshua, Haggai, and Zechariah	The names of the leaders rebuilding the temple were taken and sent to the king for a decision regarding this matter *(Ezra 4:24–5:17)*	Continued the reconstruction of the temple and named themselves the servants of the God of heaven and earth *(Ezra 5:11–16)*	The king protected the rebuilding of the temple and even supported it from his taxes so that it was completed *(Ezra 6:1–15)*
Ezra	Potential harm from enemies on the journey from Babylon to Jerusalem *(Ezra 8:21–22)*	Refused to ask the king for protection, having said God would help them; prayed and fasted for God's protection *(Ezra 8:21–23)*	God strengthened and protected his people from the power of the enemy and from ambush along the way *(Ezra 8:31)*
Nehemiah	Unknown potential consequences for sadness of heart in the king's presence, causing overwhelming fear *(Neh 2:1–2)*	Explained his sadness, prayed silently to the God of heaven, and then requested to leave the king's service and go and rebuild his city; also asked for supplies to do so *(Neh 2:3–8)*	The king granted his requests, for he was graciously strengthened by God; returned to Jerusalem and rebuilt the wall *(Neh 2:8–6:16)*
Jesus	The shame and death of a cross *(Heb 12:2)*	Endured the cross and despised the shame for the joy that lay before him *(Heb 12:2)*	Now seated at the right hand of the throne of God *(Heb 12:2)*

KEY VERSE

"If you keep silent at this time, relief and deliverance will come to the Jewish people from another place, but you and your father's family will be destroyed. Who knows, perhaps you have come to your royal position for such a time as this."

ESTHER 4:14

Job

Genre | **HISTORICAL NARRATIVE, POETRY, WISDOM**

The book of Job is a narrative about God's mysterious sovereignty and wisdom over suffering that focuses on the ruinous events that befall a righteous man named Job.

INTRODUCTION

AUTHOR The author of Job is unknown, but he was a learned man whose knowledge embraced the heavens (22:12; 38:32–33) and earth (26:7–8; 28:9–11; 37:11,16).

BACKGROUND Although Job is set in the patriarchal period, its date of writing is unknown. Jewish tradition places the authorship of Job in the time of Moses. The author was doubtless an Israelite as confirmed by his frequent use of God's covenant name (*Yahweh*, usually rendered as the LORD).

MESSAGE AND PURPOSE The book of Job demonstrates that a sovereign, righteous God is sufficient and trustworthy for every situation in life, even in the most difficult of circumstances. The book of Job teaches that suffering comes to everyone, the righteous and unrighteous alike. God does not always keep the righteous from danger or suffering. Ultimately God controls all of life's situations, including limiting the power of Satan. God's comfort and strength are always available to the trusting soul. Although the book of Job does take note of the problem of suffering, it focuses more on the nature of human conduct before a sovereign and holy God.

SUMMARY The book of Job is named after the central character and speaker. The narrative deals with a man who lost everything and the subsequent discussions he had about the reason for his suffering. God alone had the final word and eventually restored all that Job had lost.

STRUCTURE The writer was a skilled storyteller, artistically characterizing the distinctions between the protagonist (Job), antagonist (Satan), and literary foils (the three friends and Elihu). The characterization demonstrates that God himself is the ultimate protagonist (or "hero") of the story.

Outline

I. Prologue: The Setting of the Test (1:1–2:13)
- A. Job's life before the test (1:1–5)
- B. Satan's first accusation and proposed test (1:6–12)
- C. Job's response to the first test (1:13–22)
- D. Satan's second accusation and proposed test (2:1–7)
- E. Job's response to the second test (2:8–10)
- F. The arrival of Job's comforters (2:11–13)

II. Development: Examining Job's Condition (3:1–27:23)
- A. Job's lament over his condition (3:1–26)
- B. Dialogues about Job's condition (4:1–27:23)

III. Denouement: Explaining Job's Condition (28:1–37:24)
- A. Job's speeches about his condition (28:1–31:40)
- B. Elihu's speeches about Job's condition (32:1–37:24)

IV. Resolution: Job's Condition and God's Greatness (38:1–42:6)
- A. God's first speech: his sovereign power (38:1–40:2)
- B. Job's response: his self-renunciation (40:3–5)
- C. God's second speech: Job's impotence (40:6–41:34)
- D. Job's response: his repentance (42:1–6)

V. The Scene after the Test (42:7–17)
- A. Job and his three comforters (42:7–9)
- B. Job and his family (42:10–17)

WORD STUDY

satan

Hebrew pronunciation:
[sah TAHN]

CSB translation:
adversary, Satan

Uses in Job: 14
Uses in the OT: 26

Focus passage:
Job 1:6–9,12

Satan denotes *adversary* (1 Sam 29:4) or *enemy* (1 Kgs 5:4). Even the angel of the Lord could be one who *opposes* (Num 22:22). *Satan* refers to military (1 Sam 29:4) and political (1 Kgs 11:25) *enemies.* OT evidence favors the connotation "accuser." The related noun *sitnah* means *accusation* (Ezra 4:6). A judicial setting shows an *accuser* at someone's right hand to give him his own treatment, which was verbal attack (Ps 109:2–7). In a heavenly courtroom, someone standing at Joshua's right hand opposes him before the angel of the Lord (Zech 3:1–2). Here and 17 other places *satan* seems to identify a particular supernatural being by the name or title *Satan,* as in Arabic; once the article is absent from *satan* (1 Chr 21:1). The verb *satan* (6x, *oppose, be an enemy*) may derive from the noun and appears alongside it (Zech 3:1). The verb form *satan* occurs in five of the psalms.

ruach

Hebrew pronunciation:
[RU ahkh]

CSB translation:
wind, breath, spirit

Uses in Job: 31
Uses in the OT: 378

Focus passage:
Job 4:9,15

Ruach, related to *rawach* (14x, *be relieved, smell*; Gen 8:21), denotes *breath* (Gen 6:17) and *wind* (Job 21:18). *Ruach* implies *air* (Job 41:16), *breeze* (Gen 3:8), or nostril *blast* (Exod 15:8). *Wind* can represent meaninglessness (Eccl 2:17), *emptiness* (Job 16:3), or divine judgment (Jer 4:11–12). *Ruach* can be the four *winds* that signify compass directions (Jer 49:36) and a building's four sides (Ezek 42:20). *Breath* is associated with a creature's *spirit* (Gen 45:27). *Ruach* may be untranslated because one's *spirit* is oneself (Gen 41:8). *Ruach* indicates God's *Spirit* (Num 11:29) and demonic *spirits* (1 Kgs 22:21). It can be impersonal, a *spirit* of justice (Isa 28:6). *Ruach* connotes *mind* (Ezek 20:32), *will* (Isa 30:1), *courage* (Josh 2:11), or *emotions* (Prov 16:32). It is a *feeling* (Num 5:14), an *urge* (Isa 29:10). *Ruach* suggests *anger* (Job 15:13) or *despair* (Isa 61:3; lit. "faint *spirit*"). It represents one's *strength* (Judg 15:19) or *life* (Gen 26:35).

derek

Hebrew pronunciation:
[DEH rek]

CSB translation:
way, road, path

Uses in Job: 33
Uses in the OT: 712

Focus passage:
Job 24:4,13,18,23

Derek, from verbal *darak* (*tread*), indicates *way,* either as physical *path* (Num 22:22) or metaphor for *conduct* (Ezek 16:27). It occurs alongside other words for *roadway* and implies *highway* (Num 20:17), *road* (1 Sam 6:9), *route* (Deut 1:22), or *passageway* (Ezek 42:11). It suggests *journey* (Gen 24:21) or *trip* (Exod 3:18), especially when modified temporally. *Derek* can mean *distance* (Exod 8:27). With compass points it is untranslated or suggests *direction* (1 Kgs 8:44) or *toward* (Ezek 42:7). Ethically, "walk in his *ways*" (Deut 10:12) implies *instruction* (Deut 5:33) or *custom* (Gen 19:31). *Anything you do* is literally "your *ways*" (Deut 28:29). *Derek* signifies one's *course* (Job 29:25), *works* (Job 40:19), or *life* (Ps 119:26). In comparisons it can be *like* (Amos 4:10). Scripture contrasts *ways* of life and death (Jer 21:8), the evil *way* (Prov 28:10) and the *way* of integrity (Ps 101:6).

Job Timeline

2300–2100 BC

2285–2250
Enheduanna, the daughter of Sargon of Akkad, is the world's oldest known author whose works are written in cuneiform.

2280–2050
The Dispute between a Man and His Ba, Egyptian parallel to Job

2200
The Great Ziggurat at Ur

2100–2000 BC

2166–1991
ABRAHAM

2100?–1900?
JOB

2066–1866
ISAAC

2095
Death in combat of Ur-Nammu (king of Sumer, Ur, and Akkad), who standardized the weights and measures and formulated a system of law that tried to establish justice for the underprivileged

2000–1900 BC

2006–1859
JACOB

2000
The Protests of the Eloquent Peasant, Egyptian parallel of Job

2000
Man and His God, Sumerian parallel to Job

1900–1850 BC

1915–1805
JOSEPH

1900
Potter's wheel introduced to Crete

1900
Egyptian town of El Lahun gives evidence of town planning with streets at right angles.

1900
Mesopotamian mathematicians discover what later came to be called the "Pythagorean theorem."

1900
Multiplication tables appear in Mesopotamia.

1900
Khnumhotep II, an architect of Pharaoh Amenemhet II, develops encryption.

1850–1100 BC

1826–1406
MOSES

1490?–1380?
JOSHUA

1850–1600
The Admonitions of Ipuwer, Egyptian parallel of Job

1700
Ludlul Bel Nemeqi, Tabu-utul-Bel, Babylonian parallel to Job

1360
Epic of Keret, Canaanite, extant copy (original date unknown)

1290
I Will Praise the Lord of Wisdom, Mesopotamian

1100
The Babylonian Theodicy, Mesopotamian

Friends of Job

ELIPHAZ

Eliphaz's name means "God is victorious." The Scriptures provide no details about his life or family. He was the kindest of the three friends. Before coming to see Job, Eliphaz had a dream that affected him greatly (4:12–21), which likely set the tone for all three of his speeches. Eliphaz believed that all suffering was punishment for sin. Therefore, in Eliphaz's mind, because Job was suffering greatly, he must have sinned grievously against God.

BILDAD

Bildad's name may mean "son of Hadad," but this is not certain.

As with Eliphaz, the Bible gives no information about Bildad's family. Most Bible commentators believe he was younger than Eliphaz, as it was customary for the oldest person to speak first. Bildad was a consummate traditionalist (8:8–10). He expressed amazement that Job would question the traditional belief that suffering is the result of sin. The book of Job includes three speeches by Bildad (chaps. 8; 18; and 25). Exhibiting little concern for Job's feelings, Bildad's speeches instead focused on traditional theological claims.[7]

ZOPHAR

Zophar's name may mean "young bird" or "little bird."

The fact that Zophar spoke third suggests he was the youngest of the friends. He valued common sense and found no delight in many words (11:2). He showed little patience with Job. Like his friends, Zophar focused on Job's disobedience as the cause of his suffering. In his speeches Zophar insisted that Job must have sinned; otherwise, he would not be suffering. Zophar came to the discussion with preconceived ideas, and he refused to adjust his thinking to Job's situation.

Wisdom Literature

WISDOM LITERATURE	STYLE	PURPOSE
JOB	Narrative prologue and epilogue, with poetic dialogues making up most of the book	Provides spiritual insight for "the problem of evil"—God is sovereign and receives glory as we "fear . . . the LORD," even in our suffering *(Job 28:28)*
PSALMS	An anthology of Hebrew poetry; psalm types include praise, thanksgiving, lament, trust, wisdom, and royal psalms	Poetic expressions of praise and faith to guide God's people to approach him in "the fear of the LORD" *(Ps 111:10)*, regardless of their circumstances
PROVERBS	A few extended wisdom poems, but largely consists of unrelated proverbs strung together—proverbs are general rules, not absolute promises	Gives positive and negative principles for successful living in the world God has created, chiefly the need to "fear . . . the LORD" *(Prov 1:7)*
ECCLESIASTES	A mixture of poetry and prose; overtly pessimistic about life "under the sun," or apart from God	Answers the question "What is the meaning of life?" and the answer is "Fear God and keep his commands" *(Eccl 12:13)*
SONG OF SOLOMON, OR SONG OF SONGS	A song composed entirely of Hebrew poetry, featuring a bride, a groom, and a chorus of "friends"	Answers the question "Should a husband and wife enjoy the sexual dimension of their relationship?" and the answer is yes

NEW TESTAMENT REFERENCES	POINTS TO JESUS	WISDOM LITERATURE
James 5:11—Job given as an example of faithful endurance in the face of suffering	The ultimate answer to the problem of evil is found in Jesus's death on the cross—the righteous for the unrighteous—to bring us to God *(1 Pet 3:18)*	JOB
Ephesians 5:19; Colossians 3:16—The psalms are to be part of our worship to God and encouragement for each other	Some psalms prophesy specifically about Jesus's crucifixion *(Ps 22)*, resurrection *(Ps 16)*, ascension, and second coming *(Ps 110)*	PSALMS
• Hebrews 12:5–7 *(Prov 3:11–12)* • James 4:6 *(Prov 3:34)* • 1 Peter 4:8 *(Prov 10:12)* • Romans 12:20 *(Prov 25:21–22)*	All the treasures of wisdom and knowledge are found in Jesus Christ, who created all things and holds all things together *(Col 1:15–17; 2:3)*	PROVERBS
Luke 12:15–21—Jesus's parable of a rich fool echoes Ecclesiastes: we should be rich toward God, not store up treasure for ourselves	To fear God is to know him and the One he has sent—Jesus *(John 17:3)*; we are to obey him and teach others to do the same *(Matt 28:18–20)*	ECCLESIASTES
—	This ideal romance, as with every marriage, is a picture of the greater relationship between Christ and his bride, the church *(Eph 5:22–33)*	SONG OF SOLOMON, OR SONG OF SONGS

Psalms

Genre | **POETRY, WISDOM**

The book of Psalms contains songs and prayers directed to God from a varying range of situations and contexts, many of which are associated with King David.

INTRODUCTION

AUTHOR Since the book is a collection of many different psalms written over a long time, there is not just one author for this collection. By far the most common designation in the titles is "Of David," which may refer to David as the author of those psalms. Other titles include the designations of Solomon (Pss 72; 127), Asaph (Pss 50; 73–83), the sons of Korah (Pss 42; 44–49; 84–85; 87–88), Ethan the Ezrahite (Ps 89), Heman the Ezrahite (Ps 88), and Moses (Ps 90). All of these use the same Hebrew preposition as appears with David's name and therefore have the same ambiguity about authorship.

BACKGROUND The book of Psalms consists of many different hymns and prayers composed by individuals but used by the community. If one were to take the names in the titles as authors, the date of composition ranges from the time of Moses (fifteenth century BC) to a time following the exile (sixth century BC or later). Some of the titles do contain historical information that might indicate the setting of the composition, although even this (like the authorship) is ambiguous.

MESSAGE AND PURPOSE There are myriad messages scattered through the 150 psalms, but overall, this record of the responses of God's people in worship and prayer serves the purpose of teaching us how to relate to God in various circumstances of life. The psalms also demonstrate God's sovereignty and goodness for his people in order to instill confidence in those who trust in him.

SUMMARY The word for *psalms* in Hebrew is *tehilîm*, which means "praise." The English title is derived from the Greek translation (LXX) *Psalmoi*, which means "Songs of Praise." Praise directed to the Lord, the God of Israel, is certainly the primary emphasis in the Psalms. Some have referred to the Psalms as Israel's hymnbook, which is partially true but overall is insufficient to account for all that is in the Psalms. More than one-third of the collection is made up of prayers to God. Therefore, it contains both hymns and prayers that were used in the context of Israel's worship.

STRUCTURE The book of Psalms is, from first to last, a book of poetry. Hebrew poetry lacks rhyme and regular meter but uses parallelism wherein two (or three) lines are balanced and complete a thought. The psalms can be divided into classes. There are hymns (145–150) and songs of thanksgiving (30–32). Psalms of lament (38–39) are prayers or cries to God during distressful situations. Royal psalms (2; 110) are concerned with the earthly king of Israel. Enthronement psalms (96; 98) celebrate the kingship of the Lord. Penitential psalms (32; 38; 51) express contrition and repentance, and wisdom or didactic psalms (19; 119) tend to be proverbial.

Outline

Psalms is unlike most other biblical books since it contains many writings collected and compiled over a period of time and finally organized into its present form. For this reason, it is not possible to outline the book in the standard way. However, there is clearly a structure to the collection. The book is divided into five parts, also known as books. According to Jewish tradition, this fivefold division was based on the arrangement of the Torah (or Pentateuch), the first five books of the Bible. The book divisions are Book I (Pss 1–41), Book II (Pss 42–72), Book III (Pss 73–89), Book IV (Pss 90–106), and Book V (Pss 107–150).

Another part of the structure is that psalms are generally grouped together by their titles, such as the Asaph psalms and those of the sons of Korah. Following the close of each of the first four books is a doxology or statement identifying the end of one book and the beginning of another. The psalms containing these statements are known as "seam" psalms because they show the "piecing together" of these psalms to form the collection as it now stands.

WORD STUDY

'ashrey

Hebrew pronunciation: [ash RAY]

CSB translation: happy, blessed

Uses in Psalms: 26

Uses in the OT: 44

Focus passage: Psalm 1:1

'Ashrey, an interjection especially frequent in Psalms, means *happy* (Ps 1:1) and implies *blessed* (Eccl 10:17). It is similar to *baruk* ("blessed") but probably more secular. *'Ashrey* is never used of or by God. Though it announces a *happy* condition (2 Chr 9:7), it often requires that people do things like waiting (Dan 12:12), obeying divine decrees (Ps 119:2), and showing kindness (Prov 14:21). *'Ashrey* may have produced the verb *'ashar* (10x), which would mean to "say *'ashrey*" to someone. *'Ashar* in intensive forms signifies *consider* or *declare fortunate* (Song 6:9; Mal 3:12) and *call blessed* (Ps 72:17). It can be *bless* (Job 29:11). The passive is *be blessed* (Ps 41:2); the passive participle indicates *happy* (Prov 3:18). Scholars disagree whether it is the same verb as the *'ashar* meaning "proceed" (Prov 4:14). The noun *'osher* (Gen 30:13) and interjection *'esher* (Prov 29:18) are translated as *happy*.

kavod

Hebrew pronunciation: [kah VOHD]

CSB translation: glory, honor, wealth

Uses in Psalms: 51

Uses in the OT: 200

Focus passage: Psalm 24:7–10

Kavod relates to verbal *kaved* and adjectival *kaved*, which indicate heaviness. *Kavod* describes God's *glory* (Exod 16:7). The King of *glory* (Ps 24:10) is Israel's *Glory* (Jer 2:11), manifesting *glory* (Exod 24:17). The ark of the covenant represents Israel's *glory* (1 Sam 4:22). People give *glory* to God (Jer 13:16). Earthly kings (Isa 8:7) and thrones (Jer 17:12) have *kabod*. It is associated with natural (Isa 60:13) or manufactured (Exod 28:2) beauty. Especially in Proverbs, *kabod* signifies *honor* (Prov 3:35). An antonym is *disgrace* (Hab 2:16). *Kavod* means *wealth* (Gen 31:1), *riches* (Isa 61:6), *abundance* (Nah 2:9), *splendor* (Isa 14:18), or *reward* (Num 24:11). A nation's *kavod* is its *nobility* (Mic 1:15) or *dignitaries* (Isa 5:13). *Kavod* indicates the self, translated as *soul* (Ps 57:8) or *whole being* (Job 29:20; Pss 16:9; 108:1). Adjectivally, *kavod* is *glorious* (Isa 3:8); rendered as a noun, it is *honor* (Prov 20:3).

selah

Hebrew pronunciation: [see LAH]

CSB translation: selah

Uses in Psalms: 71

Uses in the OT: 74

Focus passage: Psalm 46:3,7,11

Selah, an expression found in Psalms and Hab 3:3,9,13, remains obscure. Always occurring with "choir director" or *mizmor* ("psalm"), *selah* may specify musical or recitation style. It could be a later addition, for the Septuagint translation *diapsalma*, possibly a new word representing *selah* and indicating musical pause, appears 81 times. *Selah* might derive from *salal* ("lift up, exalt") and call worshippers to lift their eyes to heaven and repeat the psalm, or raise their voices and repeat a refrain. Alternatively, musicians might lift their instruments to perform a musical interlude. An ancient theory suggests that *selah*, read and pronounced *netsah* ("forever"), called worshippers to respond with a praise refrain. If from the root *sl* ("bow, pray"), *selah* could ask worshippers to bow in prayer. *Selah* could indicate the sound of the strings if related to a Persian word for *song*. *Selah* could abbreviate a phrase signaling a change in voice.

WORD STUDY *(continued)*

torah

Hebrew pronunciation:
[toe RAH]

CSB translation:
law, instruction, teaching

Uses in Psalms: 36
Uses in the OT: 223

Focus passage:
Psalm 119:1,18,29,34,44

Singular (Lev 14:32) or plural (Prov 7:2), ***torah*** indicates particular *laws* or *instructions. Torah* as a collective denotes *instruction* for particular individuals (Deut 17:11) or nations (Deut 33:4). *Torah* describes civil (Exod 18:16) and religious (Lev 6:9) *laws,* the book of Deuteronomy (Deut 1:5), all of Moses's writings (Josh 8:31), the Prophets (Dan 9:10), or the whole Word of God (Ps 19:7). The focus of *torah* is not a specific literary form but divine authority; any communication from God constitutes *torah. Torah* also pictures a parent's *teaching* (Prov 6:20). It appears as *instructions* (Num 5:30), *revelation* (2 Sam 7:19), *ruling* (Hag 2:11), *legal* (Num 19:2), and *legally required* (Neh 12:44). *Torah* derives from *yarah* (47x), which means *teach* (Exod 4:12), *instruct* (Deut 17:10), or *show* (Exod 15:25). Once *yarah* is *determine* (Lev 14:57), *prepare* (Gen 46:28), and *gesture* (Prov 6:13). *Yarah* and *torah* appear together seven times (Deut 17:11).

chesed

Hebrew pronunciation:
[KHEH sed]

CSB translation:
faithful love, kindness, loyalty

Uses in Psalms: 129
Uses in the OT: 249

Focus passage:
Psalm 136:1-26

The etymology of ***chesed*** is unknown. Half the word's occurrences are in Psalms, where it is closely associated with God. *Chesed* is *faithful love* (Exod 34:6), *love* (Isa 54:8), or *constant love* (Ps 40:10). It is a quality that binds people together: *kindness* (Gen 19:19), *loyalty* (Job 6:14), *goodness* (Isa 40:6), or *faithfulness* (Mic 6:8). *Chesed* implies *favor* (Esth 2:9) and *grace* (Ezra 9:9). Adjectivally, it appears as *gracious* (Dan 9:4), *kind* (Prov 11:17), *faithful* (Isa 57:1), and *loving* (Prov 31:26). It occurs with *'asah* ("do") as *deal kindly* (1 Sam 20:8), *show kindness* or *loyalty* (2 Sam 9:1; 22:51). The plural implies *acts/deeds of faithful love* (Pss 107:43; Neh 13:14). *Chasiyd* (34x) denotes *faithful* (Pss 86:2; 89:19; 145:17; Mic 7:2) and functions nominally. *Chasad* (2x) means *prove oneself faithful* (Ps 18:25).

Psalms Timeline

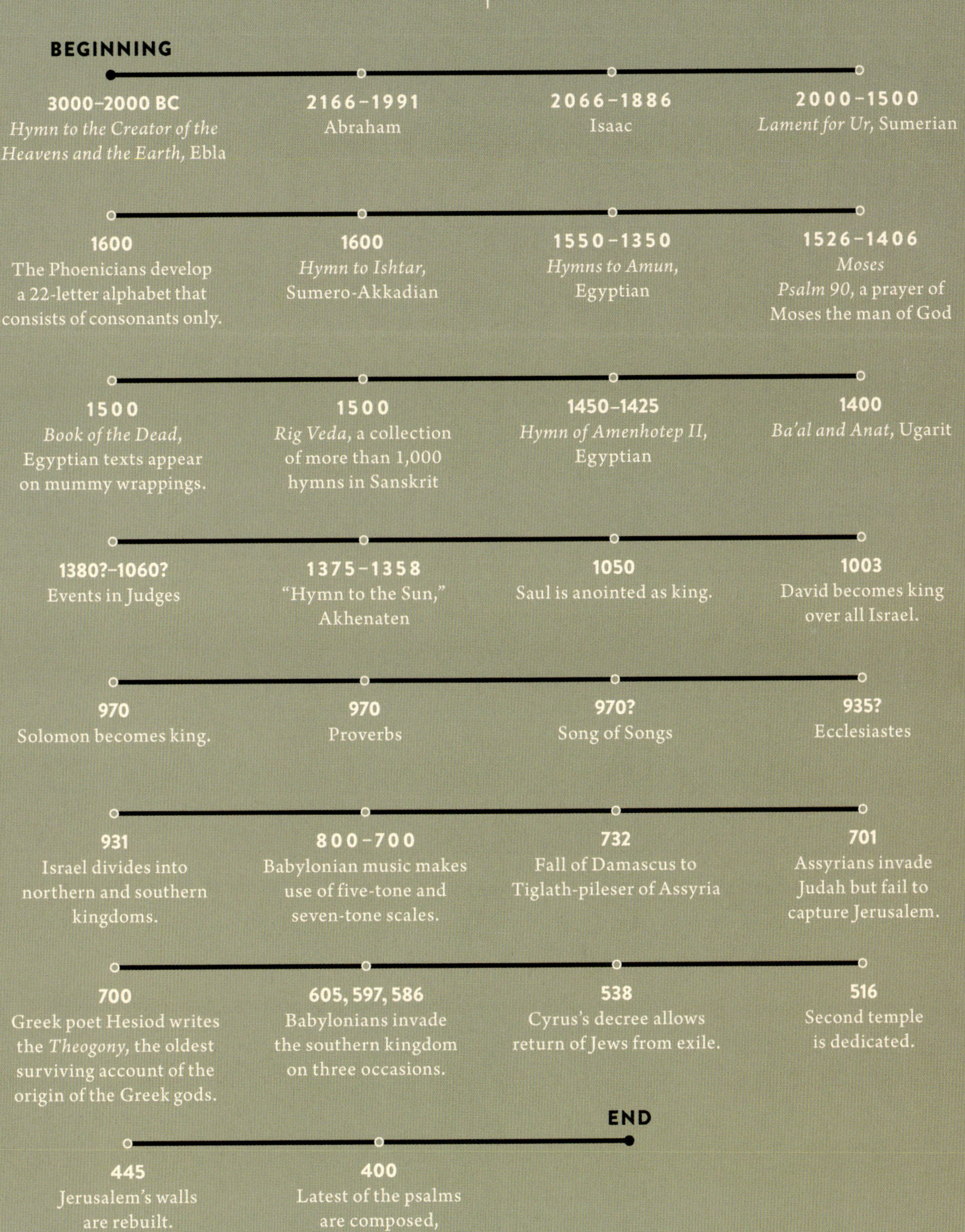

Authorship of the Psalms

The Psalter was not completed until late in Israelite history. But it contains hymns written over a period of hundreds of year. Many individual psalms are far older than the whole book.

AUTHOR	PSALM(S)
David	75 total psalms: Psalm 2 (see Acts 4:25); Psalm 95 (see Heb 4:7); Psalms 3–9; 11–32; 34–41; 51–65; 68–70; 86; 101; 103; 108–110; 122; 124; 131; 133; 138–145
Asaph	Psalms 50; 73–83
The sons of Korah	Psalms 42; 44–49; 84–85; 87–88
Heman the Ezrahite	Psalm 88
Solomon	Psalms 72; 127
Moses	Psalm 90
Ethan the Ezrahite	Psalm 89
Anonymous	The 48 remaining psalms

Types of Psalms

Scholars debate the forms and classifications of individual psalms. Many psalms are not neatly or easily categorized. However, identification helps the reader gain insight into the use of that psalm and its possible original context or a fitting present context in worship.

For the purpose of this overview, individual psalms were grouped into the following categories: hymns, laments, songs of thanksgiving, royal psalms, enthronement psalms, penitential psalms, and wisdom or didactic psalms.

These classifications, however, should not be taken with a determined dogma. The religious feelings and expressions found in the Psalms may at times overlap between classifications. A few psalms *(Pss 25; 34; 37; 111; 112; 119; 145)* are acrostically arranged according to the Hebrew alphabet, probably to aid memorization.

LAMENT

A lament can be expressed by the community *(Pss 44; 74; 79)* or the individual *(Pss 22; 39; 41; 54)*. Both types of laments are prayers or cries to God on the occasion of distressful situations. Differences are related to the types of trouble and the experiences of salvation. For the community, the trouble may be an enemy; for an individual, it may be an illness. The basic pattern includes an invocation of God, a description of the petitioner's complaint(s), a recalling of past salvation experiences (usually in community laments), petitions, a divine response (or oracle), and a concluding vow of praise.

THANKSGIVING

The thanksgiving psalms are also spoken by the community *(Pss 106; 124; 129)* and the individual *(Pss 9; 30)*. These psalms are related to the laments in that they are responses to liberation occurring after distress. They are expressions of joy and are fuller forms of the lament's vow of praise.

HYMN

The hymn is closest in form to a song of praise as sung in modern forms of worship. These psalms are uniquely liturgical and can be sung antiphonally; some have repeating refrains *(Pss 8; 136)*. The hymn normally includes a call to praise. Then the psalm describes the reasons for praising God. The structure is not as clear-cut as other types of psalms.

ROYAL

These psalms are concerned with the earthly king of Israel. Again, these are usually understood as mixed psalms. They were used to celebrate the king's rule. They may have included an oracle for the king. In some cases *(Ps 72)*, prayers were made to intercede on behalf of the king. Some royal psalms have messianic implications/fulfillments *(Pss 2; 89; 110)*.

ENTHRONEMENT

Enthronement psalms celebrate Yahweh's kingship. They are closely related to the hymns; the main difference is a celebration of Yahweh as King over all creation.

PENITENTIAL

Penitential psalms are expressions of contrition and repentance. The psalmist pleads to be restored to a right relationship with God.

WISDOM/DIDACTIC

This type has poetic form and style but is distinguished because of content and a tendency toward the proverbial. These psalms contemplate questions of theodicy *(Ps 73)*, celebrate God's Word *(the Torah; Ps 119)*, or deal with two different ways of living—that of the godly person or the evil person *(Ps 1)*.

Messianic Psalms

IN PSALMS, THE MESSIAH WAS PROPHESIED TO BE . . .	
Rejected by Gentiles	*Psalm 2:1; Acts 4:25–28*
Conspired against by political/religious leaders	*Psalm 2:2; Matthew 26:3–4; Mark 3:6*
King of the Jews	*Psalm 2:6; John 12:12–13; 18:32–33*
The Son of God	*Psalm 2:7; Matthew 3:16–17; Luke 1:31–35; Hebrews 1:5–6*
Resurrected and crowned King	*Psalms 2:7; 16:8–10; Matthew 28:6; Acts 2:25–32; 13:30–33; Romans 1:3–4*
In complete authority over all things	*Psalms 2:8; 8:6; Matthew 28:18; Hebrews 1:1–2*
For all people	*Psalm 18:49; Ephesians 3:4–6*
Forsaken by God at his crucifixion	*Psalm 22:1; Mark 15:34*
Despised and rejected by his own	*Psalm 22:6; Luke 23:21–23*
Called by God while in the womb	*Psalm 22:10; Luke 1:30–33*
Abandoned or betrayed by his own disciples	*Psalms 22:11; 41:9; 55:12–14; Mark 14:17–18,50; Luke 22:47–48*
Crucified	*Psalm 22:14; Matthew 27:35*
Accused by false witnesses	*Psalms 27:12; 35:11; Matthew 26:59–61; Mark 14:55–59*
God's sacrificial lamb for redemption of all mankind	*Psalm 40:6–8a; Hebrews 10:10–13*
A messenger of mercy	*Psalm 45:2; Luke 4:22*
Sitting on an eternal throne	*Psalm 45:6–7; Luke 1:31–33; Hebrews 1:8–9*
Condemned for God's sake	*Psalm 69:7,9; Matthew 26:65–67; Romans 15:3*
Rejected by the Jews	*Psalm 69:8a; John 1:11*
Brokenhearted	*Psalm 69:20a; John 19:34*
Exalted to the right hand of God	*Psalms 80:17; 110:1,5; Matthew 22:41–46; Mark 16:19; Acts 5:31; 1 Peter 3:21–22*
From the lineage of David	*Psalms 89:3–4,19–37; 132:11–17; Matthew 1:1*
God's only begotten Son	*Psalm 89:27; Mark 12:6; Colossians 1:18; Revelation 1:5*
The Creator of all things	*Psalm 102:25–27; John 1:3; Ephesians 3:9; Hebrews 1:10–12*
Coming in the name of the Lord	*Psalm 118:26; Matthew 21:9*

God in the Psalms

GOD IS OUR . . .	
Shield	*Psalms 3:3; 28:7; 119:114*
Rock	*Psalms 18:2; 42:9; 95:1*
King	*Psalms 5:2; 44:4; 74:12*
Shepherd	*Psalms 23:1; 80:1*
Judge	*Psalm 7:11*
Refuge	*Psalms 46:1; 62:7*
Fortress	*Psalms 31:3; 71:3*
Avenger	*Psalm 26:1*
Creator	*Psalm 8:1,6*
Deliverer	*Psalm 37:39–40*
Healer	*Psalm 30:2*
Protector	*Psalm 5:11*
Provider	*Psalm 78:23–29*
Redeemer	*Psalm 107:2*

Proverbs

Genre | **POETRY, WISDOM**

The book of Proverbs is a collection of wise sayings and observations about the nature of life in God's world.

INTRODUCTION

AUTHOR Solomon is credited with the proverbs in chapters 1–29 of the book of Proverbs (1:1; 10:1). There is biblical evidence that Solomon was wise and a collector of wise sayings (1 Kgs 3:5–14; 4:29–34; 5:7,12; 10:2–3,23–24; 11:41). Chapters 1–24 of Proverbs may have been written down during his reign, 970–931 BC. The proverbs in chapters 25–29 were Solomon's proverbs collected by King Hezekiah, who reigned 715–687 BC (25:1). The last two chapters are credited to Agur and Lemuel (30:1; 31:1), about whom nothing else is known. An editor was inspired to collect the proverbs of Solomon, Agur, and Lemuel into the book we now have.

BACKGROUND Solomon addressed his teaching to his son or sons, but these inspired wise sayings are applicable to all people. The book of Proverbs, like the rest of the Bible, contains stories, teaching, and examples. People should make appropriate application of these truths to their own situations (1 Cor 10:11).

MESSAGE AND PURPOSE Because these proverbs are in the Bible, they do not just entertain; they exhort, encourage, and offer hope. Solomon called readers, especially youth, to pursue wisdom rather than foolishness. He encouraged the inexperienced to become wise rather than mockers, to be teachable rather than incorrigible, to live rather than to die. He predicted that people who pursued wisdom would generally find success and happiness in this life, but he promised that they would absolutely find joy and blessing in eternity.

SUMMARY A proverb is derived from astute observations about how life usually works; the creator of a proverb shows himself very knowledgeable and perceptive, able to see what is generally true and to draw conclusions from it: "The pen is mightier than the sword." In addition to all this, the proverbs in the book of Proverbs are also divinely inspired. Since they come from God, we know they are true and we can be certain they are beneficial.

STRUCTURE The book of Proverbs is in the wisdom genre. Wisdom books consist of the intelligent author's observations on the world and the people in it. However, without an inspired, godly perspective, the world would be depressing and hopeless, as parts of Job and Ecclesiastes show. Ultimately, biblical wisdom is informed by and founded on faith in God.

Outline

I. **Solomon's Exhortations and Warnings (1:1–9:18)**
   A. Contrast between wisdom and riches (1:1–3:20)
   B. Praise of wisdom, love, and worthy conduct (3:21–4:27)
   C. Warnings against lust, idleness, and deceit (5:1–7:27)
   D. A portrayal of wisdom (8:1–9:18)

II. **Solomon's Proverbs (10:1–29:27)**
   A. Collected proverbs (10:1–22:16)
   B. Thirty sayings of the wise (22:17–24:22)
   C. More sayings of the wise (24:23–34)
   D. Hezekiah's collection (25:1–29:27)

III. **Other Proverbs (30:1–31:31)**
   A. Words of Agur (30:1–33)
   B. Words of Lemuel (31:1–9)
   C. Praise of a capable wife (31:10–31)

WORD STUDY

da'ath

Hebrew pronunciation: [dah ATH]

CSB translation: knowledge

Uses in Proverbs: 39
Uses in the OT: 88

Focus passage: Proverbs 8:9–10,12

Fundamentally, ***da'ath*** (*knowledge*) refers to a relational awareness of people or objects gained through the senses. *Knowledge* is gained through practical involvement with the object of knowledge, and *da'ath* only infrequently expresses the concept of abstract intellectual *knowledge* apart from relationship. In Proverbs, there are two understandings of *knowledge*. In chapters 1–9, *knowledge* focuses more on insight gained through theological reflection (1:7,29; 2:5–6,10; 3:20; 9:10), while in chapters 10–29, *knowledge* focuses primarily upon the ability to handle interpersonal relationships (10:14; 11:9; 12:1; 14:6; 17:27; 19:25; 21:11; 23:12). In theological contexts, God possesses *knowledge* (Job 10:7; Prov 3:20), and he disseminates it to men (Job 21:22; Pss 94:10; 119:66; Isa 40:14). The fear of the Lord is the beginning of *knowledge* (*da'ath,* Prov 1:7; 2:5), and the perception of God's plans and purposes through relationship with him is referred to as *knowledge* (Isa 5:13; 11:2).

'ewiyl

Hebrew pronunciation: [eh VEEL]

CSB translation: fool

Uses in Proverbs: 19
Uses in the OT: 26

Focus passage: Proverbs 10:8,10,14,21

In Proverbs, ***'ewiyl*** (*fool*) refers to one who is morally deficient from the standpoint of being able to make reasoned moral judgments. He willfully refuses to make moral choices, neither choosing good nor rejecting evil. He arrogantly refuses to receive moral instruction and to learn from his mistakes (1:7; 12:15; 15:5). The *fool* is characterized by *foolishness* (*'iwwelet*), an internal moral corruption that renders the *fool* impotent to make reasonable moral judgments in life (15:21; 16:22). While he is young, there is hope that a youth can be separated from his foolishness (22:15), but later in life the *fool* is irrevocably marked by his folly (27:22). His moral deficiency manifests itself in matters of speech, morality, discipline, religion, and daily life. He speaks either the wrong thing or at the wrong time (10:8,10,14,21; 14:3), and he is quick to show his anger (12:16; 20:3) and to refuse resolution (29:9).

chakam

Hebrew pronunciation: [khah KHAM]

CSB translation: wise

Uses in Proverbs: 47
Uses in the OT: 138

Focus passage: Proverbs 14:1,3,16,24

Chakam (*wise*) describes one with a high degree of knowledge and skill in a particular area. *Chakam* may describe a skilled craftsman in a task such as sewing (Exod 28:3; 35:25) or construction (Exod 31:6; 36:1–2,4,8). Second, *chakam* may refer to skillfulness in exercising good judgment in managing interpersonal relations. The *wise* can manage people and affairs of state (Gen 41:33,39; 1 Kgs 5:7; Prov 20:26) and adjudicate impartially (Deut 1:13,15; 16:19; 1 Kgs 2:9; Prov 24:23). Third, *chakam* may refer to skillfulness in devising a scheme or plan (*shrewd, wise, cunning, clever*, 2 Sam 13:3; 14:2; 20:16). In Proverbs and Ecclesiastes, *chakam* carries both intellectual and moral connotations and describes the skill of right living. In contrast to the fool, the *wise* have ethical, religious, and pragmatic wisdom. They foresee the ramifications of their actions and consequently change them. The *wise* obey the Lord (Ps 107:43; Hos 14:9), exercise discernment (Prov 16:21; Eccl 2:14), and turn from evil (Prov 14:16).

kesiyl

Hebrew pronunciation: [keh SEEL]

CSB translation: fool

Uses in Proverbs: 49
Uses in the OT: 70

Focus passage: Proverbs 17:10,12,16, 21,24–25

Kesiyl indicates someone foolish because of laziness and complacency. The *kesiyl* has a stupidity stemming from apathy toward moral issues, not willful disregard of them. This apathy distinguishes him from the *'ewiyl*, a *fool* who is intentionally immoral. The *kesiyl* harbors anger, is easily provoked (Eccl 7:9), and in consequence becomes careless (Prov 14:16). He is amused by purposeless activity (Eccl 7:4–6) and speaks without thinking (Prov 15:2). Being self-indulgent (Prov 19:10), he squanders resources (Prov 21:20). Like the *'ewiyl*, he displays his foolishness (Prov 13:16), loves ignorance (Prov 1:22), and repeats foolish behavior (Prov 26:11). He brings harm to companions (Prov 13:20), is self-deceived (Prov 14:8), and is self-destructive (Eccl 4:5). *Kesel* (6x) is *confidence* (Prov 3:26) but also *stupidity* (Eccl 7:25) or *arrogance* (Ps 49:13). *Kislah* denotes *foolish ways* (Ps 85:8) or *confidence* (Job 4:6), and *kesiylut* signifies *folly* (Prov 9:13). *Kasal* means *be foolish* (Jer 10:8).

Solomon Timeline

3000–2200 BC

2166–1991
ABRAHAM

2686–2160
The Instruction of Prince Hardjedef, Egyptian Old Kingdom

2600
The Instructions Addressed to Kagemni, Egyptian

2575–2134
The Instructions of Ptah-Hotep, Egypt's Old Kingdom

2450–2250
Collections of proverbs found among the royal archives at Ebla

2200–1700 BC

1526–1406
MOSES

2160
The Royal Instruction of Khety to Merikare, Egyptian

2040–1640
The Instruction of a Man for His Son, Egyptian Middle Kingdom

1925
The Instruction of King Amenemhet I for His Son Sesostris I, Egyptian

1900–1700
Instructions of Shuruppak, Sumerian Proverb Collection

1700–1200 BC

1050?–970
DAVID

1600
The Phoenicians develop a 22-letter alphabet that consists of consonants only. It is read from right to left and becomes an important step in the development of the modern Western alphabet. This is the world's first purely phonetic alphabet. It is based on sounds and not symbolic representations of objects.

1500–1200
The Counsels of Wisdom, Akkadian

1380?–1060?
Events in Judges

1200–900 BC

990?–931
SOLOMON

1186–1069
The Instruction of Amenemope, Egyptian

1050
Saul anointed king

1003
David becomes king over all Israel.

970
Solomon becomes king.

970
Proverbs

The Four Contributors

Though the title of Proverbs (1:1) seems to ascribe the entire book to Solomon, closer inspection reveals that the book is composed of parts and that it was formed over a period of several hundred years. It is difficult to know precisely the role Solomon and his court may have had in starting the process that culminated in the book of Proverbs. In Israel, wisdom was considered Solomonic almost by definition. Thus the titles in 1:1 and 10:1 are not strictly statements of authorship in the modern sense.

THE CONTRIBUTORS	SCRIPTURE REFERENCE	DATE	BACKGROUND
Solomon	Proverbs 1–24	Approximately 1000–950 BC	Solomon was the tenth son of David and the second son of Bathsheba. Solomon became the third king of Israel and reigned 40 years, about 1000 BC.
Hezekiah's men, or the court of Hezekiah	Proverbs 25–29	About 700 BC	Influenced by the court of Egypt; used the literary expertise of the scribes and traditional wisdom of Israel
Agur	Proverbs 30	No evidence has been discovered to support dating this writing.	Agur is distinguished by the presence of seven numerical sayings (vv. 7–9,15a,15b–16,18–19, 21–23,24–28,29–31). Numerical sayings are found in second millennium ancient Near Eastern literature and continue well into the first millennium.
King Lemuel	Proverbs 31	No evidence has been discovered to support dating this writing.	A king who received words of wisdom from his mother concerning wine, women, and the legal rights of the weak and poor. Exactly where his kingdom of Massa was is not known. This section of Proverbs apparently comes from a non-Israelite woman.

Wisdom in Proverbs

PROVERBS ON WISDOM

The fear of the LORD is the beginning of knowledge;
fools despise wisdom and discipline.
Proverbs 1:7

Trust in the LORD with all your heart, and do not rely on your own understanding; in all your ways know him, and he will make your paths straight. Don't be wise in your own eyes; fear the LORD and turn away from evil.
Proverbs 3:5–7

Happy is a man who finds wisdom
and who acquires understanding,
for she is more profitable than silver,
and her revenue is better than gold.
She is more precious than jewels;
nothing you desire can equal her.
Long life is in her right hand;
in her left, riches and honor. . . .
She is a tree of life to those who embrace her,
and those who hold on to her are happy.
Proverbs 3:13–16,18

Don't abandon wisdom, and she will watch over you;
love her, and she will guard you.
Wisdom is supreme—so get wisdom.
And whatever else you get, get understanding.
Cherish her, and she will exalt you;
if you embrace her, she will honor you.
Proverbs 4:6–8

When arrogance comes, disgrace follows,
but with humility comes wisdom.
Proverbs 11:2

A fool's way is right in his own eyes,
but whoever listens to counsel is wise.
Proverbs 12:15

The eyes of the LORD are everywhere,
observing the wicked and the good.
Proverbs 15:3

NEW TESTAMENT ON WISDOM

"Therefore, everyone who hears these words of mine and acts on them will be like a wise man who built his house on the rock. The rain fell, the rivers rose, and the winds blew and pounded that house. Yet it didn't collapse, because its foundation was on the rock. But everyone who hears these words of mine and doesn't act on them will be like a foolish man who built his house on the sand. The rain fell, the rivers rose, the winds blew and pounded that house, and it collapsed. It collapsed with a great crash."
Matthew 7:24–27

When I came to you, brothers and sisters, announcing the mystery of God to you, I did not come with brilliance of speech or wisdom. I decided to know nothing among you except Jesus Christ and him crucified. I came to you in weakness, in fear, and in much trembling. My speech and my preaching were not with persuasive words of wisdom but with a demonstration of the Spirit's power, so that your faith might not be based on human wisdom but on God's power. . . . We speak God's hidden wisdom in a mystery, a wisdom God predestined before the ages for our glory. None of the rulers of this age knew this wisdom, because if they had known it, they would not have crucified the Lord of glory. But as it is written,

What no eye has seen, no ear has heard, and no human heart has conceived—God has prepared these things for those who love him.
1 Corinthians 2:1–5,7–9

Now if any of you lacks wisdom, he should ask God—who gives to all generously and ungrudgingly—and it will be given to him.
James 1:5

The wisdom from above is first pure, then peace-loving, gentle, compliant, full of mercy and good fruits, unwavering, without pretense.
James 3:17

KEY QUOTE

Just as Job concluded with the importance of the fear of God, so the same concept brackets the beginning and ending of [these] two books, Proverbs and Ecclesiastes. Proverbs seems life-affirming; Ecclesiastes life-denying. The one sees the possibilities that life affords; the other its limitations. . . . The hermeneutical point is that the path to this wisdom [see Prov 3:18] is found in the fear of the Lord (Prov. 1:9) and the mouth of Solomon (Prov. 1:1; 10:1; 25:1). In contrast, Ecclesiastes seems to deal not with the issue of blessing but with the problem of curse. . . . The way out of the death and exile, where wisdom seems lost, is given through the line of David: fear God and keep his commandments; this is the whole duty of humanity (Eccles. 12:13).

STEPHEN G. DEMPSTER[8]

Ecclesiastes

Genre | **POETRY, WISDOM**

Ecclesiastes is Wisdom literature reflecting on life and its apparent futility in light of death.

INTRODUCTION

AUTHOR According to Ecclesiastes 1:1 and 1:12, the author was David's son and a king over Israel from Jerusalem. Also, 12:9 speaks of the author as a writer of proverbs, so Solomon appears to be the author. Many scholars believe that Ecclesiastes was written too late in Israel's history for this to be true, and they want to date the book at least 500 years after Solomon's time (later than 450 BC). However, strong evidence attests that the book does come from the age of Solomon. For instance, it displays a great knowledge of literature from early Mesopotamia and Egypt.

BACKGROUND Ecclesiastes is Wisdom literature, meaning that it is in the part of the Bible especially concerned with helping readers cope with the practical and philosophical issues of life. It has roots in the Wisdom literature of Egypt and Babylon. Ecclesiastes, in contrast to Proverbs, is for a more mature reader. It engages the question of whether death nullifies all purpose and meaning in life.

MESSAGE AND PURPOSE Ecclesiastes shows us that since we and our works are futile—that is, destined to perish—we must not waste our lives trying to justify our existence with pursuits that ultimately mean nothing. Put simply, Ecclesiastes examines major endeavors of life in light of the reality of death.

SUMMARY The book of Ecclesiastes faces the issue of how we can find meaning in life in light of the seemingly futile nature of everything. It will not allow the reader to retreat into superficial answers. It does not answer this problem by comforting us with hollow slogans. To the contrary, its motto is "Everything is futile." But by forcing us to face the futility of human existence, it guides us to a life free of empty purpose and deceitful vindication.

STRUCTURE Ecclesiastes does not have the kind of structure we usually look for in a book of the Bible. At first glance it seems to move to and fro among various topics in a way that seems almost incoherent. It has no simple hierarchical outline, and it often jumps rapidly from one topic to the next. But a closer look reveals a structure that alternates between two perspectives: that of human existence apart from God and that of existence lived before God.

Outline

I. God and the Futility of Life (1:1–2:26)
- A. The humdrum of life (1:1–11)
- B. The Teacher's quest (1:12–18)
- C. The emptiness of pleasure (2:1–3)
- D. The emptiness of possessions (2:4–11)
- E. The limits of wisdom (2:12–17)
- F. The emptiness of work (2:18–23)
- G. Pleasure, possessions, wisdom, and work in God's perspective (2:24–26)

II. Time and Eternity (3:1–22)
- A. The rhythm of time (3:1–8)
- B. Eternity in time (3:9–15)
- C. Eternity and death (3:16–22)

III. Society (4:1–16)
- A. A place of injustice (4:1–6)
- B. A place of comfort (4:7–12)
- C. The more things change (4:13–16)

IV. Religion (5:1–6:12)
- A. Authentic religion (5:1–7)
- B. Wealth: God's perspective (5:8–6:12)

V. Wise Sayings (7:1–29)
- A. Proverbs (7:1–14)
- B. The value of moderation (7:15–22)
- C. Wisdom's limitations (7:23–29)

VI. Wisdom as Prudence (8:1–10:20)
- A. Health (8:1)
- B. Authority figures (8:2–5)
- C. Timing (8:6–7)
- D. Realistic expectations (8:8–9)
- E. Reverence for God (8:10–13)
- F. Inequities (8:14)
- G. Enjoyment (8:15–9:10)
- H. Wisdom's limits (9:11–18)
- I. Wisdom preferable to folly (10:1–20)

VII. Invest in Life (11:1–10)

VIII. Aging and Death as Teachers (12:1–8)

IX. The Teacher's Objectives and Conclusion (12:9–14)

WORD STUDY

hevel

Hebrew pronunciation: [HEH vel]

CSB translation: breath, futility

Uses in Ecclesiastes: 38
Uses in the OT: 73

Focus passage: Ecclesiastes 1:2,14

Hevel may originate in the sound of *breath* (Isa 57:13). It may have produced a verb (*haval*) that occurs five times, once used as *keep up empty talk* (Job 27:12). *Haval* denotes *become worthless* (Jer 2:5) or *place false hope* (Ps 62:10). The causative means *delude* (Jer 23:16). *Breath* as transient and apparently insignificant underlies all metaphorical uses of *hevel*. It can indicate *vapor* (Ps 39:5) or *mist* (Prov 21:6), but the idea of little worth is always present. *Hevel* connotes *fraud* (Prov 13:11). It signifies *empty* (Job 27:12), *worthless* (Jer 10:3), *futile* (Job 21:34), *fleeting* (Prov 31:30), or *in vain* (Lam 4:17). It describes man (Ps 62:9). This key word in Ecclesiastes suggests *futility* except at Ecclesiastes 9:9. *Absolute futility* is literally "*futility of futilities*" (Eccl 1:2). The plural often denotes *worthless idols* (Deut 32:21) since context clarifies what the *hevel* is.

tovah

Hebrew pronunciation: [toh VAH]

CSB translation: goodness, well-being, happiness

Uses in Ecclesiastes: 7
Uses in the OT: 67

Focus passage: Ecclesiastes 6:3,6

Feminine ***tovah*** connotes *goodness* (Ps 65:11) more often than masculine *tov* and frequently contrasts with *ra'ah* ("evil"). It means *good, good things,* and *good work* or *deed*. *Tovah* indicates *friendship, grace, prosperity, happiness, well-being,* or *favor*. It suggests *well* (Judg 9:16), *kindly,* or *favorably*. The verb *tov* (44x) means *be better* (Judg 11:25; Song 4:10), *beautiful, favorable,* or *well off*. It connotes *prosper* (Deut 5:33). Infinitives signify *good* or *better*; causative verbs mean *do well* (1 Kgs 8:18). *Be good* "in the eyes" or "before" indicates *please* (Num 24:1), *meet/find approval, seem right* or *good, be agreed on,* or *prefer*. With "heart" as subject, one *feels good* (Esth 1:10) or *is in a good mood*. *Tuv* (32x), the most common word for *goodness* (Exod 33:19), signifies *goods, the best, best products, bounty,* and *prosperity*. It implies *good, glad, cheerful* (Deut 28:47), *thriving, lovely,* and *fine*.

Ecclesiastes Timeline

BEGINNING

4000 BC
Light wooden plows, Mesopotamia

4000
Copper smelting, Mesopotamia

3500
Irrigation developed, Mesopotamia

2700–1400
Epic of Gilgamesh

2575–2134
The Instruction of Ptah-Hotep, Egypt's Old Kingdom

2166–1991
Abraham

2000–600
Chinese literature, first of seven periods

1990–1800
The Man Who Was Tired of Life, Egyptian

1900
The Complaints of Khakheperre-sonb, Egyptian

1900
Egyptians develop an alphabet of 24 signs.

1900
Egyptians use the flooding of the Nile to their agricultural advantage by building systems of irrigation.

1600–1400
The Admonitions of Ipuwer, Egyptian

1570–1070
The Satirical Letter of Hori, Egyptian

1530–1500
Declarations of Innocence from the Egyptian *Book of the Dead*

1526–1406
Moses

1500–1000
Heavy import and export trade, Egypt

1500–500
Words of Ahiqar, Egyptian

1406–1380?
Events in Joshua

1380?–1060?
Events in Judges

1200
Epic of Gilgamesh is recorded.

1160
The Harper's Song for Inherkhway, Egyptian

1100
The Babylonian Theodicy, Mesopotamian

1003
David becomes king over all Israel.

970
Solomon becomes king.

970
Proverbs

970?
Song of Songs

935?
Ecclesiastes

END

KEY VERSE

"Absolute futility," says the Teacher.
"Absolute futility. Everything is futile."

ECCLESIASTES 1:2

KEY VERSE

When all has been heard, the conclusion of the matter is this: fear God and keep his commands, because this is for all humanity. For God will bring every act to judgment, including every hidden thing, whether good or evil.

ECCLESIASTES 12:13–14

KEY QUOTE

Ecclesiastes announces the vanity of the pursuit of pleasure divorced from the knowledge of God. Life is vain unless one lives for God. This is a condemnation, a judgment, of godless living. People who do not fear God and live for him are condemned to vain lives, and along with this the audience of Ecclesiastes is taught that God will bring all things to final judgment (3:17; 12:14). Satisfaction under the sun and salvation at the final judgment depend upon fearing God and obeying his commandments (12:13). Salvation comes to those who heed the announcement of present vanity and coming judgment.

JAMES M. HAMILTON JR.[9]

Song of Songs

Genre | **POETRY, WISDOM**

The Song of Songs is romantic Hebrew love poetry describing the intimate goodness of the marriage relationship.

INTRODUCTION

AUTHOR

The Song claims authorship by Solomon in its title, "The Song of Songs, which is Solomon's." The church has long accepted this at face value, but modern critics raise objections to Solomon as author. However, no evidence supports these objections. Moreover, the structure of the book suggests that the title is integral to the book's composition and is thus original.

BACKGROUND

A compelling historical reason to date the Song as coming from the time of Solomon is its nearest literary parallel—the Egyptian love songs. No one doubts their origin before or contemporaneous with the time of Solomon.

MESSAGE AND PURPOSE

The central theme of the Song of Songs is a celebration of the goodness and beauty of romantic love. The Song's romantic ideals are as captivating as its imagery: emotional intimacy, sensitive communication, delightful sexuality, profound companionship, common perspective, willing forgiveness, respect, integrity, security, love's devotion through bleak seasons of winter, and love's renewal in new seasons of spring.

SUMMARY

The Song of Songs celebrates the love of Solomon and his bride, who is called Shulamith or the Shulammite (6:13). The excitement of courtship, the beauty of the wedding night, the sexuality of the first night and subsequent nights, as well as tender friendship—all of these elements make this book a celebration of romance and marital sensuality as God intended them.

STRUCTURE

The Song of Songs is a poem whose components form a chiastic structure. The author intended to emphasize the central elements of the structure, the day and night of the wedding. When God inspired Solomon to write this song, he gave divine approval to romantic love.

Outline

Section A: Their Story Begins (1:2–2:7)
- A. The Shulammite, Solomon, and the daughters of Jerusalem (1:2–4)
- B. Her brothers, their vineyards, and her appearance (1:5–6)
- C. Her character and beauty (1:7–11)
- D. Love's expression (1:12–2:5)
- E. Refrains conclude Section A and begin Section B (2:6–7)

Section B: Invitation to Enjoy a Spring Day (2:6–17)
- A. Refrains of longing and patience (2:6–7)
- B. Her beloved's invitation to come from her house to enjoy spring (2:8–14)
- C. Refrains (after caution) of unity and invitation to her breasts (2:15–17)

Section C: Night of Separation preceding Wedding (3:1–5)
- A. She is awakened, alone, and longing for him (3:1)
- B. Leaves home to find him (3:2)
- C. Is found by guards (3:3a)
- D. Asks for help (3:3b)
- C′. Finds Solomon (3:4a)
- B′. Returns home with him (3:4b)
- A′. Is reunited with him through the night (3:4b); transition (3:5)

Section D: Wedding Day and Night (3:6–5:1)
- A. Songwriter's own words (3:6–11)
- B. Celebration of the wedding's beginning (3:6–11)
- C. Wedding night (4:1–5:1)
- B′. Celebration of the wedding's consummation (5:1a)
- A′. Songwriter's own words (5:1b)

Section C′: Night of Separation following Wedding Night (5:2–7:9)
- A. She is awakened, alone, and reluctant (5:2–8)
- B. Awakened to give tenfold praise (5:9–16)
- C. Aware of his presence in the garden (6:1–3)
- D. Receives his praise in the garden (6:4–10)
- C′. Recounts her journey to the garden (6:11–13)
- B′. Receives tenfold praise (7:1–5)
- A′. Delightfully make love, together drift off to sleep (7:6–9)

Section B′: Invitation to Enjoy a Spring Day (7:10–8:4)
- C′. Enjoyment of breasts and refrain of unity (7:7–8,10)
- B′. Her invitation to come enjoy spring then return to her house (7:11–8:2)
- A′. Refrains of longing and patience (8:3–4)

Section A′: Their Story Complete (8:3–14)
- E′. Refrains conclude Section B′ and begin Section A′ (8:3–4)
- D′. Love's devotion (8:5–7)
- C′. The Shulammite's character and beauty (8:8–9)
- B′. Her brothers, their vineyards, and her appearance (8:10–12)
- A′. The Shulammite, Solomon, and the Shulammite's companions (8:13–14)

The design of the Song underscores its central theme: a celebration of the goodness and beauty of romantic love.

WORD STUDY

dod

Hebrew pronunciation: [DOHD]

CSB translation: love, uncle

Uses in Song of Songs: 39
Uses in the OT: 61

Focus passage: Song of Songs 1:2,4, 13–14,16

Dod has two distinct meanings that likely developed from a single verb *yadad* (*love*). In Song of Songs, *dod* refers to Solomon and always has a pronominal modifier identifying Solomon as the woman's romantic *love* (Song 1:13). Elsewhere, this sense of *dod* appears only when Isaiah refers to Yahweh as his *loved one* (Isa 5:1). The concept of romantic relationship occurs in the abstract plural use of *dod* to indicate sexual *love* (Song 5:1) or *lovemaking* (Prov 7:18). *Dod* also denotes the important *uncle* on the father's side (Lev 10:4). If a father died, the paternal *uncle* or his son became the widow's guardian and took the place of the deceased (Esth 2:7,15). The *uncle* held redemption rights for kinsmen (Lev 25:49). A cousin was called "son of a *dod*" (Jer 32:9). *Dod* may connote *relative* (Amos 6:10). Feminine *dodah* specifies an *aunt* married to a father's brother (Lev 18:14).

yapheh

Hebrew pronunciation: [yah FEH]

CSB translation: beautiful

Uses in Song of Songs: 13
Uses in the OT: 42

Focus passage: Song of Songs 4:1,7

The adjective ***yapheh*** generally describes someone physically *beautiful* (Gen 12:11). It is part of a word family applying regularly to feminine beauty but also to men and other things. Frequently the words "form" (*to'ar*) or "appearance" (*mar'eh*) modify *yapheh*. These phrases indicate *shapely* and *beautiful* women (Gen 29:17) or *well-built* and *handsome* men (Gen 39:6). The second phrase covers *healthy-looking* cows (Gen 41:2). *Yapheh* alone depicts *beautiful* eyes (1 Sam 16:12), voice (Ezek 33:32), or tree branches (Ezek 31:3). Describing a city's elevation, *yapheh* implies *splendidly* (Ps 48:2). Twice it connotes *appropriate* (Eccl 3:11; 5:18). The noun *yopi* (19x) is usually *beauty* (Ps 45:11) but characterizes wisdom as *magnificent* (Ezek 28:7). The verb *yapah* (8x) means *be beautiful* (Ezek 16:13) or *handsome* (Ps 45:2). Love *is delightful* (Song 4:10). The reflexive denotes *beautify oneself* (Jer 4:30), the intensive *decorate* (Jer 10:4). The reduplicated adjective *yephehpiyyah* signifies *very beautiful* (Jer 46:20).

Interpreting Song of Songs

No other book of the Bible (except perhaps Revelation) suffers under so many radically different interpretations as the Song of Songs. The major approaches are as follows:

ALLEGORICAL INTERPRETATION

From early times both Christians and Jews have allegorized the Song of Songs. Jews have taken it to picture the love between the Lord and Israel, and Christians have regarded it as a song of the love between Christ and the church. (Traditional Roman Catholic interpreters have often identified the woman with the virgin Mary.) The allegorical approach was standard from the medieval period through the Reformation, but it has few adherents now.

Common allegorical identifications include that the man is Christ and the woman is the church, his kisses (1:2) are the Word of God, the woman's dark skin (1:5) is sin, her breasts (7:7) are the church's nurturing doctrine, her two lips (4:11) are law and gospel, and the "army with banners" (6:4) represents the church as the enemy of Satan. Advocates of this approach claim that the New Testament supports their case, since Ephesians 5:22–33 and other texts describe the church as Christ's bride.

But the New Testament never gives the Song an allegorical interpretation. New Testament passages that speak of the bride of Christ do not refer to Song of Songs. The material of Song of Songs is grossly inappropriate for worship. It is impossible to imagine a Christian praising Christ in terms of 1:2,16 or 5:10–16. It is equally bizarre to think of Jesus Christ describing his church in terms of 7:1–9. This ancient interpretation has rightly been abandoned.

DRAMATIC INTERPRETATION

For the past 200 years, many interpreters have argued that the Song is a dramatic story. Some say it is a two-character drama in which Solomon and the woman are the main actors. Others take it as a three-character drama in which Solomon, the woman, and a shepherd are the main actors. Neither approach is convincing. A romantic drama of this kind was altogether unknown in the ancient Near East. Also both interpretations are at many points forced and unnatural.

WEDDING SONG INTERPRETATION

Some have argued that Song of Songs is a wedding song. Some scholars have studied Near Eastern wedding ceremonies and have pointed out similarities between those rituals and the lyrics of the Song. Even so, it is difficult to read the Song of Songs as an order of service for a wedding. But even though the Song is not the text of a wedding ceremony, it indicates that the couple was getting married.

LOVE SONG INTERPRETATION

The preferred interpretation is the most simple and obvious. Song of Songs is a love song in three parts—a man, a woman, and a chorus of women. It has no secret allegories or identifications. It tells no story and has no plot. It is a lyrical expression of romantic love between a couple who are in the process of marrying. Its language and imagery, which go from royal pomp and majesty to the rustic, pastoral setting of the meadow, are meant to convey all the grandeur and glory as well as the simplicity and natural beauty of love.

KEY QUOTE

The one-flesh union of man and woman remains good, and part of God's order for our created existence. But the ultimate peace/wholeness (shalom) is not to be found there, nor is the final return to Eden. Sex is good, but not the greatest good, and that is why it can be forgone, if need be, for the sake of the kingdom. The true and final triumph over death and the grave, the complete release from the curse of the fall, is found in the cross of Christ, and in the new relationship between God and his people that it brings about. The relationship is depicted in gospel terms as a relationship between a bridegroom and his bride, and the final joy as a marriage. . . . From a New Testament perspective, the love depicted in the Song is not only a taste of what was given in creation, but a sign of what will be consummated in the new creation—a sign of the gospel [see Eph 5:31–32]. . . . True love—love as strong as death—is not simply a matter of the mind or of the will, but of the affections as well. And that is true whether we speak of the love between a man and a woman, or that between Yahweh and Israel, or that between Christ and the church.

BARRY G. WEBB[10]

Isaiah

Genre | **PROPHECY (PRE-EXILE), POETRY, PROSE**

The book of Isaiah is a collection of oracles declaring the people's sin against God and their need for repentance in light of both impending judgment and future restoration.

INTRODUCTION

AUTHOR Isaiah's authorship of the whole book has been vehemently contested in the modern period. Many scholars have argued that the historical Isaiah could not have written chapters 40–66. For those who believe that God knows the future and can reveal it to his servants, it is not problematic that God through Isaiah predicted the rise of Babylon, its victory against Judah, the exile, and the return.

BACKGROUND The book presents itself as the writing of one man, Isaiah son of Amoz. The superscription to the book dates his prophetic activity as spanning the reigns of four kings of Judah: Uzziah, Jotham, Ahaz, and Hezekiah. Uzziah's reign was a particularly prosperous time in the history of Judah, but storm clouds were on the horizon. Assyria was on the rise again in the person of Tiglath-pileser III (745–727 BC). Isaiah 37:38 suggests that the prophet lived until the death of Sennacherib in 681 BC.

MESSAGE AND PURPOSE Isaiah's message is relatively simple. First, Isaiah accused God's people of sin: rebelling against the one who made them and redeemed them. Second, Isaiah instructed these sinners to reform their ways and act obediently. Third, Isaiah announced God's judgment on the people because of their sin. Finally, God revealed his future restoration of the people, or at least of the faithful remnant who survived the judgment. As part of the restoration of God's people, Isaiah foresaw both judgment on the nations (chaps. 13–23) and a future turning of the nations to God (2:1–4). The first part of the book (chaps. 1–39) emphasizes sin, the call to repentance, and judgment; the second part (chaps. 40–66) emphasizes the hope of restoration.

SUMMARY Isaiah was an eighth-century BC prophet. His book is the first of the Prophets in the English canon and the first of the Latter Prophets in the Hebrew canon. Isaiah is powerful in its poetic imagination, intriguing in its prophetic vision, and complex in its structure. One can never read or study the book without gaining new insights into the nature of God and our relationship with him. The authors of the New Testament read the book of Isaiah in light of the coming of Christ and realized that this prophet anticipated the Messiah's coming with remarkable clarity. For this reason they quoted or alluded to Isaiah more than any other Old Testament book.

STRUCTURE The book of Isaiah is a combination of both prose and poetry. The prose is found primarily in chapters 36–39, a section that forms a bridge between the two sections of the book (see "Message and Purpose"). Isaiah's poetry is rich and varied. He wrote hymns, wisdom poetry, and even poetry that resembles a love song (5:1–7). The richness is seen in Isaiah's vocabulary. He used over 2,200 different Hebrew words, far more variety than is found in any other Old Testament book.

Outline

I. **Rebuke and Promise from the Lord (1:1–6:13)**
   A. Rebellion met with judgment and grace (1:1–31)
   B. Chastisement will bring future glory (2:1–4:6)
   C. Judgment and exile for the nation (5:1–30)
   D. Isaiah cleansed and commissioned (6:1–13)

II. **The Promise of Immanuel (7:1–12:6)**
   A. Immanuel rejected by worldly wisdom (7:1–25)
   B. God's deliverance and the coming Deliverer (8:1–9:7)
   C. Exile is coming for proud Samaria (9:8–10:4)
   D. Promise of a future glorious empire (10:5–12:6)

III. **Coming Judgment upon the Nations (13:1–23:18)**
   A. Babylon (13:1–14:23)
   B. Assyria (14:24–27)
   C. Philistia (14:28–32)
   D. Moab (15:1–16:14)
   E. Damascus and Aram (17:1–3)
   F. Israel (17:4–14)
   G. Cush (18:1–7)
   H. Egypt (19:1–20:6)
   I. Babylon, additional judgment (21:1–10)
   J. Dumah (21:11–12)
   K. Arabia (21:13–17)
   L. Jerusalem (22:1–25)
   M. Tyre (23:1–18)

IV. **First Cycle of General Judgment and Promise (24:1–27:13)**
   A. Universal judgment for universal sin (24:1–23)
   B. Praise to the Lord as Deliverer (25:1–12)
   C. A song of comfort for Judah (26:1–21)
   D. Promise of preservation for God's people (27:1–13)

V. **Woes upon the Unbelievers of Israel (28:1–33:24)**
   A. God's dealings with drunkards and scoffers (28:1–29)
   B. Judgment for those who try to deceive God (29:1–24)
   C. Confidence in man vs. confidence in God (30:1–33)
   D. Deliverance through God's intervention (31:1–32:20)
   E. Punishment of deceivers and triumph of Christ (33:1–24)

VI. **Second Cycle of General Judgment and Promise (34:1–39:8)**
   A. Destruction of the Gentile world powers (34:1–17)
   B. The ultimate bliss of God's redeemed (35:1–10)
   C. Deliverance for King Hezekiah (36:1–39:8)

VII. **Comfort for God's People (40:1–66:24)**
   A. The purpose of peace (40:1–48:22)
   B. The Prince of Peace (49:1–57:21)
   C. The program of peace (58:1–66:24)

WORD STUDY

shaphel

Hebrew pronunciation: [shah FAIL]

CSB translation: be low, humbled

Uses in Isaiah: 15
Uses in the OT: 30

Focus passage: Isaiah 2:9,11,17

Isaiah has half the uses of ***shaphel***, which means *be lowly* (Prov 16:19) or *sink* (Isa 32:19). People *are humbled* (Isa 2:9) or *brought down* (Isa 29:4). Trees *are felled* (Isa 10:33) and mountains *leveled* (Isa 40:4). Causative verbs mean *humiliate* (Job 40:11), *humble* (Prov 29:23), *demote* (Prov 25:7), *bring down* or *low* (Isa 25:11–12), *stoop down* (Ps 113:6), and *send down* (Isa 57:9). *Shephelah* (20x) is the name for the *Judean foothills* (Josh 9:1). The adjective *shaphal* (17x) denotes *low* (Ezek 17:6), *lowly* (Isa 57:15), *humble* (Ezek 17:14), or *humiliated* (Mal 2:9). Once it is *lowliest* (Ezek 29:15). The phrase "*lower* than" is translated *beneath* (Lev 13:20). The noun *shephel* means *humiliation* (Ps 136:23) or *lowly position* (Eccl 10:6). *Shiphlah,* meaning *depths,* occurs with the verb *shaphel* (Isa 32:19). "*Lowness* (*shiphlut*) of hands" suggests *negligent* hands hanging down (Eccl 10:18). The adjective *shaphel* implies *humbled* (Isa 2:12).

WORD STUDY *(continued)*

kaved

Hebrew pronunciation: [kah VAID]

CSB translation: be heavy, honor

Uses in Isaiah: 20
Uses in the OT: 114

Focus passage: Isaiah 25:3

Kaved, related to *kavod* (*glory*) and adjectival *kaved* (*heavy*), means *be heavy* (Neh 5:18), *weigh, weigh down,* or *be heavily loaded.* One *receives honor* (Job 14:21). Fighting *is fierce* or *intensifies.* Sin *is serious.* Ears *are deaf,* and eyesight *is poor.* The "hand *being heavy* on" (Ps 32:4) implies *getting the upper hand* or *severely oppressing.* Passive-reflexive verbs denote *be honored* or *glorified.* Something *is a burden.* Springs *are filled.* God *reveals* or *displays glory*; people *honor themselves* and *receive* or *enjoy glory.* Participles indicate *dignitaries* and signify *honored, important, high in rank, glorious,* or *highly respected.* The intensive verb means *honor* (Exod 20:12), *glorify, show respect for,* or *reward.* It is also *harden.* The causative verb involves *loading, heavily burdening, weighing down,* or *making heavy.* One *deafens* or *closes* ears and *hardens* hearts. God *brings honor,* and people *get glory.* The reflexive-passive verb signifies *act important* or *multiply oneself.*

yatsar

Hebrew pronunciation: [yah TSAR]

CSB translation: form

Uses in Isaiah: 27
Uses in the OT: 63

Focus passage: Isaiah 43:1,7,10,21

This common Semitic verb means *form* (Gen 2:7), especially regarding pottery. The participle denotes *potter* (Isa 29:16) or *craftsman* (Hab 2:18); *pottery* is sometimes literally "article of a *potter*" (Ps 2:9). ***Yatsar*** signifies *make* (Isa 44:9), *plan* (Isa 46:11), or *form* (Ps 33:15). Men *make* evil laws (Ps 94:20). The participle describes God as *Creator* or *Maker* (Isa 27:11; 45:9). So comparing God to a *potter* is natural (Jer 18:2–6). God *forms* mountains (Amos 4:13), locust swarms (Amos 7:1), and man's spirit (Zech 12:1). *Yatsar* occurs alongside *bara'* ("create," 5x) (Isa 45:18) and *'asah* ("make," 21x) (Jer 33:2). Twice *yatsar* accompanies related *yetser* (9x), where the noun means *shape* (Hab 2:18) or *what is formed* (Isa 29:16). *Yetser* also indicates *intention* (1 Chr 28:9), *inclination* (Gen 6:5; 8:21), *mind* (Isa 26:3), *desire* (1 Chr 29:18), and *what* someone *is made of* (Ps 103:14).

bara'

Hebrew pronunciation: [bah RAH]

CSB translation: create

Uses in Isaiah: 21
Uses in the OT: 48

Focus passage: Isaiah 45:7–8,12,18

Bara', occurring in the active and passive, is theological in that it has no clear subject other than God. *Bara'* always connotes *create,* though occasionally it is better translated *be done* (Exod 34:10) or *bring about* (Num 16:30). It suggests *creating* something new (Jer 31:22). The participle refers to God as *Creator* (Isa 40:28). He *created* not only the whole universe (Gen 1:1) but such particulars as sea creatures (Gen 1:21), heavenly bodies (Isa 40:26), and wind (Amos 4:13). *Bara'* most frequently describes the creation of human beings (Isa 45:12), both peoples and individuals (Ezek 21:30; 28:15). *Bara'* applies to providential acts such as new generations (Ps 102:18). God *creates* disaster as well as words of praise (Isa 45:7; 57:19). Spiritually, he *creates* clean hearts (Ps 51:10) and will create Jerusalem to be a joy (Isa 65:18). The related noun *beriy'ah,* translated *something unprecedented,* indicates circumstances that God would create (Num 16:30).

Isaiah Timeline

750–725 BC

740
Death of King Uzziah of Judah

740
Isaiah's call to be a prophet

734–732
Tiglath-pileser III's invasions of Israel

734
Pekah of Israel and Rezin of Damascus form a mutual defense alliance against Assyria and invite Ahaz of Judah to join them.

734
Ahaz refuses Isaiah's counsel and seeks protection from Assyria by paying tribute to them, creating a heavy financial burden on Judah for years to come.

732–722
Alliance between Aram and Israel collapses with the fall of Damascus and the fall of Samaria.

725–700 BC

715–701
Hezekiah of Judah initiates reforms and shows resistance to Assyria.

715–701
Hezekiah prepares for war against Assyria, strengthens Jerusalem's defenses, and receives Merodach-baladan's envoys from Babylon.

701
Sennacherib of Assyria defeats the Phoenicians, Philistines, and Egyptians; destroys most cities in Judah; and besieges Jerusalem.

701
God delivers Jerusalem from the Assyrian forces.

700–600 BC

687
Manasseh succeeds his father, Hezekiah, as king of Judah.

668–631
Ashurbanipal rules over a declining Assyrian Empire that experiences revolts in 642, contributed to the assassination of Amon of Judah (641) and the rise of his son Josiah (641–609).

609
Josiah killed by the Egyptians at Megiddo

605
Babylonians defeat Pharaoh Neco of Egypt at Carchemish.

600–500 BC

605, 597, 586
Babylonians attack Jerusalem and take citizens of Judah into exile.

539
Cyrus captures Babylon without resistance.

538
Cyrus issues a decree allowing the Jews to return to Judah.

537–536
Work begins on rebuilding the temple in Jerusalem.

520–518
Renewed work on the temple

515
New temple dedicated

The Kings Isaiah Served

UZZIAH

Also known as Azariah, he was the son and successor of King Amaziah of Judah. "All the people of Judah" declared Uzziah as king when he was 16 years old (2 Kgs 14:21; 2 Chr 26:1). Uzziah is remembered not so much as the leader who brought Judah to a golden age rivaling David's and Solomon's empires but as the "leper king." The brief account of Uzziah's reign in 2 Kings 15:1–7 portrays the king as one who "did what was right in the LORD's sight" (v. 3). No explanation for the king's affliction is given in 2 Kings other than "the LORD afflicted the king, and he had a serious skin disease until the day of his death" (v. 5).

AHAZ

The Bible characterizes Ahaz as an evil man who participated in the most monstrous of idolatrous practices (2 Kgs 16:3, 11). His 16-year reign was contemporary with the prophets Isaiah and Micah. Isaiah gave counsel to Ahaz during the Syro-Ephraimitic crisis, when Rezin, king of Aram, and Pekah, king of Israel, joined forces to attack Jerusalem.

JOTHAM

The 16-year period given for his reign may include the time he acted as regent for his father when Uzziah contracted leprosy and could not perform the functions required of royalty. Jotham evidently was an effective ruler. His reign was marked by building projects, material prosperity, and military successes.

HEZEKIAH

The son and successor of Ahaz as king of Judah, Hezekiah began his reign when he was 25 years old. At this time in history, the nation of Assyria had risen to power. Hezekiah began his reign by bringing religious reform to Judah. Hezekiah was not willing to court the favor of the Assyrian kings. The temple in Jerusalem was reopened, and the idols were removed. The critical time for Hezekiah came in 705 BC when Sennacherib became king of Assyria. Hezekiah's faith and physical recovery from illness (Isa 38:1–21) brought him recognition from the surrounding nations (2 Chr 32:33). His dependence upon prayer to God protected his nation from Sennacherib's army. Hezekiah died in 687/86 BC, and his son Manasseh succeeded him. They are listed in Jesus's genealogy (Matt 1:9–10).

Isaiah's Messianic Prophecies

OLD TESTAMENT REFERENCE	NEW TESTAMENT AFFIRMATION
Isaiah 2:2–4	Luke 24:47
Isaiah 6:9–10	Matthew 13:14–15
Isaiah 7:14	Matthew 1:22–23
Isaiah 8:14–15	Romans 9:33
Isaiah 9:1–2	Luke 2:32
Isaiah 9:6–7	Matthew 1:21,23
Isaiah 11:1–10	Romans 15:12
Isaiah 16:4–5	Luke 1:31–33
Isaiah 22:21–25	Revelation 3:7
Isaiah 25:6–12	1 Corinthians 15:54
Isaiah 28:16	1 Peter 2:6
Isaiah 29:18–19	Matthew 5:3
Isaiah 32:1–4	Revelation 19:16; 20:6
Isaiah 33:22	1 Timothy 1:17; 6:15
Isaiah 35:4–10	Matthew 11:5; 12:22
Isaiah 40:3–5	Matthew 3:3; Mark 1:3
Isaiah 40:10–11	Hebrews 13:20
Isaiah 42:1–16	Luke 2:32

OLD TESTAMENT REFERENCE	NEW TESTAMENT AFFIRMATION
Isaiah 49:6–12	2 Corinthians 6:2
Isaiah 50:6	Luke 22:63–65
Isaiah 52:13–53:12	Matthew 8:7; 27:1–2, 12–14,38
Isaiah 53:4–5	Acts 10:43; 13:38–39
Isaiah 53:7	John 1:29; 11:49–52
Isaiah 53:9	Mark 15:3–4,27–28
Isaiah 53:12	John 12:37–38
Isaiah 55:4–5	Romans 9:25–26
Isaiah 59:16–20	Romans 11:26–27
Isaiah 60:1–3	Luke 2:32
Isaiah 61:1–3	Luke 4:17–19
Isaiah 62:1–2	Revelation 3:12
Isaiah 62:11	Matthew 21:5
Isaiah 63:1–3	Revelation 19:13
Isaiah 63:8–9	Matthew 25:34–40
Isaiah 65:9	Hebrews 7:14
Isaiah 65:17–25	Revelation 21:1

Isaiah 53 in the New Testament

ISAIAH 52:13–53:12

- "He said to him, 'Am I to come and heal him?'" *Matthew 8:7*
- "When daybreak came, all the chief priests and the elders of the people plotted against Jesus to put him to death. After tying him up, they led him away and handed him over to Pilate, the governor." *Matthew 27:1–2*
- "While he was being accused by the chief priests and elders, he didn't answer. Then Pilate said to him, 'Don't you hear how much they are testifying against you?' But he didn't answer him on even one charge, so that the governor was quite amazed." *Matthew 27:12–14*
- "Then two criminals were crucified with him, one on the right and one on the left." *Matthew 27:38*

ISAIAH 53:4–5

- "All the prophets testify about him that through his name everyone who believes in him receives forgiveness of sins." *Acts 10:43*
- "Everyone who believes is justified through him from everything that you could not be justified from through the law of Moses." *Acts 13:39*
- "For I passed on to you as most important what I also received: that Christ died for our sins according to the Scriptures." *1 Corinthians 15:3*
- "In him we have redemption through his blood, the forgiveness of our trespasses, according to the riches of his grace." *Ephesians 1:7*
- "He did not commit sin, and no deceit was found in his mouth; when he was insulted, he did not insult in return; when he suffered, he did not threaten but entrusted himself to the one who judges justly." *1 Peter 2:22–23*
- "If we walk in the light as he himself is in the light, we have fellowship with one another, and the blood of Jesus his Son cleanses us from all sin. . . . If we confess our sins, he is faithful and righteous to forgive us our sins and to cleanse us from all unrighteousness." *1 John 1:7,9*

ISAIAH 53:7

- "The next day John saw Jesus coming toward him and said, 'Here is the Lamb of God, who takes away the sin of the world!'" *John 1:29*
- "Jesus was going to die for the nation, and not for the nation only, but also to unite the scattered children of God." *John 11:51b–52*

ISAIAH 53:9

- "Pilate questioned him again, 'Aren't you going to answer? Look how many things they are accusing you of!'" *Mark 15:4*
- "They crucified two criminals with him, one on his right and one on his left." *Mark 15:27–28*
- "Wanting to release Jesus, Pilate addressed them again, but they kept shouting, 'Crucify! Crucify him!' A third time he said to them, 'Why? What has this man done wrong? I have found in him no grounds for the death penalty. Therefore, I will have him whipped and then release him.' But they kept up the pressure, demanding with loud voices that he be crucified, and their voices won out. So Pilate decided to grant their demand and released the one they were asking for, who had been thrown into prison for rebellion and murder. But he handed Jesus over to their will." *Luke 23:20–25*
- "Two others—criminals—were also led away to be executed with him. When they arrived at the place called The Skull, they crucified him there, along with the criminals, one on the right and one on the left." *Luke 23:32–33*

ISAIAH 53:12

- "This was to fulfill the word of Isaiah the prophet, who said: Lord, who has believed our message? And to whom has the arm of the Lord been revealed?" *John 12:38*
- "In his humiliation justice was denied him. Who will describe his generation? For his life is taken from the earth." *Acts 8:33*

Names of God in Isaiah

- IMMANUEL (7:14)
- WONDERFUL COUNSELOR (9:6)
- MIGHTY GOD (9:6)
- PRINCE OF PEACE (9:6)
- ETERNAL FATHER (9:6)
- LIGHT (10:17)
- SONG (12:2)
- HOLY ONE OF ISRAEL (12:6)
- MOST HIGH (14:14)
- MAKER (17:7)
- RIGHTEOUS ONE (24:16)
- LORD GOD (25:8)
- CROWN OF BEAUTY (28:5)
- DIADEM OF SPLENDOR (28:5)
- CORNERSTONE (28:16)
- ROCK (30:29)
- JUDGE (33:22)
- LAWGIVER (33:22)
- LIVING GOD (37:17)
- LORD OF ARMIES (23:9)
- GLORY OF THE LORD (40:5)
- CREATOR (40:28)
- EVERLASTING GOD (40:28)
- CHOSEN ONE (42:1)
- SERVANT (42:1)
- SAVIOR (43:3)
- REDEEMER (43:14)
- KING (44:6)
- ARM OF THE LORD (53:1)
- MAN OF SUFFERING (53:3)
- GOD OF THE WHOLE EARTH (54:5)
- HUSBAND (54:5)
- COMPASSIONATE (54:10)
- COMMANDER (55:4)
- LEADER (55:4)
- WITNESS (55:4)
- HIGH AND EXALTED ONE (57:15)
- MIGHTY ONE (60:16)
- GROOM (62:5)
- HOLY SPIRIT (63:10)
- POTTER (64:8)
- GOD OF TRUTH (65:16)

Primary Idols in the Old Testament

NAME OF DEITY	MAJOR REFERENCES	DESCRIPTIONS
Asherah (plural, Asherahs)	2 Kings 23; Isaiah 17:8; 27:9	Canaanite goddess, mother of Baal
Ashtoreth (plural, Ashtoreths)	1 Kings 11:5,33; 2 Kings 23:13	Canaanite goddess of fertility, love, and war, daughter of El and Asherah
Bel, Marduk	Isaiah 46:1; Jeremiah 50:2; 51:44	Babylonian god, originally known as city patron of Nippur, later identified as high god of Babylon
Baal	Judges 3:7; 1 Kings 16; 18	Storm-god, also associated with fertility and vegetation
Chemosh	Judges 11:24; 1 Kings 11	Moabite war god
Dagon	1 Samuel 5:1–7	Philistine god of agriculture whose name means "little fish," also Baal's father
Molech	1 Kings 11:7; Jeremiah 32:35 (cp. Lev 18:21; 20:5)	Ammonite god, to whom human sacrifices were offered
Nebo	Isaiah 46:1	Babylonian god of speech, writing, and water

Jeremiah

Genre | **PROPHECY (PRE-EXILE), POETRY, PROSE**

With the Babylonian exile looming, the book of Jeremiah is a set of oracles presented to announce the coming destruction of Jerusalem, certain judgment against the nations, and assurances to people going into exile.

INTRODUCTION

AUTHOR Jeremiah was a priest from the town of Anathoth (1:1). At the Lord's command, he neither married nor had children because of the impending judgment that would come upon the next generation. His ministry as a prophet began in 626 BC and ended after 586 BC. He was a contemporary of Habakkuk and possibly Obadiah.

BACKGROUND The book of Jeremiah discusses the last days of Judah. King Hezekiah reigned for 29 years (715–686 BC) and began to reverse Judah's spiritual bankruptcy. But when Hezekiah's son Manasseh came to the throne, idolatrous and superstitious cultic practices and rites came back like a flood. Josiah's reign followed Amon's two-year rule, and during Josiah's reign, a copy of the law of Moses was found. On the basis of hearing this word, the young king and all his people renewed the covenant with the Lord. However, this reformation failed to overcome the effects of the wickedness Manasseh and Amon had instituted.

MESSAGE AND PURPOSE Jeremiah is the prophet of the "word of the LORD" (1:2). Of the 429 times the OT uses the phrase "This is what the LORD says," Jeremiah accounts for 155 of them. Further, the best known passage in Jeremiah is the new covenant text in 31:31–34. Not only is it the largest Old Testament text quoted in the New Testament (Heb 8:8–12; 10:16–17), but arguably better than any other passage, it links God's ancient promises to Eve (Gen 3:15), Abraham (Gen 12:1–3), and David (2 Sam 7:16–19) with New Testament assurances that God in Christ grants believers new hearts, salvation, and fellowship with him.

SUMMARY The book of Jeremiah holds at least two great distinctions among all the Old Testament Prophetic Books: (1) This is the longest Prophetic Book in the Bible (1,364 verses). (2) The prophet Jeremiah's life is more fully described than any of the other 15 writing prophets. Into the tumultuous times of the last half of the seventh century and the first quarter of the sixth century BC came this prophet bearing a word from God for the stubborn people of Judah. The book's contents span roughly from 640 to 580 BC.

STRUCTURE The significant dateline "the fourth year of Jehoiakim" was placed at 25:1; 36:1; and 45:1, thereby dividing the prophet's book into three main sections: the prophet's faithfulness in carrying out God's commission (chaps. 2–24), the fierce opposition to his ministry (chaps. 25–35), and the collapse of Judah (chaps. 36–45). The book of Jeremiah includes poetic sections (especially in chaps. 2–25) and prose accounts as well.

Outline

I. **Prologue: Jeremiah's Call and Vision (1:1–19)**

II. **Jeremiah Calls for Repentance (2:1–25:38)**
  A. Six early messages (2:1–20:18)
  B. Four indictments on Israel's leadership (21:1–24:10)
  C. Judgment against the nations (25:1–38)

III. **Jeremiah Stands Firm Despite Harassment (26:1–36:32)**
  A. The temple sermon repeated (26:1–24)
  B. The yoke of Babylon (27:1–22)
  C. The false prophet Hananiah (28:1–17)
  D. Letters to the exiles (29:1–32)
  E. The book of consolation/comfort (30:1–33:26)
  F. Judgment for Zedekiah (34:1–22)
  G. The obedience of the Rechabites (35:1–19)
  H. The writing and rewriting of the scroll (36:1–32)

IV. **Jeremiah Sees Destruction Ahead (37:1–45:5)**
  A. Jeremiah and King Zedekiah (37:1–21)
  B. Jeremiah rescued by Ebed-melech (38:1–28)
  C. Jeremiah's fate at the fall of Jerusalem (39:1–18)
  D. Post-fall Judah and Governor Gedaliah (40:1–41:18)
  E. Jeremiah asked about going to Egypt (42:1–22)
  F. Jeremiah's counsel and God's word rejected (43:1–44:30)
  G. Summary: God's word to the scribe Baruch (45:1–5)

V. **Prophecies against the Nations (46:1–51:64)**
  A. Egypt (46:1–28)
  B. The Philistines (47:1–7)
  C. Moab (48:1–47)
  D. The Ammonites (49:1–6)
  E. Edom (49:7–22)
  F. Damascus (49:23–27)
  G. Kedar and Hazor (49:28–33)
  H. Elam (49:34–39)
  I. Babylon (50:1–51:64)

VI. **Epilogue: The Fall of Jerusalem (52:1–34)**

WORD STUDY

saraph

Hebrew pronunciation: [sah RAFF]

CSB translation: burn, burn up

Uses in Jeremiah: 23
Uses in the OT: 117

Focus passage: Jeremiah 7:31

Saraph describes *firing* bricks (Gen 11:3) and *burning* cooking fuel (Isa 44:16) but usually implies negative events. One *burned up* sacrificial refuse (Lev 4:21), leftover meat (Exod 12:10), contaminated fabric (Lev 13:55), and idols (Deut 7:25). People *burned* down enemy cities (Josh 11:11). Idolaters *burned* children (Deut 12:31). *Saraph* suggests *set on fire* (Judg 9:52); it indicates people destroyed by fire (Num 16:39). *Saraph* concerned funereal *burning ceremonies* (Jer 34:5), for which a relative was responsible (Amos 6:10). *Misraphah* was this or any *burning* of people (Isa 33:12; Jer 34:5). *Serephah* (13x) also denotes this *fire* (2 Chr 21:19). It implies *burning* (Isa 9:5), *burning debris* (Num 16:37), or a *charred* mountain (Jer 51:25). With *saraph* it is *ignite* or *make a fire* (Lev 10:6; 2 Chr 16:14). The noun *saraph* (7x) is *poisonous snake* (Deut 8:15) or *seraphim*, angels who were fiery (Isa 6:6).

galah

Hebrew pronunciation: [gah LAH]

CSB translation: uncover, exile

Uses in Jeremiah: 27
Uses in the OT: 185

Focus passage: Jeremiah 18:7,18

Galah in several conjugations means *remove* (Isa 22:8). It denotes *depart* (1 Sam 4:21) and especially *go into exile* (Isa 5:13). *Galah* indicates *uncover,* and *uncovering ears* (Job 33:16) involves *instructing* (Job 36:15), *informing* (1 Sam 9:15), or *telling* (1 Sam 20:2). Active participles suggest *captives* (Amos 6:7). Passive participles convey *uncovered* (Num 24:4) or *distributed* (Esth 3:14). Causative verbs signify *drive out* (2 Kgs 17:11), *exile* (Amos 1:6), or *deport* (2 Kgs 15:29). Reflexive-passives include *uncover oneself* (Gen 9:21) and *show off* (Prov 18:2). Passive-reflexives mean *be exposed* (Exod 20:26) or *revealed* (1 Sam 3:7) and *reveal oneself* (Gen 35:7). Intensive verbs imply *expose* (Lev 20:18), *strip* (Isa 57:8), *strip off* (Job 41:13), *flaunt* (Ezek 23:18), or *betray* (Isa 16:3). One *opens* eyes (Num 22:31) or *presents* cases (Jer 11:20). "*Uncovering* nakedness" entails *sexual intercourse* (Lev 18:6) or *violate* another's *intimacy* (Lev 20:11). The intensive passive participle connotes *open* (Prov 27:5).

megillah

Hebrew pronunciation: [meh gil LAH]

CSB translation: scroll

Uses in Jeremiah: 14
Uses in the OT: 21

Focus passage: Jeremiah 36:2,4,6,14, 20–21

Megillah, from the verb *galal* (*roll*), refers to *scrolls,* which were unrolled from side to side (not top to bottom). Vertical lines might mark columns, with writing placed on horizontal lines. *Megillah* could be a late word, the earlier term being *seper* ("writing, book"); both refer to Scripture in Psalm 40:7. An Egyptian tomb held a papyrus scroll dating to about 3000 BC. Many Dead Sea Scrolls are leather; they are up to 12 inches high and 29 feet long, the Isaiah Scroll being 17 sheepskin sheets sewn together by linen. But some Dead Sea Scrolls are papyrus. The *scroll* Jehoiakim burned indoors during winter might have made the room uninhabitable had it been leather (Jer 36:23). Ezekiel ate a divine *scroll* to picture his mission of sharing God's word (Ezek 3:1–3). A visionary flying *scroll* 30 by 15 feet, written front and back, detailed God's laws (Zech 5:1–4).

gur

Hebrew pronunciation: [GUR]

CSB translation: live for a while, be a resident alien

Uses in Jeremiah: 14
Uses in the OT: 82

Focus passage: Jeremiah 44:8,12,14,28

Gur denotes *live for a while* (Jer 44:8). One *is a resident alien* (Gen 21:23), *living/staying* (Gen 21:34; 26:3) *as a foreigner/alien* (2 Sam 4:3). *Gur* occurs with *ger, alien,* as *reside* (Exod 12:48) or *live.* It connotes *stay* (Isa 16:4), *linger* (Judg 5:17), *reside* (Isa 23:7), or *dwell* (Ps 5:4; Isa 33:14). *Gur* suits Levites, who had no tribal territory (Deut 18:6), and someone *dwelling* in another's tent, even if forever (Ps 61:4). Participles mean *resident aliens* (Isa 5:17), *alien who resides* (Lev 25:6), *resident alien* (Ps 105:12), *guest* (Job 19:15), and *human habitation* (Job 28:4). The reflexive-passive means *whirl* (Jer 30:23). *Magor* (11x) suggests *home* (Ps 55:15), *pilgrimage* (Gen 47:9), *where one lives as an alien* or *foreign resident* (Ezek 20:38), and *where one lives, stays,* or *resides* (Job 18:19). *Earthly life* represents "house of *pilgrimage*" (Ps 119:54). *Megurah* (Hag 2:19) and *mammegurah* (Joel 1:17) denote *granary.*

KEY VERSE

Then the LORD reached out his hand, touched my mouth, and told me: I have now filled your mouth with my words. See, I have appointed you today over nations and kingdoms to uproot and tear down, to destroy and demolish, to build and plant.

JEREMIAH 1:9–10

Jeremiah's Life

An approximation of the timeline of Jeremiah's life

REIGN OF JOSIAH

- Jeremiah was called as a prophet near the beginning of Josiah's reforms (Jer 1:1–10)
- Denounced the people of Judah for their half-hearted return to the Lord (Jer 3:6–18)

My anguish, my anguish! I writhe in agony! . . . For you, my soul, have heard the sound of the ram's horn—the shout of battle (Jer 4:19).

REIGN OF JEHOIAKIM

- Jeremiah was threatened with death for preaching judgment for Judah's disobedience (Jer 26)
- Prophesied Judah's 70-year exile in Babylon (Jer 25:1–14)
- Dictated to Baruch a scroll of the word of the Lord to be read in the temple (Jer 36:1–8)
  - *The scroll was read before the king, who cut it up and threw it in the fire (Jer 36:9–26)*
- Dictated to Baruch the scroll of the word of the Lord a second time (Jer 36:27–32)

If my head were a flowing spring, my eyes a fountain of tears, I would weep day and night over the slain of my dear people (Jer 9:1).

REIGN OF ZEDEKIAH

- Jeremiah carried a yoke, calling for Judah to submit to the yoke of the king of Babylon or be destroyed (Jer 27)
  - *The yoke was broken by Hananiah as part of his false prophecy; he died two months later for his rebellion against the Lord (Jer 28)*
- Sent a letter to the exiles in Babylon instructing them to settle in because restoration would come after 70 years of exile (Jer 29)
- Beaten and put in stocks for prophesying judgment against Judah (Jer 20:1–6)
- Twice asked by the king to inquire of the Lord about Babylon; Jeremiah responded with the message of judgment (Jer 21; 37:1–10)
- Accused of defecting to Babylon, beaten, and imprisoned in a dungeon (Jer 37:11–16)
- Asked by the king to inquire of the Lord about Babylon; Jeremiah responded with the message of judgment; imprisoned again, this time in the guard's courtyard (Jer 37:17–21)
- Bought a field, symbolizing the future restoration of the land to Judah and Israel (Jer 32–33)
- Accused of weakening morale in the city and dropped in a cistern of mud to die, but rescued by Ebed-melech; returned to the guard's courtyard (Jer 38:1–13)
- Asked by the king to inquire of the Lord about Babylon; Jeremiah responded with the message of judgment; returned to the guard's courtyard (Jer 38:14–28)

My eyes flow with streams of tears because of the destruction of my dear people (Lam 3:48).

JERUSALEM FALLS TO BABYLON

- Jeremiah was freed by Nebuchadnezzar and remained in Judah (Jer 39:1–14)
- Asked by the remnant of Judah to inquire of the Lord for their direction; Jeremiah responded: stay in Judah, do not go to Egypt; his advice was rejected, so taken to Egypt (Jer 42–43)
- Prophesied judgment on the remnant in Egypt for their disobedience and idolatry (Jer 44)

Let my eyes overflow with tears; day and night may they not stop, for my dearest people have been destroyed by a crushing blow, an extremely severe wound (Jer 14:17).

THE WEEPING PROPHET:
Jeremiah prophesied a difficult message of judgment for Judah and Jerusalem. He experienced anguish for his people and was persecuted by them. His ministry bore little fruit, but he was faithful to the Lord.

KEY VERSE

"Look, the days are coming"—this is the LORD's declaration—"when I will raise up a Righteous Branch for David. He will reign wisely as king and administer justice and righteousness in the land. In his days Judah will be saved, and Israel will dwell securely. This is the name he will be called: The LORD Is Our Righteousness."

JEREMIAH 23:5–6

Allusions to Jeremiah in Revelation

JEREMIAH		REVELATION
51:7	Drinking the cup of God's wrath	18:3
51:9	Babylon's sins piled up to heaven	18:5
51:33	Judgment as a harvest	14:14–15
51:25–26	Babylon as a volcano	18:8–9
51:36	Sea will become dry	21:1
51:48	Heaven and earth rejoice	18:20
51:59–64	Scroll thrown into Euphrates River	18:21

KEY VERSE

"Look, the days are coming"—this is the LORD's declaration—"when I will make a new covenant with the house of Israel and with the house of Judah. This one will not be like the covenant I made with their ancestors on the day I took them by the hand to lead them out of the land of Egypt—my covenant that they broke even though I am their master"—the LORD's declaration. "Instead, this is the covenant I will make with the house of Israel after those days"—the LORD's declaration. "I will put my teaching within them and write it on their hearts. I will be their God, and they will be my people. No longer will one teach his neighbor or his brother, saying, 'Know the LORD,' for they will all know me, from the least to the greatest of them"—this is the LORD's declaration. "For I will forgive their iniquity and never again remember their sin."

JEREMIAH 31:31–34

The New Covenant

COVENANTS OF SCRIPTURE	RECIPIENTS	COMMANDS	PROMISES/ CONDITIONS	COVENANT SIGN
Creation Covenant *(Gen 1–3)*	Adam and Eve	Be fruitful, multiply, fill the earth, and subdue it; do not eat from the tree of the knowledge of good and evil	Eternal life for obedience; death for disobedience (including spiritual alienation, exile from the garden)	—
Noahic Covenant *(Gen 6–9)*	Noah and all his descendants and every living creature	Be fruitful, multiply, fill the earth, and rule it; do not eat meat with its lifeblood in it; do not murder	Never again shall all life be destroyed by a flood; "permanent covenant" *(Gen 9:16)*	Rainbow
Abrahamic Covenant *(Gen 12; 15; 17)*	Abraham, Isaac, and Jacob and their descendants	Keep the covenant; circumcise every male	Land (Canaan); offspring (nations and kings); blessing (a great name and blessing to others); "permanent covenant" *(Gen 17:7)*	Circumcision
Mosaic (Old) Covenant *(Exod 19–24)*	The people of Israel	Keep the covenant; obey the law (Ten Commandments on tablets and other laws)	Blessing for obedience; curse for disobedience (agricultural plight, military defeat, exile from the land)	The Sabbath
Davidic Covenant *(2 Sam 7; Ps 89)*	David and his descendants	Keep the covenant; obey the law	A great name; stability for God's people; an eternal house, kingdom, and throne; "permanent covenant" *(2 Sam 23:5)*	—
New Covenant *(Jer 31:31–34; Ezek 36–37; Luke 22:14–20; Heb 8–10)*	Believers in the Messiah; Gentile believers are branches grafted onto the tree of Israel	Repentance and faith	A new heart indwelled by God's Holy Spirit and having God's teaching within, written on hearts instead of tablets; cleansing and forgiveness of sin; a Davidic king forever; "permanent covenant" *(Ezek 37:26)*	The cross (Lord's Supper)

Lamentations

Genre | **PROPHECY, POETRY**

Lamentations is a set of five poems reflecting on the destruction of Jerusalem and the burning of the temple in light of the people's covenant history with God.

INTRODUCTION

AUTHOR Jeremiah's name has long been associated with this book. A rich tradition links Jeremiah to Lamentations, making it seem safe to conclude he did indeed write this book.

BACKGROUND The sad background for these five poems of lament was the sacking of Jerusalem and the burning of the temple in 586 BC by the Babylonian army.

MESSAGE AND PURPOSE Lamentations does not offer a complete or understandable explanation for the suffering and pain found in the writing, but it was important that the pain and suffering be connected to the actual events of 586 BC. If these pent-up feelings of agony could not be attached to some datable event, the pain could threaten to take on cosmic proportions. This is why history is necessary. When sorrow becomes detached from history, suffering gets out of hand because perspective is lost, tempting a suffering person to lose touch with reality.

SUMMARY This is a book about pain but with hope in God. The author vividly addresses the extremes of human pain and suffering as few other authors have done in history. For this reason, Lamentations is an important biblical source expressing the hard questions that arise during our times of pain. The suffering the author discusses was brought on by the brutal overthrow of Jerusalem in 586 BC, one of the darkest times in Jewish history.

STRUCTURE The book of Lamentations exhibits a remarkably fine artistic structure. Each of its five chapters (five poems) is a structurally unified text. The fact that there is an uneven number of poems allows the middle poem (chap. 3) to be the midpoint of the book. Thus, there is an ascent (or crescendo) up to a fixed climax for the entire book, thereby making chapter 3 central in its form and the message it imparts. Lamentations also uses the form of the alphabetic acrostic with the 22-letter Hebrew alphabet.

Outline

I. **The City: An Outside View (1:1–22)**
   A. Description of Jerusalem's afflictions (1:1–7)
   B. Explanation of Jerusalem's afflictions (1:8–18)
   C. Effect of Jerusalem's afflictions (1:19–22)

II. **The Wrath of God: An Inside View (2:1–22)**
   A. Jerusalem's adversary (2:1–8)
   B. Jerusalem's agony (2:9–16)
   C. Jerusalem's entreaty (2:17–22)

III. **The Compassions of God: An Upward View (3:1–66)**
   A. The rod of God's wrath (3:1–20)
   B. The multitude of God's mercies (3:21–39)
   C. The justice of God's judgments (3:40–54)
   D. The prayer of God's people (3:55–66)

IV. **The Sins of All Classes: An Overall View (4:1–22)**
   A. The vanity of human glory (4:1–12)
   B. The vanity of human leadership (4:13–16)
   C. The vanity of human resources (4:17–20)
   D. The vanity of human pride (4:21–22)

V. **The Prayer: A Future View (5:1–22)**
   A. Jerusalem invokes God's grace (5:1–18)
   B. Jerusalem invokes God's glory (5:19–22)

WORD STUDY

tsar

Hebrew pronunciation:
[TSAR]

CSB translation:
adversary, foe, enemy

Uses in Lamentations: 9
Uses in the OT: 69

Focus passage:
Lamentations 2:4,17

This root in other languages denotes "enemy," "hostility," "opposition," and "damage." ***Tsar*** occurs most often in poetry and 18 times as a synonym for *'oyeb,* the most common word for "enemy" (Esth 7:6). *Tsar* signifies *foe* (Deut 32:27), *adversary* (Num 10:9), or *enemy* (Gen 14:20). It derives from and appears with the verb *tsarar* (26x), which means *attack* (Num 10:9), *harass* (Num 33:55), or *oppress* (Amos 5:12). *Tsarar* most often functions as a participle indicating *foe* (Exod 23:22), *adversary* (Ps 7:6), *enemy* (Ps 6:7), or *one who attacks* (Ps 143:12). The participle appears with the related verb *tsur* (4x), which implies *being a foe* (Exod 23:22) or *hostile* (Esth 8:11) and *showing hostility* (Deut 2:9). *Tsarah,* a feminine form of *tsar,* denotes a second wife who is a *rival* in a bigamous marriage (1 Sam 1:6).

haphak

Hebrew pronunciation:
[hah FAK]

CSB translation:
turn, change

Uses in Lamentations: 5
Uses in the OT: 95

Focus passage:
Lamentations 5:2,15

Haphak means *turn* into (Deut 23:5), *change* (Exod 10:19), *transform, pervert* (Jer 23:36), or *restore* (Zeph 3:9). People *return, turn back,* or *turn* around. *Haphak* denotes *demolish* (Gen 19:25), *overturn,* or *overwhelm.* It connotes *healing* (Ps 41:3) or *destruction* (Job 12:15). People *retrace* steps; they *get down* from chariots (2 Kgs 5:26). Passive-reflexive forms imply *becoming* (Isa 60:5) or *having a change* (Hos 11:8). Labor pains *come* (1 Sam 4:19). Hearts *are broken* (Lam 1:20). Faces *grow* pale. *The opposite happens* (Esth 9:1). Things *become warped, drained* (Ps 32:4), *turned over,* or *turned loose.* Speech is *deceitful* (Prov 17:20). Reflexive-passive verbs mean *whirl* (Gen 3:24) and *tumble. Tahpuchah* (10x) implies *perversity* (Prov 2:14), *contrariness, deception,* and *absurdity. Mahpechah* (5x) signifies *demolish* (Jer 50:40) or *fall. Hephek* (3x) denotes *the opposite* (Ezek 16:34) or *turning* things *around. Haphekah* is *demolish* (Gen 19:29). *Haphakpak* means *crooked* (Prov 21:8).

Ezekiel

Genre | **PROPHECY (EXILE)**

Ezekiel is a series of oracles and visions presented to exiles in Babylon describing judgment of sin and promising restoration.

INTRODUCTION

AUTHOR There is sufficient reason for maintaining that the prophet Ezekiel composed the book of Ezekiel in Babylon. The work demonstrates such homogeneity and literary coherence that it is reasonable to conclude that all editorial work was carried out by a single person, the prophet himself. The inclusion of historical dates at the beginning of many of the oracles and prophecies in Ezekiel is another important unifying factor.

BACKGROUND Ezekiel, son of Buzi, was among the approximately 10,000 citizens of Judah deported to Babylon when King Nebuchadnezzar invaded Jerusalem in 598/597 BC (2 Kgs 24:10–17). His prophetic call came to him five years later (the fifth year of King Jehoiachin's exile), in 593 BC. He received his call at the age of 30 (Ezek 1:1), the year he should have begun his duties as a priest (Num 4:3). The last dated oracle in the book occurs in the twenty-seventh year of King Jehoiachin (Ezek 29:17), thus indicating that Ezekiel's ministry lasted 22 or 23 years.

MESSAGE AND PURPOSE The message of the book revolves around a pivotal event in the history of Israel—the fall of Jerusalem in 586 BC. Before the announcement of Jerusalem's fall, Ezekiel's message was characterized by judgment. In his scathing review of Israelite history, Ezekiel exposed the nation's moral depravity and absence of spiritual concern (2:1–8; 8:7–18; 13:1–23; 17:1–21; 20:1–32). After the destruction of Jerusalem was complete and the nation was in exile, his message changed. He turned to a proclamation of hope, which is what the people then needed most.

SUMMARY The book of Ezekiel contains the divinely inspired prophecies of the prophet of the same name. These prophecies consist of oracles in the first person, giving the reader a sense of access to Ezekiel's private memoirs. Written primarily to the exiles in Babylon, the prophecies equally emphasize judgment of sins and the promise of hope and restoration.

STRUCTURE The prophet Ezekiel displayed a distinct style throughout his prophetic work. The phrase "son of man" occurs 93 times as a title for Ezekiel, focusing on the prophet's human nature. The introductory oracle phrase "the word of the LORD came to me" occurs 49 times in the book and alerts the reader to the beginning of a separate section. The phrase "I, the LORD, have spoken" also occurs frequently in Ezekiel (5:13,15,17; 17:21,24; 21:17,32; 22:14; 24:14; 26:14; 30:12; 34:24; 36:36; 37:14). Another feature for which Ezekiel is well known is his performance of symbolic, dramatic actions.

Outline

I. Israel, a Rebellious House, Will Fall (1:1–24:27)

A. Ezekiel sent as God's spokesman (1:1–3:27)
B. First series of symbolic actions (4:1–7:27)
C. Vision of Israel's doom (8:1–11:25)
D. Second series of symbolic actions (12:1–14:23)
E. Parables of doom (15:1–19:14)
F. Rebukes and threats (20:1–22:31)
G. Two final parables and last symbolic action (23:1–24:24)
H. News of the fall of the rebellious house (24:25–27)

II. Pagan Foreign Nations Will Be Destroyed (25:1–32:32)

A. Ammon (25:1–7)
B. Moab (25:8–11)
C. Edom (25:12–14)
D. Philistia (25:15–17)
E. Tyre (26:1–28:19)
F. Sidon (28:20–26)
G. Egypt (29:1–32:32)

III. Disciplined Israel Will Be Restored (33:1–48:35)

A. Basis of this message of hope (33:1–20)
B. News of Jerusalem's fall arrives (33:21–33)
C. The promises of restoration (34:1–39:29)
D. The vision of restoration (40:1–48:35)

WORD STUDY

'adam

Hebrew pronunciation: [ah DAHM]

CSB translation: man, mankind, person

Uses in Ezekiel: 132
Uses in the OT: 561

Focus passage: Ezekiel 12:2–3,9,18,22,27

'Adam, which never occurs in the plural, broadly signifies *man* (Gen 1:27), encompassing male and female as *mankind* (Gen 6:1), *humanity* (Isa 5:15), or *human being* (Ps 39:5). It is a collective indicating *individuals* (Job 34:29), *mankind* (Ps 22:6), or *people* (Jer 47:2); it can be translated as the noun *humans* (Exod 4:11). It specifies the *man* (Gen 4:1). It denotes *one, someone, anyone*, or *everyone* (Neh 2:10,12; Prov 17:18; Zech 11:6) and means *person* (Lev 6:3). "Son of *man*" is synonymous with other words for "man" (*'iysh*, Num 23:19; *'enosh*, Isa 51:12; *geber*, Job 16:21). "Sons of *man*" appears as *human race* (Deut 32:8), *men* (Ps 45:2), *people* (Ps 36:7), and *descendants of Adam* (Ps 90:3). *'Adam* often contrasts with animals (Num 31:26) or God (Isa 31:3). "Sons of *'adam*" opposes "sons of *'iysh*" as *low* versus *high* (Ps 49:2).

shabath

Hebrew pronunciation: [shah VATH]

CSB translation: rest, cease, stop

Uses in Ezekiel: 13
Uses in the OT: 71

Focus passage: Ezekiel 12:23

Shabath, related to *shabbath* (*Sabbath*), means *rest* or *cease* (Gen 2:2; 8:22). Land *has rest* (Lev 26:35). Things or people *quiet down, become quiet* (Isa 14:4), *go* (Prov 22:10), or *leave* (Lam 5:14–15) when ceasing activity. Accompanying other verbs, *shabath* suggests *quit* (Job 32:1). With *shabbath, shabath* yields *observe a Sabbath* (Lev 25:2). Passive-reflexive verbs denote *disappear* (Isa 17:3), *be obliterated* (Ezek 6:6), or *come to an end* (Ezek 30:18). Causative verbs describe *stopping, removing* (Exod 5:5; 12:15), *omitting* (Lev 2:13), *preventing, eliminating* (Ezek 34:10,25), or *ending* (Prov 18:18) things. Someone *rids* another of something (Isa 30:11). Causatives suggest *leave without* (Ruth 4:14) or *cause to be without*. One *silences* someone (Ps 8:2). God *blots out* memory (Deut 32:26). Killers *do away with* people (Amos 8:4). One *puts a stop/end to, makes cease,* or *causes to stop* (Josh 22:25). *Shebeth* involves ending disputes (Prov 20:3). *Mishbath* is *downfall* (Lam 1:7).

to'evah

Hebrew pronunciation: [toh ay VAH]

CSB translation: detestable thing, abomination, abhorrent

Uses in Ezekiel: 43
Uses in the OT: 118

Focus passage: Ezekiel 16:2,22,36,43,47, 50–51,58

To'evah means *detestable practices* (Ezra 9:1; Ezek 16:22), *things* (Deut 7:26; 12:31), or *acts* (Jer 7:10). *To'evah* describes what is culturally, ethically, or religiously *detestable* (Exod 8:26) and *repulsive* (Ps 88:8). The wicked and righteous are *detestable* to one another (Prov 29:27). God detests idolatry (Deut 27:15), related practices (Deut 18:10–12), prostitution (Deut 23:18), transvestism (Deut 22:5), homosexuality (Lev 18:22), child sacrifice (Deut 12:31), false prophecy (Jer 6:14–15), empty religious ritual (Isa 1:13), and other sins (Prov 6:16–19). *Ta'av* (22x), apparently from *to'evah,* means *abhor* (Deut 7:26), *despise* (Deut 23:7), or *loathe* (Ps 107:18). Passive-reflexive verbs denote *be detestable* (1 Chr 21:6), *worthless* (Isa 14:19), or *revolting* (Job 15:16). Causative verbs signify *commit a detestable act* (1 Kgs 21:26) or *what is vile* (Ps 14:1) and *commit detestably* (Ezek 16:52).

ra'ah

Hebrew pronunciation: [rah AH]

CSB translation: shepherd, feed, graze

Uses in Ezekiel: 32
Uses in the OT: 168

Focus passage: Ezekiel 34:2–3,5,7–10, 12–16

This root in many languages denotes *shepherd*. ***Ra'ah*** most often, as a participle, indicates a *shepherd* (Jer 51:23) or *herdsman* (Gen 13:7). The feminine is *shepherdess* (Gen 29:9). *Ra'ah* denotes *tending* (Gen 37:2) or *pasturing* (Gen 37:12) sheep or other animals (Gen 36:24). Animals *graze* (Gen 41:2) or *feed* (Song 4:5). *Ra'ah* suggests *sustain* (Hos 9:2), *chase* (Hos 12:1), *live* (Ps 37:3), or *take charge of* (Jer 22:22). It describes people *feeding* themselves (Ezek 34:10), *eating* (Jonah 3:7), and *being well fed* (Isa 14:30). Fire (Job 20:26), animals (Ps 80:13), and people (Isa 44:20) *feed on* things. *Ra'ah* metaphorically describes God (Gen 49:24) and political leaders (Ezek 34:2). *Ra'ah* connotes *ruler* (Jer 2:8). Death *shepherds* (Ps 49:14). Related noun *re'iy* means *range* (1 Kgs 4:23). *Mir'eh* (13x) is *pasture* (Lam 1:6) or lions' *feeding ground* (Nah 2:11). *Mar'iyt* (10x) is *pasture* (Isa 49:9) and once *flock* (Jer 10:21).

Ezekiel–Daniel Timeline

650–600 BC

649
Under Ashurbanipal, Assyrians capture and destroy Babylon.

623
Birth of Ezekiel

620
Birth of Daniel

612
Under Nabopolassar, Asshur and Nineveh fall, ending the Assyrian Empire.

605
The Babylonians hold the balance of power in the region after defeating Pharaoh Neco at Carchemish.

605
First siege of Jerusalem by the Babylonians and first wave of exiles, including Daniel, taken to Babylon

604–603
Daniel trains to serve Nebuchadnezzar.

602
Nebuchadnezzar's dream and Daniel's interpretation

599–586 BC

597
Babylonians' second siege of Jerusalem; King Jehoiachin and ten thousand citizens of Judah, including Ezekiel, exiled to Babylon

593
God calls Ezekiel, then 30 years old, to prophesy.

592
Ezekiel prophesies against pagan practices at the temple.

588
The Lord tells Ezekiel to inform the captives that the king of Babylon has again laid siege to Jerusalem.

587
Ezekiel prophesies Egypt's ruin and the destruction of Pharaoh and his army.

586
Ezekiel prophesies the downfall of Tyre.

586
Jerusalem falls to the third Babylonian siege and the temple is destroyed.

585–550 BC

585
Ezekiel's lament for Pharaoh

573
Ezekiel's vision of the new temple

571
The Lord shows Ezekiel that Egypt will be given over to the Babylonians.

569
Nebuchadnezzar invades Egypt in fulfillment of both Jeremiah's and Ezekiel's prophecies.

562
Evil-merodach, Nebuchadnezzar's son, succeeds him as king of Babylon.

561
Evil-merodach releases Jehoiachin from prison.

560
Nergal-sharezer becomes king of Babylon.

559
Cyrus the Great founds the Persian Empire.

549–500 BC

539
Daniel interprets the handwriting on the wall for Belshazzar.

539
Cyrus captures Babylon without resistance.

539
Gabriel visits Daniel with the message of 70 weeks.

538
Cyrus issues a decree allowing the Jews to return to Judah.

536
Work begins on rebuilding the temple in Jerusalem.

536
Daniel, now 84 years old, is thrown into the lions' den.

535
Daniel receives a vision of future events.

520–518
Renewed work on the temple

515
New temple dedicated

The Temple in Ezekiel 40–48

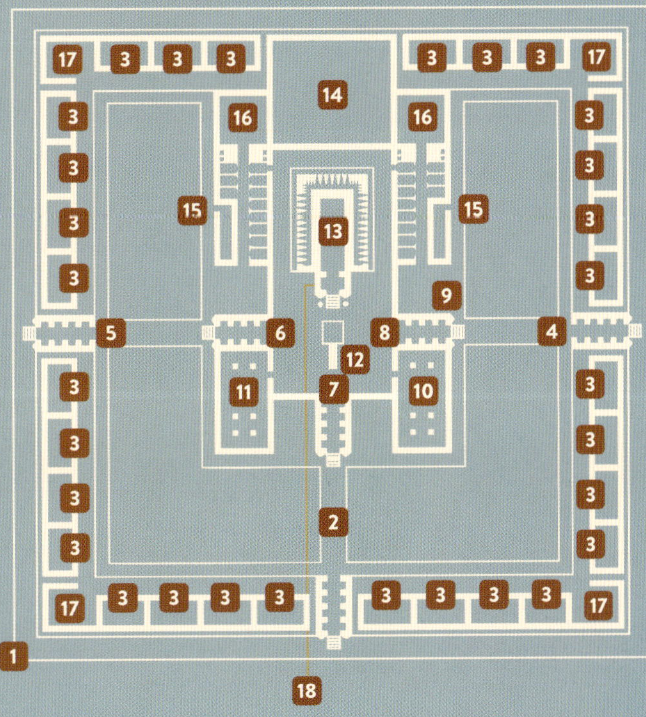

The temple described by Ezekiel was never built, and it may be that its significance was intended to be purely symbolic. This can be inferred from the fact that many of the features of this temple and its surroundings do not reflect the geographical realities of the site of Jerusalem and the Temple Mount in the land of Israel. Its distinctively cross-shaped plan is noteworthy.

FEATURES ARE LISTED IN THE ORDER IN WHICH EZEKIEL FIRST MENTIONS THEM

1. Outer Wall
40:5
2. Eastern (Main) Outer Gate
40:6–16; 42:15–43:5
3. Chambers of Outer Court (30)
40:17
4. Northern Outer Gate
40:20–22
5. Southern Outer Gate
40:24–26
6. Southern Inner Gate
40:27–31
7. Eastern Inner Gate / "The Prince's Gate"
40:32–34; 44:1–3; 46:1–8
8. Northern Inner Gate
40:35–37
9. Sacrificial Tables (4 outside gate, 4 inside)
40:38–43
10. Singers'/Priests' Chamber (south-facing door)
40:44–45
11. Singers'/Priests' Chamber (north-facing door)
40:44,46
12. Altar
40:47; 43:13–27
13. Temple (including portico, sanctuary, and surrounding rooms)
40:48–41:26
14. Building toward West (purpose not mentioned)
41:12,15
15. Priests' Chambers
42:1–14
16. Priests' Kitchens
46:19–20
17. People's Kitchens
46:21–24
18. River
47:1–12

Daniel

Genre | **PROPHECY (EXILE), APOCALYPTIC**

The book of Daniel contains narratives and visions about God's sovereign purposes for history to encourage faithfulness during a time of exile.

INTRODUCTION

AUTHOR The traditional view maintains that Daniel the prophet did indeed write this book sometime shortly after the end of the Babylonian captivity (sixth century BC). Internal testimony supports this claim. In the text itself, Daniel claimed to have written down visions given by God (8:2; 9:2,20; 12:5). Passages that contain third-person references to Daniel do not disprove his authorship. After all, authors commonly refer to themselves in the third person; for instance Moses did this in the Pentateuch. Moreover, God spoke of himself in the third person (Exod 20:7,11). Finally, Jesus Christ attributed the book of Daniel to Daniel himself (Matt 24:15).

BACKGROUND The historical setting of the book of Daniel is the Babylonian captivity. The book opens after King Nebuchadnezzar's first siege of Judah (605 BC) when he brought Daniel and his friends to Babylon along with other captives among the Judean nobility. Nebuchadnezzar assaulted Judah again in 597 and brought 10,000 captives back to Babylon. In 586 he once again besieged Jerusalem, this time destroying the city and the holy temple and exiling the people of Judah to Babylon. Daniel's ministry began in 605 when he arrived at Babylon with the first Jewish captives, extended throughout the Babylonian captivity (which ended in 539), and concluded sometime after the third year of Cyrus the Great, the Medo-Persian king who overthrew Babylonia (see Dan 1:21; 10:1).

MESSAGE AND PURPOSE The theme of the book of Daniel is the hope of the people of God during the times of the Gentiles. The phrase "the times of the Gentiles," used by Jesus (Luke 21:24), refers to the time between the Babylonian captivity and Jesus's return. It is a time when God's people live under ungodly world dominion. The book promotes hope by teaching that at all times "the Most High God is ruler over human kingdoms" (Dan 5:21). Daniel's purpose was to exhort Israel to be faithful to the sovereign God of Israel during the times of the Gentiles. He accomplished this by recounting examples of godly trust and prophecies of God's ultimate victory.

SUMMARY Daniel, "God's Judge," was a sixth-century BC prophet living in exile in Babylon. Daniel recounts key events firsthand that occurred during the Jewish captivity and also shares visions that were given to him by God.

STRUCTURE The genre of the book of Daniel is narrative, recounting historical events for the purpose of present and future instruction. The narrative contains history, prophecy, and apocalyptic visions. Apocalyptic literature refers to revelation by God given through visions and symbols with a message of eschatological (end-time) triumph. Although Daniel contains apocalyptic elements, it is not an apocalyptic book; rather, it is a narrative that includes apocalyptic visions. Noting that the book of Daniel contains both history (chaps. 1–6) and prophecy (chaps. 7–12), some divide the book into two sections. A better way to view the book's structure is based on the two languages it uses: 1:1–2:3 (Hebrew); 2:4–7:28 (Aramaic); and 8:1–12:13 (Hebrew).

Outline

I. **The Godly Remnant in the Times of the Gentiles (1:1–21)**
   A. Daniel and his friends in the Babylonian captivity (1:1–7)
   B. Daniel and the king's food (1:8–16)
   C. Daniel and the Lord's reward (1:17–21)

II. **God's Sovereignty over the Times of the Gentiles (2:1–7:28)**
   A. Daniel and the king's dream (2:1–49)
   B. Daniel's friends and the fiery furnace (3:1–30)
   C. Nebuchadnezzar's pride, madness, and repentance (4:1–37)
   D. Belshazzar's feast and the writing on the wall (5:1–30)
   E. Daniel in the lions' den (6:1–28)
   F. Daniel's vision of the four beasts, the Ancient of Days, and the Son of Man (7:1–28)

III. **God's People in the Times of the Gentiles (8:1–12:13)**
   A. Daniel's vision of the ram and the male goat (8:1–27)
   B. Daniel's prayer and vision of the seventy weeks (9:1–27)
   C. Daniel and his final visions (10:1–12:13)

WORD STUDY

peshar

Hebrew pronunciation:
[peh SHAR]

CSB translation:
interpretation

Uses in Daniel: 32
Uses in the OT: 32

Focus passage:
Daniel 2:4–7,9,16,24

The Aramaic noun ***peshar***, occurring only in Daniel, relates to an Akkadian word for interpreting dreams and omens, one connected with divination and magic and that could describe one's profession. True *interpretation* of dreams and divine messages requires God's enablement (Dan 2:30). The Aramaic verb *peshar* (2x) denotes *interpret* or *give interpretations* (Dan 5:12,16). These words link with two Hebrew word families. Similar-sounding *pesher* means *interpretation* (Eccl 8:1) and need not involve divine messages. Ecclesiastes 8:1 is the only OT passage where the root lacks the association with interpreting divine messages. Genesis 40–41 uses the verb *patar* (9x), which varies in spelling due to standard differences occurring between languages. It suggests Joseph's *interpreting* (8x) or *explaining* (Gen 40:8,22) dreams. The related noun *pithron* (5x) in that narrative signifies *interpretation* (Gen 40:8) or *meaning* (Gen 40:5; 41:11). Commentaries among the Dead Sea Scrolls use this root of interpreting Scripture.

charats

Hebrew pronunciation:
[chah RATZ]

CSB translation:
decide, decree, determine

Uses in Daniel: 3
Uses in the OT: 11

Focus passage:
Daniel 9:26–27

This root in several languages suggests cutting, and in Akkadian it also indicates determining. The former concept appears in the idiom "*sharpening* the tongue," which suggests dogs *snarling* (Exod 11:7) or people *threatening* others (Josh 10:21). Otherwise ***charats*** denotes *decide* (1 Kgs 20:40) and *determine* (Job 14:5). Once it means *act decisively* (2 Sam 5:24). In Isaiah and Daniel it implies judgments *decreed* by God against someone in the future (Isa 10:22–23). The noun *charuts* represents *threshing board/sledge* (4x, Job 41:30; Isa 28:27), *decision* (Joel 3:14), *moat* (Dan 9:25), and *maimed* animal (Lev 22:22).

Daniel's Life

REIGN OF NEBUCHADNEZZAR

- Daniel was exiled from Judah, taken to Babylon to be educated and to serve in the king's palace (1:3–6)
  - *Hananiah, Mishael, and Azariah also exiled with Daniel*
- Given the Babylonian name Belteshazzar (1:7)
  - *Daniel's friends given the names Shadrach, Meshach, and Abednego*
- Requested vegetables and water as his diet so as not to defile himself with the king's meat and wine (1:8–16)
- Blessed by God with knowledge and understanding in every kind of literature and wisdom; also understood visions and dreams of every kind (1:17)
- Served in the king's court and excelled in counseling the king in every matter of wisdom and understanding (1:19–20)
- Told and interpreted the king's dream by the wisdom of God (2:26–45)
- Promoted to ruler over the entire province of Babylon and chief governor of all the wise men of Babylon (2:48)
  - *Requested the king appoint Shadrach, Meshach, and Abednego to manage the province of Babylon (2:49)*
- Shadrach, Meshach, and Abednego refused to worship the king's statue; thrown in the furnace but saved by God (3:8–30)
- Interpreted the king's dream regarding God's punishment for his pride (4:19–27)

REIGN OF BELSHAZZAR

- *First Year:* Daniel's vision of four beasts representing four kings of the earth (7:1–28)
- *Third Year:* Daniel's vision of a ram and a goat representing the kings of Medo-Persia and Greece; interpreted by Gabriel, but Daniel could not understand it (8:1–27)
- Called before the king and interpreted the handwriting on the wall (5:13–31)
- Promoted to third ruler in the kingdom (5:29)

REIGN OF DARIUS THE MEDE/CYRUS THE PERSIAN

- *First Year:* Daniel prayed for conclusion of Jeremiah's 70 years; received understanding from Gabriel of God's decree of "seventy weeks" (9:1–27)
- *Third Year:* Daniel's vision of a glorious man dressed in linen and of the last days, which he did not understand (chaps. 10–12)
- Appointed as an administrator over the satraps of the kingdom (6:1–2)
- Ignored the king's edict and prayed to God as was his custom, so accused by his enemies before the king (6:10–15)
- Thrown in the lions' den but saved by God (6:16–23)
- Told to go to his end when he would rest in death and to await his resurrection at the end of the days (12:13)

TREASURED BY GOD: Daniel, a man greatly loved, was faithful to his God even in the midst of exile from his homeland. He experienced both blessing and extreme hardship in the land of Babylon. For his faithfulness, he was given knowledge and understanding by God and granted the ability to understand visions and dreams, which he used to serve and even rebuke the foreign kings who ruled over him. He was recognized as someone who had "a spirit of the gods in him" (Dan 5:4), but he always attributed his wisdom to God in heaven, the Most High God.

Kings of the Exile

	KING	SIGNIFICANCE	PROCLAMATIONS AND DECREES
BABYLON	**Nebuchadnezzar** *2 Kings 24–25; Daniel 1–4*	The Lord's servant to bring judgment against the people of Judah for their sin *(Jer 25:9)*	• Decree for the execution of all his wise men *(Dan 2:13)* • Proclaimed God is God of gods and Lord of lords and a revealer of mysteries *(Dan 2:47)* • Decree for leaders to worship the king's statue or die in the furnace *(Dan 3:10–11)* • Praised the God of Shadrach, Meshach, and Abednego and decreed honor for him; no other god is able to rescue like this *(Dan 3:28–29)* • Praised the Most High God, whose works are true and ways are just, and proclaimed his wonders to all the earth *(Dan 4)*
BABYLON	**Belshazzar** *Daniel 5*	The last king of Babylon by the judgment of God *(Dan 5:25–31)*	—
MEDO-PERSIA	**Darius the Mede / Cyrus the Persian** *2 Chronicles 36; Ezra 1–4; Daniel 6*	The Lord's shepherd to return the people from exile and rebuild the temple *(Isa 44:24–45:7)*	• Decree for the exiles of Judah to return to Jerusalem and rebuild the temple *(Ezra 1:2–4)* • Irrevocable decree that no one petition any god or man except the king for 30 days *(Dan 6:6–9)* • Decree for everyone in the kingdom to tremble in fear before the living God of Daniel, who rescued him from the lions *(Dan 6:26–27)*
MEDO-PERSIA	**Darius** *Ezra 5–6*	The Lord's decree for rebuilding the temple fulfilled through the decree of Darius *(Ezra 6:14)*	• Decree affirming and supporting the rebuilding of the temple of God in Jerusalem *(Ezra 6)*
MEDO-PERSIA	**Ahasuerus / Xerxes** *Esther*	Made Esther his queen, a position ordained "for such a time as this" *(Esth 2:17; 4:14)*	• Irrevocable decree drafted by Haman for the destruction of the Jews *(Esth 3:7–15)* • Irrevocable decree drafted by Mordecai for the defense of the Jews *(Esth 8:8–14)*
MEDO-PERSIA	**Artaxerxes** *Ezra 4; 7–10; Nehemiah*	The Lord put it into the king's mind to glorify the house of the Lord in Jerusalem *(Ezra 7:27)*	• Decree to stop the rebuilding of Jerusalem until a further decree is given *(Ezra 4:17–23)* • Decree permitting Ezra and others to return to Jerusalem and reinstitute the sacrifices and the law of God *(Ezra 7:11–26)* • Permission granted to Nehemiah to go to Jerusalem and rebuild it *(Neh 2:1–8)*

Nebuchadnezzar's Dream

HEAD OF GOLD

CHEST AND ARMS OF SILVER

STOMACH AND THIGHS OF BRONZE

LEGS OF IRON

FEET OF IRON AND FEET OF CLAY

"The head of the statue was pure gold, its chest and arms were silver, its stomach and thighs were bronze, its legs were iron, and its feet were partly iron and partly fired clay." –Daniel 2:32–33

Visions in Daniel

	A GREAT STATUE DANIEL 2	FOUR BEASTS DANIEL 7	A RAM AND A GOAT DANIEL 8
Babylon (609–539 BC)	Head of pure gold // The king of Babylon *(2:32,38)*	First beast: Like a lion with eagle's wings // An earthly kingdom *(7:4,17)*	—
Medo-Persia (539–330 BC)	Chest and arms of silver // A kingdom inferior to Babylon *(2:32,39)*	Second beast: Like a bear raised up on one side // An earthly kingdom *(7:5,17)*	A two-horned ram, one horn longer // The kings of Media and Persia *(8:3–4,20)*
Greece (330–63 BC)	Stomach and thighs of bronze // A third kingdom to rule the whole earth *(2:32,39)*	Third beast: Like a leopard with four wings and four heads // An earthly kingdom *(7:6,17)*	A goat with one large horn, later replaced by four horns (2) // The king of Greece; four weaker kingdoms arose after him *(8:5–8,21–22; see also 11:2–20)*
ROME (63 BC–)	Legs of iron; feet partly iron and partly fired clay // A fourth kingdom, strong but divided *(2:33,40–43)*	Fourth beast: Strong, with iron teeth; different from the others; ten horns (1) // A fourth earthly kingdom, different from the others; ten kings *(7:7,23–24)*	—
Types of the Antichrist *(see 2 Thess 2:1–12; 1 John 2:18–23; Rev 13:1–18)*	—	(1) A little horn with an arrogant mouth emerged; it successfully warred against God's holy ones until it was killed and burned // A king different from the others; it spoke against God and his holy ones until the appointed time for his judgment *(7:8–11,20–22,24–26)*	(2) A little horn emerged and acted arrogantly against the Prince (God) and his sanctuary; for a time, it was successful // A ruthless king who successfully destroyed God's people until he was broken, but not by human hands *(8:9–12,23–26; see also 11:21–45)*
Visions of the Christ *(see Matt 24:30–31; 26:64; Luke 20:9–18; Rev 1:1–20)*	A stone, dislodged without human hands, crushed the statue and became a mountain filling the earth // God will set up a kingdom that will crush all other kingdoms and never be destroyed *(2:34–35, 44–45)*	One like a son of man on the clouds of heaven received an everlasting, worldwide dominion from the Ancient of Days // The kingdoms of earth will be given to God's holy ones, and his kingdom will be everlasting *(7:13–14,27)*	—

KEY VERSE

I continued watching in the night visions, and suddenly one like a son of man was coming with the clouds of heaven. He approached the Ancient of Days and was escorted before him. He was given dominion and glory and a kingdom, so that those of every people, nation, and language should serve him. His dominion is an everlasting dominion that will not pass away, and his kingdom is one that will not be destroyed.

DANIEL 7:13–14

Seeing Jesus in the Exile and Return

THE LORD | *Will Send His Messenger to Prepare His Way (Mal 3:1)*	**JESUS, THE LORD** | *His Ways Are Prepared by John the Baptist (Luke 1:76–77)*
DANIEL Determined Not to Defile Himself with the King's Food or Wine *(Dan 1:8)*	**JESUS** Came to Take Away Sins, and There Is No Sin in Him *(1 John 3:5)*
THE FOURTH MAN One "Like a Son of the Gods" in the Furnace with the Exiles *(Dan 3:25)*	**THE SON OF GOD** The One Who Endured the Fire of God's Wrath for Us *(Rom 3:25)*
DANIEL A Man of Wisdom, Said to Have "a Spirit of the Gods" in Him *(Dan 5:11–14)*	**CHRIST JESUS** The Man of Wisdom, God-Given Wisdom for Our Salvation *(1 Cor 1:30)*
ONE LIKE A SON OF MAN Coming on the Clouds to Rule *(Dan 7:13–14)*	**THE SON OF MAN** Jesus Coming on the Clouds with Power and Glory *(Matt 24:30)*
CYRUS THE PERSIAN Anointed by God to Rule and Rebuild the Temple *(Isa 44:24–45:7)*	**JESUS THE MESSIAH** Anointed by God to Rule—He Is the Temple *(John 1:41; 2:21)*
ZERUBBABEL A Descendant of Jehoiachin; Returned from the Exile *(1 Chr 3:17–19)*	**JESUS CHRIST** A Descendant of Zerubbabel; the End the Exile *(Matt 1:12–17)*
ESTHER Chosen as Queen "for Such a Time as This" to Save Her People *(Esth 4:14)*	**JESUS** Born in the Fullness of Time to Redeem Those under the Law *(Gal 4:4–5)*
EZRA Devoted Himself to Studying, Obeying, and Teaching the Law of the Lord *(Ezra 7:10)*	**JESUS** The Scriptures, Including the Law of the Lord, Testify about Him *(John 5:39,46)*
NEHEMIAH A Man of Prayer *(Neh 1:5–11; 2:4; 4:9; 5:19; 6:9,14; 13:14,22,29,31)*	**JESUS** A Man of Prayer *(Matt 26:36–44; Luke 11:1–13; John 17; Rom 8:34; Heb 7:25)*
THE SUN OF RIGHTEOUSNESS Will Rise with Healing in Its Wings *(Mal 4:2)*	**THE DAWN** Jesus Will Visit Us and Guide Us into the Way of Peace *(Luke 1:78–79)*

Kingdom Visions

DANIEL'S PROPHETIC OUTLOOK ON THE COMING MESSIAH AND THE EVERLASTING KINGDOM

DREAM/VISION	MEANING	FULFILLMENT IN CHRIST
"The God of the heavens will set up a kingdom that will never be destroyed, and this kingdom will not be left to another people. It will crush all these kingdoms and bring them to an end, but will itself endure forever." *(Dan 2:44–45)*	The kingdom of God will ultimately and permanently triumph despite the temporary dominion of other worldly kingdoms.	"The kingdom of the world has become the kingdom of our Lord and of his Christ, and he will reign forever and ever." *(Rev 11:15; see also Luke 1:33; 1 Cor 15:24; 2 Pet 1:11)*
"Suddenly one like a son of man was coming with the clouds of heaven. He approached the Ancient of Days and was escorted before him. He was given dominion and glory and a kingdom, so that those of every people, nation, and language should serve him. His dominion is an everlasting dominion that will not pass away, and his kingdom is one that will not be destroyed." *(Dan 7:13–14)*	The Ancient of Days (God) gives the Son of Man dominion and power to rule over the earth and an everlasting kingdom consisting of every people, nation, and language.	"Then the sign of the Son of Man will appear in the sky, and then all the peoples of the earth will mourn; and they will see the Son of Man coming on the clouds of heaven with power and great glory." *(Matt 24:30; see also Matt 25:31; 26:64; Mark 13:26; 14:61–62; Luke 21:27; Acts 1:9–11; Rev 1:7)*
"The kingdom, dominion, and greatness of the kingdoms under all of heaven will be given to the people, the holy ones of the Most High. His kingdom will be an everlasting kingdom, and all rulers will serve and obey him." *(Dan 7:27)*	The covenant people of God will inherit the same everlasting kingdom as the Son of Man, despite the beastly world powers that threaten them during the present age.	"I also saw the holy city, the new Jerusalem, coming down out of heaven from God, prepared like a bride adorned for her husband. Then I heard a loud voice from the throne: Look, God's dwelling is with humanity, and he will live with them. They will be his peoples, and God himself will be with them and will be their God." *(Rev 21:2–3; see also Luke 1:33; 1 Cor 15:24; Rev 11:15; 20:4; 22:5)*
"From the issuing of the decree to restore and rebuild Jerusalem until an Anointed One, the ruler, will be seven weeks and sixty-two weeks. . . . After those sixty-two weeks the Anointed One will be cut off and will have nothing. The people of the coming ruler will destroy the city and the sanctuary. . . . He will make a firm covenant with many for one week, but in the middle of the week he will put a stop to sacrifice and offering. And the abomination of desolation will be on a wing of the temple." *(Dan 9:25–27)*	After 69 weeks (roughly 483 years) from the rebuilding of the city (445 BC), the Messiah will come and be cut off. Following this, in the middle of another "week," there will be an end to sacrifice and offering. There is some ambiguity as to whether the "Anointed One" or an evil "coming ruler" will be the agent who puts a stop to sacrifice.	"Wasn't it necessary for the Messiah to suffer these things and enter into his glory?" *(Luke 24:26; see also Luke 9:21–22; 19:41–44; 24:25–27,44–47)* "'So when you see the abomination of desolation, spoken of by the prophet Daniel, standing in the holy place' (let the reader understand), 'then those in Judea must flee to the mountains.'" *(Matt 24:15–22; see also Mark 13:14–20; Luke 21:20–24; 2 Thess 2:3–8)*
"Many who sleep in the dust of the earth will awake, some to eternal life, and some to disgrace and eternal contempt. Those who have insight will shine like the bright expanse of the heavens, and those who lead many to righteousness, like the stars forever and ever." *(Dan 12:2–4)*	Two forms of bodily resurrection will take place in the future: one to eternal joy under God's blessing and another to eternal suffering under God's condemnation.	"Do not be amazed at this, because a time is coming when all who are in the graves will hear his voice and come out—those who have done good things, to the resurrection of life, but those who have done wicked things, to the resurrection of condemnation." *(John 5:28–29; see also Matt 25:34,46; Rev 20:11–15; 21:3–8)*

KEY VERSE

Many who sleep in the dust of the earth will awake, some to eternal life, and some to disgrace and eternal contempt. Those who have insight will shine like the bright expanse of the heavens, and those who lead many to righteousness, like the stars forever and ever.

DANIEL 12:2–3

Minor Prophets

(BOOK OF THE TWELVE)

Genre | PROPHECY (PRE-EXILE, EXILE, POST-EXILE), NARRATIVE

The Minor Prophets are the 12 short-form works of the writing prophets that emphasize the reality of sin and judgment as well as the promise of salvation and restoration.

INTRODUCTION

AUTHOR Historically, the books known as the Minor Prophets have been accepted as being written by the person who is named at the beginning of the book (e.g., Hos 1:1; Joel 1:1; Amos 1:1, et al.). However, the book of Jonah is an exception as an anonymous narrative about the prophet of the same name. These prophets belonged to three different eras of Israel and Judah's history: preexilic (Hosea, Amos, Jonah, Micah, Nahum, Zephaniah, Habakkuk); exilic (possibly Obadiah); and postexilic (Haggai, Zechariah, Malachi). The dating of Joel has always been difficult with suggestions ranging from premonarchic Israel to Israel in the postexilic period and sometimes well into the Hellenistic period.

BACKGROUND The "Minor" Prophets are so named not because of their lesser importance but because of their length. The longest, Hosea, occupies about 14 pages in an average English Bible. Altogether the Minor Prophets are about the size of Ezekiel. Despite having been written at different times as separate books, sometime in the development of the Hebrew canon these 12 books were all bound together on the same scroll in an order that has generally remained unchanged. Consequently, they came to be known in Jewish tradition perhaps more appropriately as "the Twelve" or "the Book of the Twelve."

MESSAGE AND PURPOSE A focus on behavioral change explains the prophets' use of messages of indictment, instruction, judgment, and hope or salvation. Indictment messages identified Israel's sins and God's attitude toward them. Instruction told them what they must do about it, and judgment and hope messages motivated the listeners to obey by explaining the consequences of disobedience (judgment) or of repentance and faith (hope). Messages of judgment involve specific applications of the covenant curses found in Leviticus 26 and Deuteronomy 28 (see, for example, Joel 1:4–20; Amos 4:6–11; Zeph 1:13; Hag 1:10–11). They serve, then, as reminders that sin has its consequences. In some cases, the judgment and salvation oracles combine in a special way to motivate right behavior by a purified remnant. Our historical perspective allows us to recognize that in some cases announcements of future judgment or salvation concerned the distant future, beyond the lifetime of the prophet's immediate audience.

SUMMARY The Minor Prophets (in Jewish tradition often called "the Book of the Twelve" as a literary unit) are shorter in length than the books known as the "Major" Prophets (Isaiah, Jeremiah, Ezekiel, Daniel). Though written at different times as separate books, they were at some point bound together on the same scroll and contain common themes and patterns, such as indictment, instruction, judgment, and hope or salvation.

STRUCTURE Some have argued that "the Book of the Twelve" exhibits an overall plot or structure, with some even observing that the first six books, Hosea–Micah, emphasize sin; the next three, Nahum–Zephaniah, stress punishment; and the last three, Haggai–Malachi, stress restoration.

Outlines

HOSEA

I. The Pain and Persistence of Divine Love (1:1–3:5)
II. Threefold Accusation and Call to Repent (4:1–7:16)
III. Alternating Lament of the Lord and Hosea (8:1–14:9)

JOEL

I. The Locust Plague (1:1–20)
II. An Invading Northern Army (2:1–11)
III. Repentance and Renewal (2:12–19)
IV. Northern Army Destroyed (2:20)
V. Physical Restoration of the Land (2:21–27)
VI. Spiritual Revival of the People (2:28–32)
VII. Vengeance on the Nations (3:1–21)

AMOS

I. Prophecies against the Nations (1:1–2:16)
II. Three Discourses against Israel (3:1–6:14)
III. Five Symbolic Visions of Israel's Condition (7:1–9:10)
IV. Promises of Israel's Restoration (9:11–15)

OBADIAH

I. An Oracle of the Lord against Edom (vv. 1–9)
II. Esau's Sin against His Brother Jacob (vv. 10–14)
III. The Wider Context: The Day of the Lord (vv. 15–18)
IV. House of Jacob Will Possess Edom's Territory (vv. 19–21)

JONAH

I. Jonah's Flight from God (1:1–17)
II. Jonah's Prayer of Thanksgiving from the Fish (2:1–10)
III. Jonah's Preaching in Nineveh (3:1–10)
IV. Jonah's Anger at God's Mercy (4:1–11)

MICAH

I. Coming Defeat and Destruction (1:1–16)
II. Corruption of the People (2:1–13)
III. Corruption of the Leaders (3:1–12)
IV. Hope for a Glorious Future Restoration (4:1–5:15)
V. Corruption of the City and Its Leaders (6:1–16)
VI. Corruption of the People (7:1–7)
VII. Future Reversal of Defeat and Destruction (7:8–20)

NAHUM

I. Prelude (1:1–10)
II. Nineveh's Destruction as Part of God's Plan (1:11–15)
III. Nineveh's Destruction to Be Complete (2:1–13)
IV. Nineveh's Destruction the Result of Sin (3:1–18)
V. Postlude (3:19)

HABAKKUK

I. Dialogue between God and Habakkuk (1:1–2:20)
II. Habakkuk's Psalm (3:1–19)

ZEPHANIAH

I. Prophecy of God's Judgments (1:1–2:3)
II. God's Judgment of the Nations (2:4–3:8)
III. Promised Blessings (3:9–20)

HAGGAI

I. Reprimand and Call to Rebuild the House of God (1:1–15)
II. Reminder of the Lord's Presence and Future Glory of the Temple (2:1–9)
III. Religious Principles about Holiness and Uncleanness (2:10–19)
IV. Restoration of Davidic Line Promised (2:20–23)

ZECHARIAH

I. Call to Conversion (1:1–6)
II. Visionary Disclosure of God's Purposes (1:7–6:15)
III. A Prophetic Message to the People (7:1–8:23)
IV. The Emerging Kingdom (9:1–14:21)

MALACHI

I. Priests Exhorted to Honor the Lord (1:1–2:9)
II. Judah Exhorted to Faithfulness (2:10–3:6)
III. Judah Exhorted to Return to the Lord (3:7–4:6)

WORD STUDY

racham

Hebrew pronunciation:
[rah KHAM]

CSB translation:
love, have compassion, pity

Uses in Hosea: 7
Uses in the OT: 47

Focus passage:
Hosea 2:1,4,23

Racham derives from *rechem* (26x, *womb*), and related languages associate "womb" and "compassion." *Racham* means *love* (Ps 18:1). Intensive verbs signify *have/show compassion* (Exod 33:19; Deut 13:17) or *show mercy* (Isa 60:10). Their participle denotes *compassionate* (Ps 116:5), and their infinitive indicates *mercy* (Hab 3:2). Their passive conveys *receive compassion* (Hos 2:23) or *find mercy* (Prov 28:13). *Rachamiym* (40x) indicates *mercy* (Deut 13:17) or *compassion* (Isa 54:7). It is *merciful acts* (Prov 12:10), *mercies* (Lam 3:22), and *merciful* (Gen 43:14). It suggests *emotion* (Gen 43:30), *pity* (Ps 106:46), and, in a prepositional phrase, *in mercy* (Zech 1:16). The same words imply *abundant compassion* (Neh 9:31) or *mercies are . . . great* (1 Chr 21:13). *Rachum* (13x) means *compassionate* (Deut 4:31) or *merciful* (2 Chr 30:9). Eleven times *rachum* occurs alongside "gracious" (*chunun*, Exod 34:6). *Rachamaniy* is *compassionate woman* (Lam 4:10).

sela'

Hebrew pronunciation:
[SEH lah]

CSB translation:
rock, cliff

Uses in Obadiah: 1
Uses in the OT: 63

Focus passage:
Obadiah 3

Sela' occurs (4x, Ps 71:3) alongside *tsur* (76x), which encompasses various kinds of rock. *Sela'* often involves *rock* faces, particularly *cliffs* (Isa 2:21), where eagles (Job 39:27–28) and hyraxes (Prov 30:26) live. People are thrown off them (Ps 141:6). *Mountain goats* is literally "goats of the *sela'*" (Job 39:1). *Sela'* identifies named *rocks* (Judg 15:8) and *rock* columns (1 Sam 14:4). Some think that Obadiah 3 specifies Sela, an Edomite fortress city, rather than *rock*. The Septuagint sometimes translates *sela'* (Isa 42:11) as *petra*, perhaps corresponding to Petra in Jordan. *Sela'* is associated with crevices and clefts (Jer 13:4; 49:16), also with fortresses (Isa 33:16). God is our *sela'* (Ps 18:2). Tyre stripped of civilization is *sela'* (Ezek 26:14). Crypts were carved in *sela'* (Isa 22:16). *Sela'* implies *stone* (Judg 6:20); the plural suggests *rocks* (1 Sam 13:6).

saq

Hebrew pronunciation:
[SACK]

CSB translation:
sack, sackcloth

Uses in Jonah: 3
Uses in the OT: 48

Focus passage:
Jonah 3:5–6,8

Saq denotes *sack* (6x, Gen 42:27), entering English through Greek and Latin. *Saq* was *sackcloth* (Isa 15:3). The thick, rough, dark-colored material was goat hair (Isa 50:3; Rev 6:12) or camel hair (Matt 3:4). It might provide blankets (2 Sam 21:10). Akkadian, the Ninevite language, used the root similarly. Ninevites wore *sackcloth* to express repentance (Jonah 3:8), as did Israelites (Neh 9:1). *Sackcloth* was worn on the skin (2 Kgs 6:30; Job 16:15) and involved self-humbling (1 Kgs 21:27–29). Mourning was the chief reason for wearing *sackcloth* (Gen 37:34; Joel 1:8). Ammonites (Jer 49:3) and Arameans (1 Kgs 20:32) wore *sackcloth*. Prophets called for it communally in the face of judgment (Jer 4:8). People might tear regular clothes and fast (Esth 4:1,3), covering themselves with dust (4x, Jer 6:26) or ashes (7x, Jonah 3:6), perhaps shaving or cutting themselves (Jer 48:37). *Sackcloth* could signal protest (Esth 4:1).

The Better Jonah

JONAH	JESUS
Jonah was a prophet *(Jonah 1:1; 2 Kgs 14:25)*	Jesus is the Prophet *(Matt 12:41; Acts 3:17–26)*
Jonah slept in the boat as a storm raged, and he was tossed into the sea to calm the waves *(Jonah 1:4–16)*	Jesus slept in the boat as a storm raged, and he spoke to calm the winds and the waves *(Matt 8:23–27)*
Jonah was in the belly of a fish for three days and three nights and then vomited out on dry ground *(Jonah 1:17; 2:10)*	Jesus was in the heart of the earth for three days and three nights and then raised from the dead *(Matt 12:38–40; 28:1–10)*
Jonah repented and prayed, "Salvation belongs to the Lord" *(Jonah 2:9)*	Salvation is in Christ Jesus and obtained through repentance and faith in him *(Acts 4:11–12; 2 Tim 2:10)*
Jonah's preaching resulted in Nineveh's repentance *(Jonah 3:4–10)*	Jesus's preaching results in repentance throughout the world *(Rev 5:9–10; 7:9–17)*
Jonah resented God's compassion for the people of Nineveh, who did not know their right hand from their left *(Jonah 4:1–11)*	Jesus reflects God's compassion for people who are like sheep without a shepherd *(Matt 9:36; 14:14; 15:32; 20:34)*

The Hebrew Prophets in History

(9TH–5TH CENTURIES BC)

PROPHET	APPROX. DATES (BC)	LOCATION/HOME	BASIC BIBLE PASSAGE	CENTRAL TEACHING	KEY VERSE
Elijah	875–850	Tishbe	1 Kgs 17:1–2 Kgs 2:18	Yahweh, not Baal, is God	1 Kgs 18:21
Micaiah	856	Samaria	1 Kgs 22; 2 Ch 18	Judgment on Ahab; proof of prophecy	1 Kgs 22:28
Elisha	855–800	Abel-meholah	1 Kgs 19:15–21; 2 Kgs 2–9; 13	God's miraculous power	2 Kgs 5:15
Jonah	786–746	Gath-hepher	2 Kgs 14:25; Jonah	God's universal concern	Jonah 4:11
Hosea	786–746	Israel	Hosea	God's unquenchable love	Hos 11:8–9
Amos	760–750	Tekoa	Amos	God's call for justice and righteousness	Amos 5:24
Isaiah	740–698	Jerusalem	2 Kgs 19–20; Isaiah	Hope through repentance and suffering	Isa 1:18; 53:4–6
Micah	735–710	Moresheth-gath/ Jerusalem	Jer 26:18; Micah	Call for humble mercy and justice	Mic 6:8
Oded	733	Samaria	2 Chr 28:9–11	Do not go beyond God's command	2 Chr 28:9
Nahum	686–612	Elkosh	Nahum	God's jealousy protects his people	Nah 1:2–3
Zephaniah	640–621	?	Zephaniah	Hope for the humble and righteous	Zeph 2:3
Jeremiah	626–584	Anathoth/ Jerusalem	2 Chr 36:12; Jeremiah	Faithful prophet points to new covenant	Jer 31:33–34
Huldah (the prophetess)	621	Jerusalem	2 Kgs 22; 2 Chr 34	God's book is accurate	2 Kgs 22:16
Habakkuk	608–598	?	Habakkuk	God calls for faithfulness	Hab 2:4
Ezekiel	593–571	Babylon	Ezekiel	Future hope for new community of worship	Ezek 37:12–13
Obadiah	580	Jerusalem	Obadiah	Doom on Edom to bring God's kingdom	Obad 21
Joel	539–531	Jerusalem	Joel	Call to repent and experience God's Spirit	Joel 2:2–29
Haggai	520	Jerusalem	Ezra 5:1; 6:14; Haggai	The priority of God's house	Hag 2:8–9
Zechariah	520–514	Jerusalem	Ezra 5:1; 6:14; Zechariah	Faithfulness will lead to God's universal rule	Zech 14:9
Malachi	500–450	Jerusalem	Malachi	Honor God and wait for his righteousness	Mal 4:2

Minor Prophets Timeline

850 BC

836–796 Joel's prophecy likely occurred

793–753 At a time the Assyrian Empire is in decline, God calls Jonah to go to Nineveh and preach repentance.

793–745 Jeroboam II, king of the northern kingdom, enjoys an era of peace, expansion, increased trade, and increased affluence.

763 Assyria experiences two severe plagues **(765 and 759)** and a total eclipse.

760–750 Amos is called to travel from Judah to Israel to prophesy in Samaria.

750 BC

760–722 Hosea's prophetic ministry

745–727 Assyria emerges from years of decline as Tiglath-pileser III invades Israel.

740 Isaiah is called to be a prophet. Nineveh repents in response to Jonah's preaching and is spared God's judgment.

735–700 Micah begins his prophetic ministry.

725–722 Assyria's Shalmaneser V besieges Samaria.

722 Samaria falls to Assyria's Sargon II; nearly 28,000 Israelites are sent into exile.

705–681 Sennacherib establishes Nineveh as the capital of the Assyrian Empire.

701 Sennacherib captures and devastates Judah, besieging but not capturing Jerusalem.

700 BC

700 Greeks establish trading posts in Philistine territory along the Mediterranean coast.

700 Philistines and Phoenicians sell the people of Judah and Jerusalem as slaves to the Greeks.

Years of prophetic silence **(698–626)** in Judah coincide with some of Judah's darkest years under the rule of Manasseh **(697–642)** and Amon **(642–640).**

689 When Babylon rebels against Sennacherib, he destroys the city. Sennacherib is murdered by his two sons, one of whom, Esar-haddon **(681–669),** succeeds him as king.

671 Esar-haddon invades Egypt.

667 Egypt rebels **(669)** and Esar-haddon's son Ashurbanipal **(668–627)** sets out to reconquer Egypt.

665 Egypt rebels again, so Ashurbanipal destroys Thebes.

Nahum **(663–612)** prophesies that just as Assyria destroyed Thebes, Nineveh (Assyria's capital) will be destroyed.

650 BC

641–609 Ashurbanipal **(668–636)** rules over a declining Assyrian Empire that experiences revolts in **642,** contributing to the assassination of Amon of Judah and the rise of his son Josiah.

640 Josiah is placed on Judah's throne at the age of eight when his father, Amon, is assassinated.

630–621 Zephaniah's years of prophecy

621 The book of the law is found and read publicly, spurring additional reform under Josiah.

612 Calah is destroyed and the combined armies of the Babylonians and the Medes lay siege to Nineveh. After two months, the city falls.

612 With the fall of Nineveh, the Babylonian Empire succeeds the Assyrian Empire as the dominant force in the ancient Near East.

610 BC

610 An Assyrian general claims the throne and rallies what is left of the Assyrian army in Haran. An alliance with Egypt brings a few troops to Assyria's aid, but as the Babylonians approach, Haran is abandoned.

609 Josiah killed by the Egyptians at Megiddo

609 Josiah's son Jehoahaz II succeeds him and is deposed, replaced by his brother Jehoiakim.

605 Nebuchadnezzar leads the Babylonians to defeat Pharaoh Neco II at Carchemish.

605 Habakkuk prophesies what the growing Babylonian strength means for Judah.

605 Jeremiah prophesies that the Babylonian exile will last 70 years.

600 BC

605, 597, 586, 582 Nebuchadnezzar attacks Jerusalem and leads the citizens of Judah into exile.

598 A reinforced Babylonian army approaches Judah; Jehoiakim dies.

597 Nebuchadnezzar plunders the temple and takes Jehoiachin and the royal family into exile; Zedekiah becomes king.

593 Ezekiel begins to prophesy.

593–571 Events in Ezekiel

587 Zedekiah rebels against Babylon. He apparently dies in captivity.

587–586 Events in Obadiah

586 Jerusalem and the temple of Solomon destroyed

582 As punishment for the uprising against Gedaliah, Nebuchadnezzar deports more citizens.

581 Cyrus the Elder, founder of the Persian Empire, is born.

550 BC

538 Cyrus's decree allows return of Jews from exile; 42,360 returned initially.

536 Second temple construction begins under Zerubbabel's and Joshua's leadership.

526 Discouragement brings work on the temple to a halt.

520–518 Haggai and Zechariah encourage the people to resume construction of the temple.

AUGUST 29, 520 Haggai's first message

SEPTEMBER 21, 520 Temple building resumes

OCTOBER 17, 520 Haggai's second message

OCTOBER/NOVEMBER 520 Zechariah's first prophetic message

DECEMBER 18, 520 Haggai's third and fourth messages

FEBRUARY 15, 519 Zechariah's night visions

DECEMBER 7, 518 Zechariah's message on fasting

515 Second temple is completed and dedicated.

500 BC

490
Greeks defeat Persians in battle of Marathon through superior military intelligence and strategy, forestalling Persian expansion into Europe.

486–465
Events in Esther

Greek victories over Persians in battle of Salamis, **480**, and Plain of Plataea, **479**, thwart Persian expansion into Europe and are keys to Greek hegemony in the Mediterranean Basin and Europe.

460–430
Malachi's prophecy

458
Second group of exiles returns to Jerusalem under the leadership of Ezra.

450 BC

445
Third group of exiles returns under Nehemiah's leadership.

445
Jerusalem's walls rebuilt under Nehemiah's leadership

432
Nehemiah returns to Persia.

431–404
Peloponnesian War between Athens and other Greek city-states

425
Nehemiah returns to Jerusalem.

Messianic Prophecies

MESSIANIC PROPHECY	MINOR PROPHET	NEW TESTAMENT
Triumphal entry	Zechariah 9:9	Mark 11:7–11
Betrayed for 30 pieces of silver	Zechariah 11:12	Matthew 26:15
Side pierced	Zechariah 12:10	John 19:34
Preceded by forerunner	Malachi 3:1	Luke 7:24–17
Preceded by Elijah	Malachi 4:1–3	Matthew 11:13–14

Contemporaries and Hearers

Listing of the prophets by age (Babylonian age, Persian age), organized by hearers

	ASSYRIAN EMPIRE 620 BC	BABYLONIAN EMPIRE 620–540 BC	PERSIAN EMPIRE 539–330 BC
TO JUDAH	**JOEL (836–796?)** Call to repent of social injustices and impure worship and to experience God's Spirit. **ZEPHANIAH (630–621)** Call to repent of idolatry. There is hope for the humble righteous.	**HABAKKUK (609–605)** God calls Judah to repent of idolatry and injustices and renew their faithfulness to him.	**HAGGAI (520)** Call to repent and rebuild the temple to worship God. God's house is the priority. **ZECHARIAH (520–518)** Call to repent and rebuild the temple to worship God. Faithfulness would lead to God's universal rule. **MALACHI (460–430)** Call to repent and God will bring restoration. Honor him and wait for his righteousness.
TO ASSYRIA/ NINEVEH	**NAHUM (663–612)** God would destroy Nineveh for their wickedness. God's jealousy protects his people.		
TO EDOM		**OBADIAH (587–586)** Edomites would receive judgment because of their role in Jerusalem's destruction. Their doom would bring God's kingdom.	

LITERARY PARALLELS IN THE MINOR PROPHETS

JOEL / AMOS

The LORD will roar from Zion and make his voice heard from Jerusalem.

JOEL 3:16

The LORD roars from Zion and makes his voice heard from Jerusalem.

AMOS 1:2

AMOS / OBADIAH

So that they may possess the remnant of Edom and all the nations that bear my name—this is the declaration of the LORD; he will do this.

AMOS 9:12

This is what the Lord GOD has said about Edom: We have heard a message from the LORD; an envoy has been sent among the nations: "Rise up, and let's go to war against her." Look, I will make you insignificant among the nations; you will be deeply despised.

OBADIAH 1B–2

JONAH / NAHUM

The word of the LORD came to Jonah son of Amittai: "Get up! Go to the great city of Nineveh and preach against it because their evil has come up before me."

JONAH 1:1–2

The LORD is good, a stronghold in a day of distress; he cares for those who take refuge in him. But he will completely destroy Nineveh with an overwhelming flood, and he will chase his enemies into darkness.

NAHUM 1:7–8

Sources

[1] Geerhardus Vos, *Biblical Theology: Old and New Testaments* (Carlisle, PA: Banner of Truth, 2012), 165.

[2] Adapted from *Holman Concise Bible Commentary* (Nashville, TN: Holman Reference, 1998), 64. Biblical citations were taken from Sandra L. Richter, *The Epic of Eden: A Christian Entry into the Old Testament* (Downers Grove, IL: InterVarsity Press, 2008), 84.

[3] Stephen G. Dempster, *Dominion and Dynasty: A Biblical Theology of the Hebrew Bible* (Downers Grove, IL: InterVarsity Press, 2003), 122–123.

[4] John D. Currid, *Against the Gods: The Polemical Theology of the Old Testament* (Wheaton, IL: Crossway, 2013), 133–34.

[5] "Prophets," *Holman Bible Dictionary* (Nashville, TN: Holman Bible Publishers, 1991), 1141–2.

[6] Adapted from W. Wayne VanHorn, "Prophet, Priest, and King," *Biblical Illustrator*, Winter 2010–11. Copyright ©2010 Lifeway Christian Resources. Used by permission.

[7] H. L. Ellison, "Bildad" in *ISBE*, vol. 1 (1979), 510.

[8] Stephen G. Dempster, *Dominion and Dynasty: A Theology of the Hebrew Bible* (Downers Grove, IL: InterVarsity Press, 2003), 206.

[9] James M. Hamilton Jr. *God's Glory in Salvation through Judgment: A Biblical Theology* (Wheaton, IL: Crossway, 2010), 320.

[10] Barry G. Webb, *Five Festal Garments: Christian Reflections on the Song of Songs, Ruth, Lamentations, Ecclesiastes and Esther* (Downers Grove, IL: IVP, 2000), 34–35.